Writing the Irish West

Writing *the*
IRISH WEST

ECOLOGIES AND TRADITIONS

*To Lynne O'Donnell
with best wishes
From Eamonn*

Eamonn Wall

University of Notre Dame Press

Notre Dame, Indiana

Manufactured in the United States of America

Library of Congress Cataloging-in-Publication Data

Wall, Eamonn, 1955–
    Writing the Irish West : ecologies and traditions / Eamonn Wall.
        p.   cm.
    Includes bibliographical references and index.
    ISBN-13: 978-0-268-04423-7 (pbk. : alk. paper)
    ISBN-10: 0-268-04423-6 (pbk. : alk. paper)
    1. English literature—Irish authors—History and criticism.
2. Ireland, West of.   3. Ireland—In literature.   4. Literature and society—
Ireland.   5. National characteristics, Irish, in literature.   I. Title.
    PR8722.W45W35   2011
    820.9'3584171—dc22
                                                                                2010049972

FOR
Matthew and Caitlin

This is not landscape, full of the somnambulations
Of poetry

And the sea. This is my father, or, maybe,
It is as he was,

A likeness, one of the race of fathers: earth
And sea and air.

—*Wallace Stevens, "The Irish Cliffs of Moher"*

CONTENTS

Acknowledgments   ix

Preface   xi

one
Adequate Steps: Tim Robinson's *Stones of Aran*   1

two
Wings Beating on Stone: Richard Murphy's Ecopoetry   51

three
Tracing the Poetry of Mary O'Malley   71

four
High Ground: John McGahern's Western World   87

five
A Wild West Show: The Plays of Martin McDonagh   113

six
Across a Blue Sound: Seán Lysaght's *Clare Island Survey*   139

seven
Carrying the Songs: The Poetry of Moya Cannon   157

Bibliography   177

Index   195

ACKNOWLEDGMENTS

Let me express debts of gratitude for the support received while I was engaged in the process of researching and writing this book. A number of these chapters began as papers delivered at American Conference for Irish Studies meetings and benefited greatly from the feedback provided by my colleagues in that organization. Special thanks are due to Pascale Guibert of the University of Caen, Basse-Normandie, for an invitation to speak at a colloquium that she organized, which helped to get this work under way; and to José Lanters for providing detailed and helpful feedback on the manuscript. Thanks are due to the staff at the Office of Research Administration, University of Missouri-St. Louis, and its director, Nasser Arshadi, who assisted greatly at the time of my application for a University of Missouri Research Award. Particular gratitude is due to Shannon McMahon for her invaluable help; to the evaluators of my proposal, who recommended it for support; and to my superiors at UM-St. Louis— Joel Glassman, director of the Center for International Studies, Mark Burkholder, former dean of the College of Arts and Sciences, and the late Barbara Kachur, former chair, Department of English—who facilitated my leave from the classroom for a year. My special thanks are due to my friend Gearoid Ó hAllmhuráin for his encouragement and good cheer during the time when this book was being written. The library staff at UM-St. Louis was courteous and helpful, even when they were asked to locate the most obscure volumes via interlibrary loan. Research was also conducted at the National Library of Ireland in Dublin and aided there by its friendly staff. A word of thanks is due to Mary Troy and Pier Davis, and also to the faculty of the UM–St. Louis MFA Program in Creative Writing for their encouragement. Thanks to Sue Maher and Al Kammerer for taking me to some the best places in the American West; to the Tolan family, our neighbors in Webster Groves, for looking after our house and animals when we were absent; to Greg Zacharias and Annie Shahan for their friendship and support; and to William Kerwin for encouragement. In Galway, I am grateful to Louis de Paor, director of the Center for Irish Studies; to Seamus O'Grady, director of the Study Abroad Programs at NUI-Galway; and to Kevin Higgins and Susan Millar DuMars for their hospitality and friendship. My greatest debts are to my families in the United States and Ireland for love, good times, and generous hospitality. My American family, exhibiting much forbearance and humor, were companions on much of the fieldwork that was part of this research (without always being aware of it), while the generosity of my Irish family has made possible our extended visits to Ireland and the completion of this book.

Earlier versions of chapters included in this book first appeared in the *South Carolina Review*, "From Macchu Picchu to Inis Mór: The Poetry of Mary O'Malley," 38:1 (Fall 2005): 118–27; and *New Hibernia Review*, "Walking: Tim Robinson's *Stones of Aran*," 12:3 (Fomhar/ Autumn 2008): 66–79. Many thanks to Wayne Chapman and James Silas Rogers, the editors of the *South Carolina Review* and *New Hibernia Review*, respectively. An earlier version of "Wings Beating on Stone: Richard Murphy's Ecology," was published in Christine Cusick, ed., *Out of the Earth: Ecocritical Readings of Irish Texts* (Cork: Cork University Press, 2010): 5–19.

The research and writing of this book was supported by a research leave grant from the University of Missouri.

PREFACE

It was late one afternoon in eastern Colorado. I was traveling with my family along the highway westward toward Denver when the decisive prod that got me started on the research and writing that culminated in this book was delivered—unexpectedly. We had been in the car for most of the day and were all looking forward to spending the night in a motel in one of the small towns where we habitually stopped on those Western sojourns. Given that we were westbound on Interstate 76, it was likely that we would stop for the night in Sterling though, if we pushed it, we might make it as far as Fort Morgan. We were all getting tired; however, we had been somewhat energized by the hour gained when we crossed the invisible line from Central to Mountain Time. Also, the gradual change in landscape brought on by the rising elevation—from Nebraska to Colorado—was for us, then living in Nebraska, a harbinger of holidays and adventures. We had entered the West.

How much longer could we hold out before stopping? Not much, I thought, when I looked at my companions in the car. They had faded into silence and had even turned off the radio, a sure sign of the kind of epic fatigue that sets in toward the end of long days on American interstates. Picking up on their mood, I began to think of how pleasant it would be to find myself in a simple roadside motel for the night, one with an outdoor pool, and close by a good local restaurant featuring hearty Western dishes: meat, potatoes, salads, apple pie and ice cream. Wouldn't a beer be nice! As these thoughts grew stronger, I decided not to drive all the way to Fort Morgan; Sterling would be good enough. It was only another thirty miles. I looked out at the dry grasslands of eastern Colorado and sang my way onward.

That evening, it occurred to me that I had spent much more time in the American West than I had ever spent in its Irish equivalent. Arriving in the States as an immigrant and then living and working in Nebraska for eight years had opened up a new world for me, and it was one that I embraced eagerly. Whenever the opportunity presented itself, I had headed into the West. On these journeys, I was fortunate to have my wife, Dru, with me; she had traveled many of these roads previously and knew a great deal about their lore and histories. She had also read the books and understood the language of the land. My children were able to teach me the basic facts of American history and topography and provided all these trips with purpose — they were learning the language of their land. Over time, my knowledge of the American West deepened and broadened, and the more I witnessed it in person, the more I wanted to read about it when I got home from these road trips. Call it fate, luck, or accident, but I had managed to acquire some decent, firsthand knowledge of the American West. All the while, time passed quickly, happily, and, because I was a parent, unconsciously. On a deeper level, the American West had become part of my inner life: I loved it, thought about it, dreamed about it.

My engagement with the physical landscape of the West of Ireland, it occurred to me as I was singing toward Sterling that summer evening, was minimal when contrasted with my time spent in its American equivalent. In the Ireland I grew up in of the 1950s and 1960s, my family did not travel far afield: our given routes took us to the homes of relatives in County Wexford and, on occasion, to Dublin, to attend the Spring Show at the RDS and hurling matches in Croke Park. We did not know many people from the West of Ireland; indeed, Westport, for example, was as remote to us as Gdansk. Even though I had visited the Irish West several time before emigrating to the United

States in the early 1980s, my most telling encounters with it had been in the form of the books that I had read. On that late summer evening in Colorado, I pledged to myself to make an effort to understand the American West more thoroughly by reading deeply of its literature, while, at the same time, engaging with the landscape of the Irish West by sojourning there. Again, fate intervened. A change of job meant that I would be required to stay some part of each year in Galway and, simultaneously, my brother and his wife had moved from Dublin to Sligo, to settle near my sister-in-law's family, and they invited us to come visit them. Now, I had family in the West and, as a result, a sense of belonging.

This comparative study has grown out of my engagements with two Wests—the Irish and the American—and the "Western-ness" that they share. However, I have never tried to push comparisons beyond what is logical because, in some important respects, these Wests are quite distinct. What I have done is place texts side by side for analysis when warranted and reasonable. I have found that West of Ireland writers share much with their American counterparts. Moreover, it is clear to me that some of the theoretical approaches that have been developed for the study of the literature of the American West will be of great use to scholars of the literature of the West of Ireland. In writing this book, I have made extensive use of some of these theories and approaches, in addition to the more familiar sources from the field of Irish Studies. In a sense, my critical landscape is regional and international rather than national. I am interested in exploring connections between parts of different countries rather than between nations. Both writing and ecology, as will be evident here, are local activities that are internationally dispersed.

Because, to a great degree, the writers under consideration here are exploring landscape and place—in the largest sense—this study is frequently underlined by scholarship in the areas of ecocriticism and ecofeminism, particularly in the chapters on the work of Richard Murphy and Moya Cannon. In the chapter on Tim Robinson, William Least-Heat Moon's *PrairyErth,* Robin Jarvis's *Romantic Writing and Pedestrian Travel,* and William J. Smyth's *Map-making, Landscapes and Memory: A Geography of Colonial and Early Modern Ireland, c. 1530–1750* have served as both guides and totems in my exploration of Robinson's mapping of Árainn or Inishmore. Research on the poetry of Mary O'Malley led to an examination of the explosive growth of Western cities (Phoenix and Galway) and how this has influenced writers. In my discussion of the role that violence plays in the works of John McGahern and Martin McDonagh, I have been guided by the historical work of Richard Slotkin and Richard White. The chapter on Seán Lysaght's work, on the other hand, probes connections between poetry and science, another area where ecology and writing go in tandem. Occasionally, this research has allowed me to pair writers profitably: John McGahern and Owen Wister, Martin McDonagh and Sam Peckinpah, Richard Murphy and Gary Snyder, for example. But, more than anything, ecocriticism is at the heart of this study because ecological visions are at the heart of Western writing, both in the United States and in Ireland. For each writer under consideration here, being from, or associated with, the West is important and singular, though how this West is defined changes from one writer to the next, or from one book to the next, within an author's work. These seven creative writers are more concerned with showing the West than with defining it. At the same time, each one is involved in a dialogue with his/her literary tradition and is writing an ecological response to Western space.

In the United States, the West is defined geographically, at least by some, as all of those states situated west of the Mississippi River. Others will argue that it begins when one crosses the Missouri River, while a minority will provide other limits. And a few, dyspeptically, will claim that California is not a Western state at all! In Ireland, some will see the West as being synonymous with the boundaries of the province of Connacht, while others will include Donegal, Kerry, Clare, and Limerick. Of course, as writers such as Gloria Anzaldúa remind us, borderlands are often pressure points of creativity. In Ireland, the work of John McGahern might be claimed by both the Midlands and the West. For the purposes of this study, however, I have concentrated on the work of writers from Connacht. I have done so in the interests of an efficient completion of the project, though I am certain that, for

example, writers such as Brian Friel and Nuala Ní Dhomhnaill do belong to the West.

In both America and Ireland, the Western regions are spaces
of great beauty that share complex histories, and the works written
by the seven authors under consideration here, from various perspectives and in multiple genres, arise from those parts of the physical and
psychic landscapes where fissures have emerged. Literary and moral
imaginations have been formed by interactions with place, space, and
a natural world that exists in free play with the human. In both Wests,
ecology is one of the roots of creativity. Today, in the United States,
scholars write of the New West, defined, for example, by the growth
of such cities as Las Vegas and Phoenix, and by such industries as the
software design and computer manufacturing that have replaced agriculture and gold mining. Ireland also possesses a New West in which
cities and towns have expanded enormously (Galway, Castlebar), and
where old industries have been replaced by the new. These New Wests
are explored by writers in both places.

The contemporary Western author, in both the United States
and Ireland, writes in the shadow of giants—in the former, Owen
Wister and Mary Austin; and, in the latter, Lady Augusta Gregory,
W. B. Yeats, and J. M. Synge. In regard to the American West, Richard White has noted that "late-nineteenth-century Americans imagined the West—that most modern of American sections—as the premodern world that they had lost. In it, life was primitive but also
simple, real, and basic. Every action in this world mattered, and the
fundamental decisions of everyday life supposedly involved clear moral
choices. Life in the West could restore authenticity, moral order, and
masculinity" (619). In Ireland, during that same period, as Declan
Kiberd has pointed out, a similar dynamic was at play:

> The tramp or wanderer in Yeats's poems is one who knows "the
> exorbitant dreams of beggary," the relation between imaginative
> sumptuousness and material destitution. If Augusta Gregory was
> impressed on her visits to Galway workhouses by the contrasts be-
> tween the poverty and the splendor of their tales, Yeats could see in
> these deracinated figures an image of Anglo-Ireland on the skids.

So did Synge, who signed his love letters to Molly Allgood "Your Old Tramp." (*Irish Classics* 444)

Just as Gregory, Yeats, and Synge associated the poverty of local Westerners with creativity and (enforced) antimaterialism, so, too, did American writers make similar claims about indigenous Western Americans, "Hemingway's appropriations of Indianness served to define and revitalize white manliness, a gesture whose genealogy can be traced, at least in part, to his western antecedent. . . . Like Hemingway, Mary Austin associated Indianness with authenticity and health, echoing Wister's desire to infuse white American identity with 'native' status" (Tuttle 106). For Yeats's beggar, we can substitute Hemingway's Indian. Also, when Wister decries, in his 1895 essay "The Evolution of a Cow-Puncher," "'the encroaching alien vermin' that infested the country and threatened to 'degrade our commonwealth from a nation into something half pawn-shop, half-broker's office,'" we are reminded of Revivalist ideology (Scharnhorst 116). As I demonstrate throughout this study, contemporary writers are engaged directly in intense dialogues with Revival writers, in part to debunk what seems unreal; though, more important to their shared purpose, are needs to define personal literary spaces that are in tune with their time in history.

Writing on the difference between local and national representations of the American West, White has noted:

The creation of an imagined West by those who lived in a place and sought to bond themselves to it seems readily understandable, but the creation of an imagined West by those who lived outside the West and have few or no ties to the place itself is more mysterious. Yet it is the critical issue, for the nationally imagined West has been far more powerful than the locally imagined West. It has, when necessary, put local traditions to its own uses and shaped local myths in its own image. (619–20)

In the Irish context, we can add international to national and agree that White's thesis holds true. Perhaps no West of Ireland work has been as widely disseminated or as influential in defining the region for audiences as John Ford's film, *The Quiet Man*. This same issue reappears in any discussion of Martin McDonagh's plays: his imagined West is the most powerful in terms of its popularity, though he is, of the seven writers considered in this study, the one who has spent the least time on the ground in the West. And, to muddy the waters a little more, Tim Robinson, who knows his area of the West better than anyone, is an Englishman. Unfortunately, essentialism has always played a role in literary discourse.

The men and women whose work is addressed here represent a mere sampling. Such has been the quality of important work produced in the West of Ireland in recent times that it would be a simple task to come up with alternative lists of writers for study, not to mention those who spend seasons in the West—summers, usually—and who have left us a wealth of distinguished material. In some instances, the conclusions reached might be similar; in others, they might be quite different. All the while, new writers are emerging throughout the West and insisting that their voices be heard. Absent from this study are the Irish-language writers who continue to occupy a prominent place. I had thought of including them; however, I found that my long absence from Ireland had degraded my ability to examine their work with confidence—my own Irish-language skills were not equal to the task. But, throughout this study, I have explored the role played by the Irish language in English-language texts. In addition to texts/authors directly quoted from or alluded to, the bibliography found at the end of this volume includes the works of other scholars whose books and articles have helped me to develop my own arguments.

Overall, my hope is that this study will persuade readers to think of the West of Ireland as a unique literary territory, where writers explore landscape and language and the human and nonhuman worlds with eyes fixed, simultaneously, on both the active world outside their windows and the inner world where tradition resides. The West is integral to Ireland, though also separate from the more abstract nation. The Western writer is always a Western writer first.

One

ADEQUATE STEPS

Tim Robinson's *Stones of Aran*

Tim Robinson's Aran Islands volumes, *Stones of Aran: Pilgrimage* (1986) and *Stones of Aran: Labyrinth* (1995), are two of the most celebrated texts to emerge from Ireland in recent decades and they have found favor and garnered influence across disciplines and readerships. Taken together, these companion volumes amount to an extraordinary and encyclopedic survey of Árainn, the largest of the Aran Islands, or Inishmore, as it is more popularly known. So wide-ranging are Robinson's objectives and interests that the reader will find multiple open doors to walk through from which he/she can begin a detailed analysis of the works themselves, and of Robinson's myriad achievements as an author. For the purposes of this essay, the following aspects present in *Stones of Aran* will be examined: the use of walking as an enabling and framing device; the issues that arise from Robinson's tangled relationships with cartography, various geographies, and debates over colonization and decolonization; the literariness of Robinson's texts and their engagements with the work of other writers who have also responded to Inishmore; the place that *Stones of Aran* occupies among writings produced by English contemporaries of Robinson who have also traveled overseas to examine community lives in distant places; and Robinson's placing of *Stones of Aran* within the organic whole of his own life as a visual and verbal artist. Also, an attempt will be made to describe the overall shape and attitude present in his work. Central here will be issues of form and genre that *Stones of Aran* bring to light, and the many linkages forged between map-making and mapping, and writing. In *Setting Foot on the Shores of Connemara,* Robinson makes the following distinction: "accumulating impressions in a diary, I became a writer; and then, noting placenames and routes and locations on paper, a cartographer" (212). This is a guiding trope of his work. In addition, this discussion will range widely into the Anglophone world and beyond to address Robinson's achievements in relation to those of his contemporaries.

Inspired by Robert Flaherty's *Man of Aran* (1932), Robinson first came to Aran in the summer of 1972 and later lived full-time on Inishmore with his partner for a number of years, learning Irish, and becoming part of island society. At the suggestion of the postmistress of Cill Mhuirbhigh, who had noticed his "hand for the drawing, an ear for placenames and legs for the boreens," Robinson set about drawing maps of the island that would be useful to visitors (*Pilgrimage* 11). Before his arrival in Ireland, Robinson, who was born and raised in Yorkshire, had studied Mathematics at Cambridge and worked as a visual artist and teacher in Istanbul, Vienna, and London. Published in 1975, Robinson's first map found favor with islanders and tourists alike and brought him into contact with various experts who visited Inishmore and sought him out as a guide. From these experts and from his own readings, Robinson developed a deep understanding of the complexity of the topography of the island, and the various ways it had been layered by the passing of time. These contacts drew him deeper into its *dinnsenachas,* or lore of place. The more he learned, the more complex the island grew for him, and the more he doubted the simple tropes that underlined the functional maps he had drawn; clearly, there was more to a place than its roads, buildings, hills, and so on. Each road, for example, was nuanced and detailed, not merely a line drawn between settlements, Robinson discovered; and landscapes, as he points out, "cannot themselves be shown or named," for the minimal language of maps, not to mention the problematic nature of language, is never quite pliable enough to convey the ineffable spirit of place (*Pilgrimage* 11). He found, as Melville had before him, that maps can conceal more than they reveal: "It's not down in any map; true places never are" (Smyth 54). To map Inishmore, or to *deepmap* it, to borrow William Least Heat-Moon's term, would require a larger narrative structure than could be provided by "simple" cartography.

Throughout his work, Robinson is engaged in various negotiations with the principles of map-making (cartography) and mapping (geography) as intense as those already taking place within these disciplines themselves. From the outset, as a result of his training in the postmodern visual arts, and even before he knows better, Robinson is prepared to dispute received practice across a variety of disciplines. In this respect, his discovery of the limits of maps is similar to that articulated by the American writer Barry Lopez in *Desert Notes*: "Your confidence in these finely etched maps is understandable, for at first glance they seem excellent, the best a man is capable of; but your confidence is misplaced. Throw them out. They are the wrong sort of map. They are too thin. They are not the sort of map that can be followed by a man who knows what he is doing—the coyote, even the crow, would regard them with suspicion" (Least Heat-Moon 4).

Looking back, Robinson understood that his early maps were "preliminary storings and sortings of material for another art, the world-hungry art of words" (*Pilgrimage* 11). Like *PrairyErth,* Least Heat-Moon's account of the landscape of the Flint Hills of Kansas, Robinson's *deepmap* of Inishmore is a prose narrative composed from disparate parts—a kind of bricolage—that looks toward literary rather than cartographic models for its form. Literary language, for all of its limitations, is the mode best suited to an intense examination that reaches for the totality of place. For Robinson, as for N. Scott Momaday in *The Way to Rainy Mountain,* the writer, in order to succeed at the task, would have to devote all of his learned faculties to the landscape under review, and to listen to its many resonant voices. Here is Momaday's injunction:

> Once in his life a man ought to concentrate his mind upon the re-
> membered earth, I believe. He ought to give himself up to a particu-
> lar landscape in his experience, to look at it from as many angles as
> he can, to wonder about it, to dwell upon it. He ought to imagine
> that he touches it with his hands at every season and listens to the
> sounds that are made upon it. He ought to imagine the creatures
> there and all the faintest motions of the wind. He ought to recollect
> the glare of noon and all the colors of the dawn and dusk. (Least
> Heat-Moon 4)

To achieve his objective, Robinson first found it necessary to unlearn
many aspects of his own cultural inheritance in order to hear the resonant, deep murmurings of place. Later, however, looking back, he
would note the extent to which his Aran explorations had had their
roots both in his own childhood and in aspects of the adult life he
had led before arriving in Ireland. Also, like his American contemporary Least Heat-Moon, he would have to find an original narrative
form for his *deepmap*, one that could somehow fuse together elements
drawn from cartography, the various sciences, and literature. He would
practice three arts on Inishmore — map-making, mapping, and writing, all three informed by his earlier years as a visual artist.

At the same time, Robinson must have felt singularly unprepared
to perform the tasks at hand. Certainly, he was possessed of bound-
less enthusiasm and a sound education. However, he did not know the
Irish language, nor was he conversant in the various disciplines that the
job required: anthropologist, historian, folklorist, geologist, natural scientist. Also, how could an outsider — an Englishman, no less — find
a way to penetrate Inishmore's oral culture where its maps are written
the deepest? It seemed unlikely that one man could successfully dupli-
cate the work of many, that Robinson could, in effect, become a one-
man Clare Island survey transposed to late-twentieth-century Inishmore. Had not T. S. Eliot persuaded us that the Renaissance man, with
his well-rounded store of knowledge, had disappeared in the early part
of the seventeenth century? It was no longer possible, given specialization and the emergence of the various sciences, for one person to know
everything required to comprehensively describe a place and its people,

and all that was connected to their history, however small or large that place happened to be. There is also an inherent element in the Robinsons' arrival on Inishmore of the 1960s hippie clarion call to get away from it all, of the naive departure from the anarchic and competitive city for the more wholesome and community-oriented remote island. Indeed, it is one thing to go to West Cork to make organic cheese, but quite another to travel unprepared to Inishmore to recreate the many-sided consciousness that the island has accrued from its pre-history to its present. It looked possible for Robinson to reinvent himself as a skillful map-maker; however, it seemed highly unlikely that he would be able to pull off his foolhardy mapping project. Yet, succeed he did, and magnificently so, on both fronts.

In recent decades, a good deal has been written in regard to the connection between walking and writing, with much of the primary focus being on the work of the Romantics, and on Dorothy and William Wordsworth, in particular. Most scholars have noted the shift that took place in the late eighteenth century when the perception of walking changed from a physical activity associated with poverty and toil to one connected with leisure and creativity. Morris Marples has pointed out that "poetry and pedestrianism seem very often to have gone hand in hand during the years when the influence of Wordsworth was supreme. They parted company as the nineteenth century advanced, and have only in a few special instances, such as that of Edward Thomas, been united again since those days" (67). And the Victorians, Marples points out, were prodigious walkers: "[Thomas] De Quincy calculated that by the age of sixty-five Wordsworth must have covered from 175,000 to 180,000 miles: he still had fifteen years of walking before him" (37). In America, we learn that two of Thoreau's most popular public lectures had walking as their subjects, talks that were eventually fused together into "Walking," an essay published in *The Atlantic Monthly* just after his death in 1862. Thoreau wrote: "I think I cannot preserve my health and spirits, unless I spend four hours a day at least—and it is commonly more than that—sauntering through the woods and over the hills and fields, absolutely free from all worldly engagements" (294). In the twentieth century in *Charles Baudelaire: A Lyric Poet in the Era of High Capitalism*, Walter Benjamin reminds us of the extent to which the walker was also an urban figure, as does Raymond Williams in *The Country and the City*. Nowadays, in a practice rooted in Romantic ideology, walking forms part of the ecological consciousness and imperative — a good example of this being Gary Snyder's essay, "Blue Mountains Constantly Walking" (Snyder 200–213). However, for the purposes of exploring the role played by walking in Robinson's Aran books, the major supporting texts will be Rebecca Solnit's *Wanderlust: A History of Walking* (2000) and Robin Jarvis's *Romantic Writing and Pedestrian Travel* (1997).

In *The View from the Horizon* (1997), a backward look at his career, Robinson focuses on the "good step" and the "adequate step" as his guiding markers. He has articulated this at length:

> But the notion of the adequate step, a momentary congruence between the culture one bears and the ground that bears one, eventually shatters against reality into uncountable fragments, the endless variety of steps that are more or less good enough for one or two aspects of the here and now. These splinters might be put together into a more serviceable whole by paying more heed to their cumulative nature, to the steps' repeatability, variability, reversibility and expendability. The step, so mobile, so labile, so nimbly coupling place and person, mood and matter, occasion and purpose, begins to emerge as a metaphor of a certain way of living on this earth. It is a momentary proposition put by the individual to the non-individual, an instant of trust which may not be well-founded, a not-quite-infallible catching of oneself in the art of falling. Stateless, the step claims a foot-long nationality every second. Having endlessly variable grounds, it needs no faith. The idea of freedom is associated in dozens of turns of phrase with that of the step. To the footloose all boundaries, whether academic or national, are mere administrative impertinences. With this freebooter's license there goes every likelihood of superficiality, restlessness, fickleness and transgression — and so, by contraries, goes the possibility of recurrency, of frequentation, of a deep, and even-deeper, dwelling in and on a place, a sum of whims and fancies totaling a constancy as of stone. (27–28)

From the outset, walking is the activity and trope that will frame the work. Instinctively, given his unpreparedness for his ambitious mapping project, Robinson has chosen the right approach, as Solnit reminds us: "The history of walking is an amateur history, just as walking is an amateur art. To use a walking metaphor, it trespasses through everybody else's field—through anatomy, anthropology, architecture, gardening, geography, political and cultural history, literature, sexuality, religious studies—and doesn't step in any of them on its long route" (4). Also, Solnit points out, "one aspect of the history of walking is the history of thinking made concrete—for the motions of the mind cannot be traced, but those of the feet can" (6).

Practically, walking was the only possible way for Robinson to examine the island in detail, to get to know it at the slowest possible pace, though, as Solnit reminds us, it was also the entryway for the amateur, his accidental method of transgression into the experts' discrete spaces. In addition, walking immediately connected the process of discovery to that of writing—the literary work being formed, at its most basic level, by the space and the foot. In his thinking, Robinson found himself in distinguished company. Edmund Husserl, according to Solnit, "described walking as an experience by which we understand our body in relationship to the world," something that dovetailed perfectly with Robinson's ambition to replicate the seals' engagement with their environment (27). And writing of Rousseau, Solnit argues:

> A solitary walker is in the world, but apart from it, with the detachment of the traveler rather than the ties of the worker, the dweller, the member of the group. Walking seems to have become Rousseau's chosen mode of being because within a walk he is able to live in thought and reverie, to be self-sufficient, and thus to survive the world he feels has betrayed him. It provides him with a literal position from which to speak. As a literary structure, the recounted walk encourages digression and association, in contrast to the stricter form of discourse or the chronological progression of a biographical or historical narrative. (21)

Even though Robinson does not, unlike Rousseau, believe that the world has betrayed him, he is, at the same time, a man who fled to Inishmore in 1972 from a London art scene in which he felt isolated. Inishmore provided him with a subject, and walking, with a mode. *Stones of Aran* is both chronological and associative: the geologic steps, for instance, are examples of the former, whereas the random nature of the landscape often calls for the latter. Like Joyce's *Ulysses,* to borrow Karen Lawrence's theory, *Stones of Aran* is another of those works that embarks on a formal and stylistic odyssey to be better able to respond to the imperatives of a changing and unpredictable landscape. In great part, *Ulysses* is shaped by Dublin; so, as the city turns, so does the novel. A similar dynamic is present in *Stones of Aran* and, because of this, Robinson, like Joyce before him, inherits an organic, though rudimentary form. Robinson's solitariness allows him to encounter place intensely, without interruption, while his detachment makes it possible for him to see these same spaces objectively—both as a scientist and as a writer interested in literary form.

Also, walking implies a faith in slowness, and it comes with a lack of ostentation: it is the ideal mode of progress—walking before running—for the beginner. It was also well-suited to Robinson's own temperament, innate abilities, and admitted weaknesses: "I cannot dance, perhaps because dancing takes place on the flat, on a surface that suggests no rhythms and leaves my will floundering in self-consciousness; instead I aspire to a compensating gift of walking, not in a way that overcomes the land but in one that commends every accident and essence of it to my bodily balance and understanding" (*Setting Foot* 5). Evident here is the connection between the physical body and the literary work, which illumines Robinson's prose and brings his reader into close contact with Inishmore. Also, we can trace a connection between walking and form. Just as walking across the landscape requires a series of realignments between the body and the terrain, so, too, must the literary form be aligned to account for the recorder's progress and discoveries. In this regard, *Stones of Aran* can also be profitably read in the light of Charles Olson's "Projective Verse," as both are focused on notions of space and accident. The more one thinks about *Stones of Aran,* the more clearly one can note its sophistication of purpose and execution and its alignment with Anglophone writing of the highest caliber. As is the case with *Ulysses, Stones of Aran* is another of those works informed and turned by random encounters with people.

Except for the recordings of personal epiphanies, Robinson's prose is plain and to the point:

> I start at the eastern end of the island. The road from Cill Rónáin through Cill Éinne continues past the last village, Iaráirne, and then makes a sharp turn north to a little bay; there is a stile in the wall at that turn from which a faint field-path continues the line of the road eastward, across smooth turf in which hosts of rabbits are digging sandpits, to the exact spot I have in mind. Here one can sit among the wild pansies and Lady's bedstraw with the low rocky shore at one's feet, and get one's bearings. Behind and to the left is level ground of sandy fields, and dunes in the distance. To the right the land rises in stony slopes to the ruins of an ancient watchtower on the skyline. A mile and half ahead across the sound is Inish Meáin; the third island, Inis Oírr, is hidden behind it, but the hills of the Burren in County Clare appear beyond, a dozen miles away. Since the three islands and that north-western corner of Clare were once continuous—before the millions of years of weathering, the glaciers of the Ice Ages and the inexhaustible waves cut the sea-ways between them—the land forms visible out there, a little abstracted as they are by distance, can be seen as images of Árainn itself in the context of its geological past, and it is valuable to read them thus before going out on a clamber among the details and complexities of the way ahead, so that an otherwise inchoate mass of impressions may find an ordering and a clarification. (*Pilgrimage* 17)

Sentence structures are as variable as the seen world—short and compact at the outset, "I start at the eastern end of the island," to longer and more meandering ones governed by semicolons and dashes, when the lens is widened to record a panorama. At the same time, Robinson's is a transgressive text—a walk across the garden of literary genres—that can play fast and loose with tradition, though for these turnings, given his training as a visual artist, Robinson came well-prepared. At its most basic level, walking is the primary building block of Robinson's methodology and underlines his style. At the levels of form, diction, and syntax, his work exhibits what Jarvis finds will occur when walking and writing are aligned: "Beyond this, there are other formal characteristics of walking—irregularity of line, seriality and progression, non-synthesizability, and so forth—that one might expect would have aesthetic repercussions in some of the most sophisticated versions of peripatetic" (70). Even though Jarvis's analysis is supported primarily by his readings of the Romantic poets, Coleridge in particular, his conclusions are certainly applicable to Robinson's work.

Writing of William Hazlitt, Jarvis notes the degree to which, for him, walking was liberating: "for Hazlitt, walking unhinges the socially constructed and maintained self, places it in suspension, allowing the mind to become a screen on which the passing image is momentarily projected, overdubbed with ideas and memories generated according to associationist principles" (193). Similarly, Robinson is allowed a similar type of suspension, a tabula rasa on which to record his Inishmore engagement, and a formula to make it work: "I had a formula to guide me and whip me on through the thickets of difficulties I encountered: while walking the land, I am the pen on the paper; while drawing this map, my pen is myself walking the land. The purpose of this identification was to short circuit the polarities of objectivity and subjectivity, and help me keep faith with reality" (*Setting Foot* 77).

At a deep level, he felt it necessary to erase huge parts of his inherited worldview to arrive at the blank slate that would be the starting point for his Aran adventure. To some degree, as Robinson points out, this choice was made for him: "If so drastic a step as abandoning a career and a home, each of them close to a sort of cultural centrality, for an unknown language, an untried art and 'a wet rock in the Atlantic' is not sufficient to shake one's deepest vocabulary, then where is there a possibility of self-transcendence?" (*The View from the Horizon* 16). Starting out, he had no sense that his work would ever be published. Attached to this, whether intentional or not, is a definite Zen consciousness. Think of Japhy Ryder in *Dharma Bums*—"The closer you get to real matter, rock air fire wood, boy, the more spiritual the world is"—and of Gary Snyder, the real Japhy, in another context—"This is Zen. To give a hundred percent and know it does not matter" (Solnit 146). Robinson knew that his work might never find a readership, but he was undeterred because, at the very least, it promised him the possibility of forging for himself a more intense engagement with Inishmore, its past and its present. *Stones of Aran* is process- rather than end-driven, concerned with establishing a fine attentiveness, facilitated by walking, and with drawing the reader into the objects of the landscape in which its spirits reside.

It is an epiphany, that most literary of inventions, that sets Robinson on his journey. One summer's day on Inishmore, he saw two or three dolphins cavorting close to shore, so he waded out among them "until they were passing and repassing within a few yards of me" (*Pilgrimage* 12). Robinson noted the ease with which the dolphins inhabited their world: "Yet their unity with their background was no jellyfish-like dalliance with dissolution; their mode of being was an intensification of their medium into alert, reactive self-awareness; they were wave made flesh, with minds solely to ensure the moment-by-moment reintegration of body and world" (*Pilgrimage* 12). At first, the dolphins' grace and connectedness to their world left Robinson feeling despondent: he thought that he could never experience such an intense degree of engagement with *his* world. Then, thinking of language as a vehicle for delivering to others our knowledge of the world, he realized that it might be possible for a man on Inishmore to replicate some parts of his own sense of belonging to a place: "A dolphin may be its own poem, but we have to find our rhymes elsewhere, between words in literature, between things in science, and our way back to the world involves us in an endless proliferation of detours" (*Pilgrimage* 12).

Thus persuaded, Robinson set out to create his *deepmap* of Inishmore, and his search for an overarching form is similar to what Least Heat-Moon searched for, and found, for *PrairyErth*:

> I am standing on Roniger Hill to test the shape of what I'm going to write about this prairie place. For thirty months, maybe more,

I've come and gone here and have found stories to tell, but, until last week, I had not discovered the way to tell them. My searches and re-searches, like my days, grew more randomly than otherwise, and every form I tried contorted them, and each time I began to press things into cohesion, I edged not so much toward fiction as toward distortion, when what I wanted was accuracy; even when I got a de-tail down accurately, I couldn't hook to the next without concocting theories. It was connections that deviled me. I was hunting a fact or image and not a thesis to hold my details together, and so I arrived at this question: should I just gather up items like creek pebbles into a bag and then let them tumble into their own pattern? Did I really want the reality of randomness? Answer: only if it would yield a landscape with figures, one that would unroll like a Chinese scroll painting or a bison-skin drawing where both beginnings and ends of an event are at once present in the conflated time of the American Indian. The least I hoped for was a topographic map of words that would open inch by inch to show its long miles. (15)

Least Heat-Moon's area is larger than Robinson's—Kansas's Chase County is thirty miles long north to south, twenty-six miles east to west on the south border, and a mile shorter on the north, whereas Inishmore is similar in size to the island of Manhattan, and Robinson's work is shaped differently. *PrairyErth* is formed and shaped by alter-nating chapters in which the author's narratives are preceded and fol-lowed by excepts from various texts—literary, historical, folk, scien-tific, governmental, and so on. The reader is guided through these chapters and asked to forge his/her own connections. Unlike Robinson in *Stones of Aran,* Least Heat-Moon in *PrairyErth* does not seek an en-cyclopedic view of the place under examination; however, he does sug-gest, persuasively and quite beautifully, that the Flint Hills are so com-plex that such a view could be easily entertained. Throughout, both men touch on and explore what is on and under the landscape, literally as well as metaphorically. The deep-rooted circular motion that Robin-son describes is also important to Least Heat-Moon. *Pilgrimage,* the first part of *Stones of Aran,* is a procession around the perimeter of In-ishmore, that pays homage to ancient and enduring traditions:

The circuit that blesses is clockwise, or, since the belief is thousands of years older than the clock, sunwise. It is the way the fireworshipper's swastika turns, and its Christianized descendent St. Bridget's cross. Visitors to holy wells make their "rounds" so, seven times with prayers. This book makes just one round of Árainn, though seven could not do justice to the place, and with eyes raised to this world rather than lowered in prayer. On Easter Fridays in past centuries the Aran folk used to walk around the island keeping as close to the coast as possible, and although nothing has been recorded on the question it is inconceivable that they should have made the circuit other than in the right-handed sense. This writing will lead in their footsteps, not at their penitential trudge but at an inquiring, digressive and wondering pace. (*Pilgrimage* 17)

Least Heat-Moon finds in *Black Elk Speaks* the following adage: "The Power of the World works in circles, and everything tries to be round" (215). The circular notion of time is explored by Peter Matthiessen in *The Snow Leopard,* another of the texts quoted by Least Heat-Moon: "Since concepts of Karma and circular time are taken for granted by almost all American Indian traditions, time as space and death as becoming are implicit in the earth-view of the Hopi, who avoid all linear constructions, knowing as well as any Buddhist that everything is Right Here Now. As in the great religions of the East, the American Indian makes small distinction between religious activity and the acts of everyday; the religious ceremony is life itself" (Least Heat-Moon 604).

For the Aran Islanders, who have fused the pagan and Christian together psychically and ceremonially, the circular motion of the walk around the island is a living link to their ancient past, where the circular was a privileged pattern, while the transubstantiation underlying the Catholic Mass is both ceremony and life itself. Walking combines the practical and the sacred; in fact, often one cannot exist without the other. For Robinson's purposes, given the nature of Inishmore's topography, walking was the necessary mode of discovery (he often bicycled to the point where his walking began), but it was also a mode that allowed him to step, quietly and reverently, onto the body of the island where he could listen to all that had accrued in its resonant heart. In *Pilgrimage,* he meanders around the coast recording and interpreting what he finds. In *Labyrinth,* he attempts the even more complex task of mapping the interior. For Robinson, Inishmore will not only be surveyed in its own right, but it will also serve as "*the* exemplary terrain" that informs our knowledge of the world as a whole, the little informing the large, the micro the macro, and vice versa (*The View from the Horizon* 25–26).

By laying down specific markers, such as the six ways that walkers experience landscape, Jarvis is able to draw connections between the act of walking and its role in the creation of literary works. He notes that the pedestrian's experience of landscape "is a *participatory* rather than a disinterested one"; that his/her "experience of the world is a slowly but continuously changing field of appearances"; that "the volitional character of walking" can clear the mind of the detritus of everyday life; that the walker will "at best feel equal, and often unequal, to his/her surroundings" though never their master, as a motorist might; that as a result of his/her walking pace, the "pedestrian is more alert to the multiplicity of appearances and the particularity of actual landscapes"; and that the walker's "dominant mental state is towards . . . the 'progressional ordering of reality'"(67–70). Clearly, all of these generalizations can be seen as underlying elements that make *Stones of Aran* succeed as a literary work. Also, they form Robinson's attitude toward Inishmore. He is intensely involved in his work while, at the same time, he maintains a level of detachment to ensure that the primary focus is on place rather than on its recorder, and what he encounters is as constantly changing as the ground under his feet. What is written follows the chosen order of the walk; therefore, it is modest in attitude but detailed in its bulk, a record of one man's fine-tuned attentiveness. Walking also serves, as Jarvis has pointed out, to clear the mind of what has been problematic and painful; in Robinson's case, his dissatisfaction with the London art scene. We can say, therefore, that *Stones of Aran* is concerned with both walking and walking away.

In a detailed examination of a passage from Coleridge's prose, recounting his Harz mountains tour of 1799, Jarvis notes the lack of

"separation here of mind and body" and observes his "body [respond-
ing] to the altering health of the mind, visual and aesthetic stimuli
apparently bringing revitalization of the walker's battered 'frame,'" a
mode of action and recognition that is also present in Robinson's work
(132–33). Also, both Coleridge and Robinson use various geometric
figures, such as cones, to account for the variability of their respective
landscapes. Moreover, Robinson, formerly a mathematician and visual
artist, draws such figures and includes them throughout his work. As
already noted, he prefers walking on uneven ground to dancing on a
level surface, the former suiting the rhythms of his body, and this is
also true of Coleridge, who preferred "'walking over uneven ground'. . .
a landscape that offered resistance to the body-in-motion" (Jarvis 134).
Coleridge, often the most troubled of men, "found this infinity of per-
ceptions exaggerated by the sensuous experience of pedestrian travel,
and seems to have found it exciting and therapeutic, a temporary escape from the 'unrelieved pain' of existential isolation," which corre-
sponds to what Robinson has written about his removal from London
(Jarvis 135). For both men, as Jarvis points out in regard to Coleridge,
walking in a new place was liberating:

> Annihilating the present tense is also to remove the ground of stable
> selfhood, suspending the subject between difference and deferral,
> memory and anticipation. However much Coleridge may have
> yearned for secure anchorage in his personal life, there was a parallel
> and contrary need to remove himself from all localizing, defining
> associations and commitments, to re-experience what he calls (in
> reflecting on his passion for solitary travel) "a sort of *bottom-wind*,
> that blows to no point of the compass, & comes from I know not
> whence, but agitates the whole of me." (Jarvis 135)

There is a similar dualism in Robinson's life, though it does not present itself as a dichotomy in the manner of Coleridge's. For Robinson,
it was the secure anchorage of his personal life—his relationship with
his Irish-born partner Máiréad, who is constantly extolled in his books
and with whom he also shares a business partnership in the Folding
Landscapes publishing house—that brought him to Ireland. At the

same time, it is equally clear from *Stones of Aran* that Robinson is, in large part, a solitary man who has spent long periods of time wandering alone through the Irish West. For both Robinson and Coleridge, walking must be as solitary as writing. For Coleridge, walking was a means of separating himself from society; for Robinson, walking has remained a mode of entering into a new society, a way of connecting with another set of individuals and the place they have marked and defined with their lives and traditions. It should be noted, however, that his most recent book, *Connemara: The Last Pool of Darkness* (2008), a journey from Killary Harbour to Slyne Head, is the most sociable work that he has published to date.

It would be unwise, as Jarvis reminds us, "to expect that all these qualities of 'the mind of the walker' will be comprehensively encoded in every piece of walking literature from the Romantic period onwards," and it would be even more foolish to claim that *Stones of Aran* is a book *about* walking Inishmore — it is not (70). For Robinson, it is a means to an end, one governed by necessity: going on foot was the only method of progress available to him. At the same time, Jarvis presents a great deal of compelling evidence, from such prosodic theorists as David Abercrombie, R. H. Stetson, and others, to show the extent to which the writing of prose is connected to, and even derived from, the movement of the body. Equally, Robinson's notion of the "adequate step" (24) is a metaphor, but it is also the literal connector between methodology, body, and prose. Instinctively, he certainly knew where he was going.

When his career is taken as a whole, Robinson will be seen as both a map-maker and a mapper. Generally speaking, his narrative volumes comprise the latter, with his work published by Folding Landscapes accounting for the former. In *Stones of Aran*, maps of Inishmore, the Aran Islands, Galway, and Clare are included at the end of each volume as part of the scholarly apparatus, seeming to carry a weight equal to the volumes' index, acknowledgments, and references. From this secondary positioning, they do not appear to be central to Robinson's explorations; instead, their presence is intended as a guide to orient the reader. The maps seem, as Robinson has articulated, inadequate when contrasted with his complex text and, perhaps ironically, even highlight the issues of omission that the text seeks to address. But both text and maps are interdependent: one cannot be read without the other. It would not have been possible for Robinson to proceed without the work that already had been undertaken by the Ordnance Survey, and this dependence drew him into the mire of colonial history, into issues and principles raised and contested within the disciplines of cartography and historical and cultural geography.

As has been already suggested, *Stones of Aran* is a transgressive text, and no more so than in respect to the inroads it makes into various academic territories. It should become clear, however, from an examination of some of the major contemporary debates taking place within the disciplines of map-making and mapping, that *Stones of Aran*, the contribution of an outsider, has been a prescient and timely work, and that Inishmore is an exemplary space for the laying out of often contending theories and approaches. As he crossed the landscape/space of Inishmore, Robinson not only walked its roads, paths, and fields but also crossed headlong into the centers of many raging debates in the field of geography. At the same time, it will become evident that Robinson's practice intersects with those of other geographers (cartographers, and cultural and human geographers in particular), such as Brian Harley, John Mannion, William J. Smyth, John Szegö, and Kevin Whelan, many of whom are also his contemporaries. *Stones of Aran* is a meeting text where contending views are subliminally aired and where Robinson achieves the sage synthesis that is at the heart of his work.

In *Mapping: Ways of Representing the World*, Daniel Dorling and David Fairbairn note that "the discipline of geography has had a long association with colonization and empire building, but it is also possible to argue that cartography has had an even deeper involvement than this. The writer who has opened up this field more than any other, Brian Harley, saw maps as weapons of imperialism which were at least the equal of guns and warships" (73). Like Robinson, Harley was the product of an English grammar-school education who went on to university and helped to redefine many aspects of the field in which he worked. As is the case in literary studies, where sharp divisions between scholars allow texts to be read in often mutually exclusive ways, so, too, do geographers respond to various geographic phenomena differently, with many of these newer modes of interpretation emerging in recent decades and having their roots in like ideologies:

> Beyond mere description, post-war geographers up to the 1960s attempted to discern order and establish rules governing spatial behaviour. Such universal laws were to be obtained by scientific investigation and to be rendered using mathematical and geometric language in a positivist manner. The neutrality of the observations undertaken by such "spatial scientists" relied on the notion of closed geographical systems within which humans operated, and the constrained nature of the map sheet and its stylized representation of reality proved the ideal source for initiating and conforming hypotheses. Of course, this view was forcibly challenged by Marxist geographers and others from the 1960s onwards who argued that such contextual issues and modifiers as social, economic, and political must be introduced and be part of the process of creating maps. These scholars reminded us that the making of maps is a subjective process and that the cartographer must carry with him an active store of received knowledge, or even bias, which will invariably find its way on his map. (Dorling and Fairbairn 2)

As Dorling and Fairbairn point out, this process has continued without pause; and we have now arrived at a point where, with the addition of feminist, social theoretical, structuralist, and other viewpoints, it is no longer possible to argue for the "prevalence of one particular paradigm" (2). In this respect, the recent history of cartography and geography mirrors that of literary studies where a similar reaction to literary formalism, called the New Criticism, erupted around the same time and was quickly challenged by even newer theoretical approaches to textual analysis. In both disciplines, it seems no longer possible to arrive at consensus. At the same time, there are aspects of the study of geography on which scholars do agree:

This lack of coherence in geography masks a fundamental observation that, although maps are viewed differently by different geographers, mapping is a vital geographic technique of study and maps are a primary tool. Some geographers (notably Hartshorne) have, in the past, considered that maps define the very nature of geography. All schools of geographic thought call attention to mapping as a geographic method. Indeed, it is so important to geography that mapping as a technique and the map as a tool are often the most critically analysed features when paradigm shifts occur in geography. (Dorling and Fairbairn 2)

Indeed, as Dorling and Fairbairn remind us: "Just as societies and civilizations vary enormously in their essential characteristics, so [do] their map representations vary—in purpose, scale, content and conceptions of accuracy. The physical creation of maps which embody the 'world-view' of such societies is the process of *map-making*. This can be distinguished from the mental interpretation of the world which is termed *mapping*" (3).

This distinction is not unlike the paradigm in literary studies, where the strict formalist, for example, will direct the reader to focus exclusively on the poem's inner workings, while his/her opposite will claim that no work can be read in this way because all works depend on their contexts (political, social, gender, etc.), and these contexts must underline any discussion of a work's value. However, just as map-makers and mappers depend on, and must begin with, the map, so, too, must literary scholars begin with the text. It is a prerequisite for scholars in both fields to be able readers of maps or poems in order to progress in any direction. Ideally, it would seem to me, the scholar should be able to read on multiple levels while remaining doctrine-neutral to all of them, because this will encourage an open mind. However, to those with horses in these various academic races, such a view will be considered naive, at best. Coming from outside the academy and lacking the strict training and sense of demarcation that it imposes on the professional student as a kind of article of faith, Robinson was able to blaze an original, though risky, path. He was entering the temple to lecture to the elders.

Robinson's relationship to map-making is complex, though it intersects with current cartographic theories in various ways. Taking a backward glance at his completed work in *Setting Foot on the Shores of Connemara*, he noted that "the making of a map, I soon found out, is many things as well as a work of art, and among others it is a political, or more exactly an ideological, act" (3). Following Harley, Robinson sees his own work in its political-postcolonial context: "the project I thought of as political, in that it aimed to undo some of the damage of colonialism and to uphold the local and vernacular against the leveling metropolitan culture of our times. But inevitably it was also a rescue-archaeology of a shallowly buried sacred landscape" (*My Time in Space* 95). He quickly understood the colonial push of the nineteenth-century Ordnance Survey, as clearly as Brian Friel had in *Translations*: "I am acutely aware of the fact that cartography has historically been associated with conquest, colonization, control. The Ordnance Survey was a function of the army. Therefore I have taken care that the mapping I have been essaying for the last quarter-century or so in the West of Ireland be one that returns the territory mapped to itself, to its inhabitants, and that I hope is not subject to the reproach of Éiru" (*My Time in Space* 99).

At the same time, like all map-makers and mappers, he has recognized and is thankful for the work produced by the Ordnance Survey, not least for the additional labor that it spared him from having to undertake:

> But I have not set myself up as a regional rival to the official map-makers, the Ordnance Survey, and this for two reasons. First, I need the Ordnance Survey's topographical accuracy as a basis for my own constructions of these landscapes; I do not want to spend my life remeasuring the toothy perimeters of these tiny fractions of geography, and my net is spread to catch other features of the world, including the otherworld itself as it shows itself through folklore and legend in this one. And secondly, the usual conventions of map-symbolism — the precise-looking smoothly sweeping contours, the generalized colour-coding of areas for height or vegetation cover,

the hard-and-fast line of high water mark, to mention but a few, all
useful in particular contexts — add up to a spurious claim of univer-
sality and objectivity, and I am ready to trade in some of this scientific legibility for a measure of freedom of expression, for room to
doubt. (*Setting Foot* 212)

He, too, like his academic colleagues, stresses the interdependence
that must bind together those men and women in the discipline. But
Robinson also admits that "although [I have] been making maps for a
dozen years now, cartography, in the sense of a general desire and com-
petence to make maps, remains alien to [me]" (*Setting Foot* 75). For
him, a map is also "a sustained attempt upon an unattainable goal, the
complete comprehension by an individual of a tract of space that will
be individualized in a place by that attempt" (77). Nor is he much interested in maps from a technical perspective: "I'm not very interested
in maps from the technical point of view, so I will be brief on how I
went about producing this one, and move on to the more interesting
questions of what it is like to make a map — insofar as I can untangle
my memories of the process — and why maps are, finally, so unsatis-
factory. For if cartography is not necessarily more helpless than other
modes of representation in the face of the world, it has its own characteristic failings, which the blanks on a map, essential to its legibility
as they are, reveal with disconcerting candour" (*Setting Foot* 78).

Despite a facility for drawing and his continuing work as a map-
maker, Robinson understood that the large scale of his endeavor —
"a rescue-archaeology of a shallowly buried sacred landscape" — could
not be achieved by means of map-making alone. To work toward his
ambitious end, he would need to resort to extended narrative; maps,
however, could provide a series of useful signposts and starting points.
In order for him to challenge the veracity of maps, he had to first understand how they worked, and this he accomplished by making them.
His views, and how he went about his *deepmapping* of Inishmore, echo
the sentiments of Doug Aberley, the western Canadian geographer,
who believes that "the making of maps has become dominated by specialists who wield satellites and other complex machinery. The result

is that although we have great access to maps, we have also lost the ability ourselves to conceptualize, make and use images of space—skills which our ancestors honed over thousands of years. In return for this surrendered knowledge, maps have been appropriated for uses which are more and more sinister" (Dorling and Fairbairn 141). By walking Inishmore and recording its presences, ancient and modern, Robinson seeks, as Aberley enjoins us, "to conceptualize, make and use images of space" (Dorling and Fairbairn 141). For Robinson, the term "space" recurs in his life and work—in the title of his autobiography, *My Time in Space*; and in his area of activity: "'landscape' has during the last decade become a key term in several disciplines; but I would prefer this body of work to be read in the light of 'Space'" (*Setting Foot* vi).

It was not until 1973 that the International Court of Justice eliminated the legality of the "concept of *terra nullius,* which was used to justify the westwards expansion of the United States of America, the settlement of Australia and the colonization of Africa," itself a theory of space similar to that faced by the writer and artist (Dorling and Fairbairn 88). Quickly, Robinson learned how full of signs and symbols was this empty space. In his visual art and writing, the canvas or page facing Robinson is only superficially blank—it is quickly encoded by the artist's/author's personality. The landscape of Inishmore—or its space, as Robinson would prefer—had already been heavily encoded by colonization, and it was one of the purposes of his *deepmapping* to give voice to those elements that had been removed.

In addition, the direction of Robinson's work reflects the principles set out by Common Ground, an organization founded in London in 1983 and facilitated by Harley's work, whose motto was "Know Your Place—Make a Map of It." This successful initiative placed nonexperts at the center of map-making, devolving the discipline in interesting ways. Further, Robinson's work as a cartographer and his general thinking as a geographer can be seen to dovetail in various ways with those of such Swedish scholars as Szegö, Torsten Hägerstrand, and Gunner Olsson. Szegö's humanist geography focuses on issues of space; Hägerstrand brings a variety of narrative forms into his work, such as short stories; and Olsson declares that "geography is a form of imagination," thereby placing cartography at the intersection of map-making, mapping, and the literary and visual arts (Olsson iii). Throughout the debate within geography, one notes many theories of those same scholars whose work has been central to contemporary literary studies, Michel Foucault and Berthold Auerbach in particular. Given that issues of power, representation, and language are important in both disciplines, this is hardly surprising.

An endlessly fascinating and quite beautiful recent work of academic scholarship in the discipline of geography is William J. Smyth's *Map-making, Landscapes and Memory: A Geography of Colonial and Early Modern Ireland, c. 1530–1750,* and it is instructive to place this work alongside Robinson's Aran volumes in order to compare the academic and "amateur" visions of map-making and mapping. From the outset, it is clear that for Smyth, as for the Swedish school, and for Robinson, the work of the geographer should be an interdisciplinary art with the interdependence of the visual and narrative spaces constantly stressed. As Smyth indicates, disciplines cross and intrude on one another in illuminating ways: "Since the task of the historical geographer is to track, map and interpret patterns and processes of geographical change, a central concern of this study involves the geographical construction of Ireland, its societies and regions before New English plantation and colonization, and a geographic exploration of the nature and varying effects of such intrusive processes on existing Irish societies and landscapes" (xix).

Like Robinson, Smyth begins with the age of the land and reminds us that "the ideology and, indeed, central values of the culture were wrapped up in the landscape—its occupation, its use, its names, stories and legends" (3). For both authors, the land/landscape/space is seen not just as being body-like, but as indeed being a body, though hardly the gendered version of more recent nationalist vintage. In common with the human body, the landscape of Ireland is a densely layered and complexly encoded space to which the map can only serve as a guide, an imperfect doorway leading into a narrative text. Smyth reminds us that, prior to the Elizabethan period, "as far as we know, the Irish did not use maps; measuring/overseeing with the eye (*do reir sultomhuis*) and walking the land may have been the critical skills for

assessing the size of the small areal units and their land-use potential" (74). Central to the Gaelic sense of mapping was memory (oral)
rather than the map (drawn), and "this land memory involved not only
a recognition of the history and landholding patterns amongst families
but also knowledge over the middle and long term of how the names
of places are actually changed to reflect these oscillations in kin-group
power" (75). When Robinson's work is examined in this context, we
can conclude that what he has achieved is a re-reading of the landscape
that privileges an ancient Irish methodology over the imperial one
introduced by the English in the sixteenth century. On a surface level,
our sense of space remains defined by Renaissance models, whereas
emotionally, psychically, and mythically, it is governed by deeper, more
convoluted, and less definable models. We should not assume, however, that ancient cartography everywhere was like that found in Ireland, that all cultures always favored mapping over map-making to
define their sense of space. The advances in cartography during the
Renaissance, made necessary by the "Discoveries" and created to fa-
cilitate inventories of lands gained, was influenced by the new knowledge that had entered from China, where for much of its history cartography had been entwined with Chinese political culture: "One of
the major accomplishments of the Qin dynasty (221–207 B.C.) was
the establishment of a centralized bureaucracy, setting a pattern for
subsequent dynasties. One of the distinguishing features of the bu-
reaucratic state was its emphasis on documentation, which played a
key role in maintaining communication and control over a large territory. Maps were part of this documentary system of administration,
whose philosophical foundations were laid during the Zhanguo period"
(Lee 71–74).

Both written and oral cartography had co-existed separately in
disparate parts of the world, all reconnected by the "Discoveries" that
made the Renaissance possible. As Smyth points out, "in the early decades of the seventeenth century, therefore, the Irish brand of 'mapping'
and territorial organization was being made redundant" (83). This
model was primarily literary and verbal, not graphic- and perspective-
based, and it is this latter process that *Stones of Aran* seeks to revive

(83). The redundancy that Smyth refers to reflects the official status of Gaelic mapping; nevertheless, the native mode retained a strong presence in the long reach of oral culture and was a resource that Robinson was easily able to tap into centuries later. Another recent study that has much in common with Robinson's and Smyth's work is Lillis Ó Laoire's *On a Rock in the Middle of the Ocean: Songs and Singers in Tory Island, Ireland,* a "book . . . specifically about this contextualized world, constituting a study of songs as they function in one community and centering upon the importance of song as an integral element of that community's culture" (xi). Furthermore, as Smyth points out, tracing was, and remains still, a vital element in the way that the Irish understand their world. It unites people with place (in the widest sense) and generations of people and families who have inhabited specific places: "'Tracing' is an ancient Irish pastime — the tracing of kinsmen and women and their land-histories. 'Tracing' the outlines of Ireland and its constituent parts via key landmarks was also part of this vital oral tradition" (83).

The map-making introduced by the English continues to serve as the foundation of official and academic cartography and is "the 'outsider' view of the perspective map that links Ptolemy, Mercator, Bartlett, Raven and Petty [and that] created a very different Ireland. It was this 'outsider' perspective — backed by innovative surveying instruments — that completed the mapping of plantation Ireland in the seventeenth century" (Smyth 84). A similar process was taking place in America (Smyth 412–50). The tool used to make these early modern maps was the chain, a good example of the meeting point of practicality and metaphor: "Henceforth the laying on of the chain was like a mystical rite, the agrarian equivalent of baptism or coming-of-age, which gave binding force (almost literally at the moment of survey, metaphorically forever) to the process of perambulation and which put the seal on one Irish townland after another as ready to be owned, occupied and civilized" (84–85).

Robinson's walking and mapping is a decolonizing act that returns landscape/space to its native mode of reckoning. The Ordnance Survey is not supplanted; however, its invincibility is questioned, its power and provenance doubted. Smyth's explanation of how this mode of accounting worked, "measuring/overseeing with the eye (*doreir sultomhuis*)" (74), is identical to Robinson's: "the maps I have so far undertaken cover all the land I can see from where I live, and are elaborated and externalized versions of the mental sketch maps one makes to situate oneself, cognitively and emotionally, in a new locality" (*Setting Foot* 75). Part of the attraction of Robinson's work, and why it has found such a broad readership in Ireland, results from its high degree of synchronicity with the ways in which the Irish continue to view their world: his work rings true to the psyche and the oral culture. Tracing remains a primary method for connecting place to people and underlines one's role in the present and past. Indeed, the Irish today do not have much interest in maps, the "tracing" being for the Irish verbal rather than drawn, and a product of or link with an older, Gaelic culture. For better or worse, Ireland is a space driven by narrative. Robinson quickly realized that he would have to densely record what he saw, that he would have to be both map-maker and mapper. Of course, in an oral and literary culture, the writer will always carry more weight than the cartographer. It is probably true in the areas of postcolonial Ireland where Robinson has lived that maps are still associated with distant, and sometimes oppressive, powers—once of London, now of Dublin.

The tone of Smyth's chapters is frequently set by epigraphs from such contemporary poets as Eavan Boland and Seamus Heaney, the inheritors and practitioners of Irish oral culture, thus suggesting the degree to which geography and literature remain aligned. History too, as J. C. Beckett has pointed out, "must be based on a study of the relationships between the land and its people. It is in Ireland itself, the physical conditions inspired by life in this country and the effect on those who have lived there, that the historian will find the distinct and continuing character of Irish history" (Evans, *The Personality of Ireland* 16). Just as one cannot separate the character of space from its inhabitants, so one cannot hope to understand the Irish by moving blindfolded through a single academic discipline. The historian of Ireland must be, and often is, in large part a historiographer and in smaller parts a literary scholar, anthropologist, linguist, and cartographer. Robinson, of course, is one such many-sided individual. Writers such as Smyth and Robinson certainly follow the injunction of E. Estyn Evans:

> I am pleading the cause of a trilogy of regional studies, of habitat, heritage, and history: that is, of geography, anthropology (in its widest sense, including the behavioural sciences, as well as prehistory) and recorded history (including social and economic history). I take the view that all these subjects can be regarded as parts of human history, as various approaches to the study of the evolution of man and society on this earth. Of course, they may all have their own objectives, and I am suggesting that they should interpenetrate rather than amalgamate. Even assuming that it were practicable to make a combined subject for educational purposes, on the model of some approaches to undergraduate studies in the humanities, I believe more would be lost than gained if academics were to be drawn away from their specialist fields, but they should be aware of what is going on beyond the fence: it is at the fences, along the borders, that discoveries are likely to be made. (*The Personality of Ireland* 2)

He describes this field more succinctly: "By habitat I mean the total physical environment, and by history the written record of the past. I would define heritage in broad terms as the unwritten segment of human history, comprising man's physical, mental, social and cultural inheritances from a prehistoric past, his oral traditions, beliefs, languages, arts and crafts" (*The Personality of Ireland* 3). This view is also present in the work of Momaday who, writing in a Native American context, has declared that "the imaginative experience and the historical express equally the traditions of man's reality. Finally, then, the journey recalled is among other things the revelation of one way in which these traditions are conceived, developed, and interfused in the human mind" (Least Heat-Moon 606).

The recovery of the buried narrative of a nation requires the invocation of a wide array of disciplines. And the best direction to be taken is regional rather than national, as is the case in both Smyth's and Robinson's work, to explore the relationship to space. The danger, as Evans reminds us, is of dilettantism, though it is clear from Smyth's and Robinson's achievements that, in the right hands, a wide reading of space is possible, particularly if the chosen space is limited in scope. Evans is influenced by, among others, Claude Lévi-Strauss, who argued that "there should be no gaps between anthropology and conventional history," regarding them as "indissociables"; and G. P. Marsh, the pioneer American conservationist, who "described Geography as both a poetry and a philosophy" (Evans, *The Personality of Ireland* 4).

It is also interesting to examine *Stones of Aran* in relation to works from the field of geography that treat of Irish and Irish diasporic space, in this instance the multi-authored *Atlas of the Irish Rural Landscape* (1997), and John Mannion's *Irish Settlements in Eastern Canada: A Study of Cultural Transfer and Adaptation* (1974). As Smyth does, F. H. A. Aalen and the other authors of the *Atlas of the Irish Rural Landscape* begin their work with a poem, calling on the literary artist to provide an invocation, in this instance a work of Cathal Ó Searcaigh's translated by Kevin Whelan:

> Here the prospect opens
> like a book before me
> from Doire Chonaire to Prochlais.
> I survey the meager farms, up and down
> snatched from the maw of the wild.
> Here is gathered the anthology of my community
> the texts inscribed through their inky sweat.
> Now, each enclosure like a verse records
> their supreme achievement in claiming the land.
> I can now read this epic of endurance
> in the green dialect of the crofts.
> And it hits home that I am only sealing a covenant
> When I also undertake to tackle the void. (1)

The *Atlas* is organized around three major themes, "The Making of the Irish Landscape," "Components of the Irish Landscape," and "The Challenge of Change," and it proceeds from pre-history to the present while also casting an eye forward to the future. Its aim is to provide a macro-introduction to Irish space. The three themes are followed by six "Regional Case Studies," with the one on Connemara written by Robinson, who describes space and landscape on a local scale. The various authors are interested in geography in the widest sense and address it by using scientific, cultural, agricultural, ecological and other approaches.

In many respects, the *Atlas* is a Common Ground text in which academic geographers empower others to become involved in the description and preservation of the local spaces that define a nation. Even though it is organized more traditionally than *Stones of Aran,* it covers much of the same ground, though it does not possess such a dense narrative structure. Also, the *Atlas* is a multi-illustrated volume in contrast to *Stones of Aran,* in which language must function almost exclusively as the tool to deliver Robinson's visual field. In Gillian Barrett's contribution to the *Atlas,* "Recovering the Hidden Landscape," she describes how "traces of early landscapes often remain buried beneath the ground surface and are revealed on aerial photography as subtle colour and height variations in the crops growing above sub-surface archaeological remains," an argument that has some bearing on Robinson's work, given that his purpose also is to uncover what has been concealed (64). However, despite a chapter on flying from Inishmore to Galway in *Pilgrimage,* Robinson does not make use of airplanes in his book; instead, he must recover the hidden landscape via narrative rather than via the aerial view, though they are connected in their shared practices, methodologies, and terminologies. Also, as a late-Romantic Englishman, Robinson treats the certainty that technology espouses with ambivalence: "In the making of maps, nowadays it is rare for the one person both to walk the terrain and make the drawing; specialization has alienated foot from hand. But by being wary about technologies one can still reunite the two functions, and on that basis claim cartography as personal expressive art — not just at the superficial level of artistry in design and execution, but at the core of the activity, which is the translation of a geography into a graphic image" (*Setting Foot* 3).

But Barrett's and Robinson's researches, divided by methodologies, are united by a shared intention to uncover what has been buried and by the results of their endeavors. The discrete technologies that propel them—the airplane and the foot—move toward a common end. Barrett must be above the land to record her vision, while Robinson must be grounded on it. In Barrett's hand is a camera; in Robinson's, a pen. For Robinson, coming to Inishmore ill prepared, it was necessary for him to learn the landscape the hard way: "that was the topographical experience—much of it a penance. But in this way I got the feeling of the place, its obdurate reality, into my bones" (*Setting Foot* 79).

In the preface to *Irish Settlements in Eastern Canada*, Mannion notes that "the bulk of this work . . . is based on field inquiry. Any study which has as its focus the reconstruction of the cultural landscape requires extensive field traverse. Two types of information were collected in the field: the first based on personal interviews, the second on observation of the cultural landscape" (vi). Again, Robinson's practice dovetails nicely with Mannion's, though the former's material is organized more intuitively, something that lends to *Stones of Aran* its immediacy. Both books are written after the fact, with Mannion's more formal academic structure suggesting a scholarly distance from his fieldwork, whereas Robinson's, in contrast, gives the impression of a more immediate and primal engagement. To be sure, Robinson keeps an objective distance; however, in order to engage the reader, his objectivity is intentionally undermined by the warm, strategic pose of the narrative. Both works succeed equally well in addressing their singular motives, but each one, in seeking different audiences, is guided by opposite narrative strategies. From an examination of Mannion's, one can discern, by contrast, that Robinson's is primarily an outdoor work. Mannion explores the interiors of houses and buildings in some detail and is most interested in material culture. Robinson, on the other hand, spends little time indoors in other people's homes, the exception being that of Máirtín Ó Direáin's sister Máire, and we do not learn a great deal about the interiors of Inishmore houses from his work. Like Wordsworth and Thoreau, he is focused almost exclusively on the outdoors.

I would suspect that this is a result of the *realpolitik* of gender and gender roles in Inishmore—during the day the man of the house was not at home. Robinson often alludes to the fact that his partner visits women in their homes, suggesting the discrete gender roles that existed then, and perhaps continue to exist, on Inishmore and elsewhere. One can never have complete access to every space. Overall, these various works—*Stones of Aran, Atlas of the Irish Rural Landscape,* and *Irish Settlements in Eastern Canada*—complement each other. Another complementary work in this area is Kent C. Ryden's *Mapping the Invisible Landscape,* his exploration of folklore and place with particular emphasis on the Coeur d'Alene mining district in Idaho. The changes that have taken place in geography in recent decades have resulted in forging a discipline that is strong and comfortable in its own academic skin as well as interdisciplinary, accommodating, and, I would add, more democratic in its outlook than many of the other academic fiefdoms. Also, Robinson's work is living proof of the benefits and energies that outsiders can bring to bear on scholarly disciplines: they breathe fresh air and offer new life.

When he decided to write about Inishmore, Robinson encountered the great shadows cast by such islanders and visitors as Liam O'Flaherty, Máirtín Ó Direáin, Lady Augusta Gregory, John Millington Synge, Patrick Pearse, Arthur Symons, Emily Lawless, Ethna Carbery, James Joyce, Edith Somerville and Martin Ross, Antonin Artaud, Seamus Heaney, Derek Mahon, and Michael Longley, to name only a few of the modern writers in whose work Inishmore is featured. The largest of the Aran Islands has been represented in a variety of ways and genres. Ironically, perhaps, both Synge and Pearse, the two writers most closely associated with the Aran Islands, found Inishmore to be too Anglicized, and they decamped for Inishmaan, though the largest island is particularly prominent in the former's work. Aran provided "the plots for four of his most successful plays: *Riders to the Sea, The Well of the Saints, In the Shadow of the Glen,* and *The Playboy of the Western World*" (Ó hEithir 7). Breandán Ó hEithir has summarized some of the interests and trials of a selection of these visitors:

> Some of the strangers—the word generally used in Aran for a tourist is the Irish word *strainséir,* a stranger—came with a purpose: antiquarians like O'Donovan and Petrie; botanists like Praeger and

> Colgan; linguists like Marstrander and Finck; cultural and revolu-
> tionary nationalists like Hyde and Pearse; writers like Synge, Joyce
> and Richard Power; film-makers like Flaherty and Mac Conghail;
> painters like Keating, Lambe, Rivers and McGonigle; an occasional
> mystic in search of the wisdom thought to exist on the fringes of
> continents like poor Antonin Artaud, founder of the Theatre of
> Cruelty, who saw his frightening vision of the horrors which were
> about to envelop Europe (at Dún Aonghasa in 1935) but could not
> pay his landlady; restless wanderers in search of their true voca-
> tions like Orson Welles; and the mildly curious like Tim Robinson,
> a Yorkshireman who came to look and stayed to learn Irish and re-
> store the place-names to their original forms, thus putting the is-
> lands definitely on his magically detailed map. (1)

The advent of cultural tourism, beginning during Victoria's reign,
influenced by ideas of the Romantic sublime and made possible by
emerging notions of how leisure time might be spent, brought people
to many of the most peripheral and impoverished outposts of Britain
and Ireland. Tourists and scholars continue to visit the Aran Islands
in even greater numbers and are viewed thus by the local inhabitants:
"The short answer is that Aran islanders now take that interest for
granted and find their own interest stimulated by the attention of others. To be an Aran islander is to be someone special, part of a long and
many-faceted tradition, growing up in a bilingual community with an
intense interest in its own history, just that trifle removed from mainland life and, perhaps, as one recent writer on island life commented
acidly, imagining oneself to be just a shade better than most" (3).

    Within many remote and often indigenous communities, as
Elizabeth Cook-Lynn has forcefully pointed out in regard to the
Lakota tribal areas of North America, strangers are seen to have had
a negative effect, particularly in the transmission of the sense of place.
Educated professional strangers, well connected to wealthy institutions and powerful publishers, have often become the sole agents for
the handing down of indigenous beliefs and practices with the result
that the voices of the local people have been marginalized and si-

lenced. In many parts of the world, not only have the lands and free-doms of indigenous peoples been appropriated, but so, too, have their deepest held beliefs been stolen from them. Ó hEithir, an Aran is-lander, suggests that the opposite has been true with regard to the Aran Islands. He sees that the local people, who appear most discrimi-nating in his account, have been stimulated by the interest shown by strangers, and they have been protected from gross exploitation by the sound sense of their own superiority.

In his discussion of Synge's relationship to the Aran Islands, Declan Kiberd provides a cautionary excerpt from Franz Fanon's work that should serve as the beginning for any discussion of interfaces be-tween writers and the more remote areas of their own countries: "The native intellectual who comes back to his people by way of cultural achievements behaves in fact like a foreigner. Sometimes, he has no hesitation in using a dialect in order to show his will to be as near as possible to the people. . . . The culture that the intellectual leans to-wards is often no more than a stock of particularisms. He wishes to attach himself to the people; but instead he only catches hold of their outer garments" (*Inventing Ireland* 186).

Unlike Seamus Deane, Kiberd concludes that Synge did not fall into the trap that was set for him. For Fanon, the result of such flimsy attachments can be nothing more than a superficial and specious lit-erature. From reading *Stones of Aran,* it is clear that Robinson never desired to be seen as an islander or sought to take on the transparent accoutrements of the local man. Throughout his book, he stresses that he is and wishes to remain the *strainséir:* he lives in a rented house, he is happiest when out walking alone or at home in the company of his partner, he is an atheist among believers, and he makes no effort to root himself on Inishmore: "though I have probably taken more steps about and on my three western marches than most of their born in-habitants, I have not put down roots in any of them. Roots are teth-ers, and too prone to suck up the rot of buried histories. I prefer the step — indefinitely repeatable and variable — as a metaphor of one's relationship to a place" (*Setting Foot* 213). Like the Aran dwellers, he understands that an island can be compulsive space:

> There is something compulsive in one's relationship to an island.
> A mainland area with its ambiguous or arbitrary boundaries doesn't
> constrain the attention in the same way. With an island, it is as if
> the surrounding ocean like a magnifying glass directs an intensified
> vision onto the narrow field of view. A little piece is cut out from
> the world, marked off in fact by its richness in significances. So an
> island appears to be mappable. Already a little abstracted from re-
> ality, already half-concept, it holds out the delusion of a compre-
> hensible totality. (*Setting Foot* 1)

While remaining an outsider, Robinson learns Inishmore's lore and
language, thereby entering into the spirit of place without becoming
intrusive.

   Throughout, Robinson is engaged with many of the other writers, artists, film-makers, and scientists—both islanders and visitors—
who have left accounts of their time spent on Inishmore. Given the
encyclopedic nature of *Stones of Aran,* this is hardly surprising. Of
these, Synge's, Liam O'Flaherty's, and Robert Flaherty's works are
treated at length while others are only alluded to. However, it is clear
that the writer to whom Robinson is most drawn is Máirtín Ó Direáin
(1910–1988), the native-born Irish-language poet, whose work is
referenced throughout both volumes. It is to Ó Direáin's poetry that
Robinson most often returns for guidance. Ó Direáin, born in the village of Sruthán on the western part of the island, left before his eighteenth birthday to take a position in the post office in Galway. In 1937
he went to Dublin, where he pursued a career as a civil servant that
continued until his retirement (*Labyrinth* 413–14). While exploring
Sruthán and the poet's work, Robinson developed a close friendship
with Ó Direáin's sister, Máire; and, in one of the few houses of women
that he is admitted to, he gives an account of a domestic interior and
material culture that matches the wonderful descriptions of island
homes that one finds in Synge's *The Aran Islands.* Máire is a treasure
trove of information, particularly in regard to plant life, and she strikes
up such a strong friendship with Robinson that she suggests that he
and his partner move into the old Ó Direáin homestead where she

and her family had been raised. However, given the disrepair that the house has fallen into, this suggestion is an impracticable one.

Within Ó Direáin's work, Robinson locates two almost mutually exclusive directions. The first is a poetry and prose of optimism, reflecting backward glances to the idyllic world of childhood. The second is a more severe poetry that explores the Ireland and Inishmore of adulthood, and it is heavy with despair and an overwhelming sense of gloom, all caused, it would seem, by the poor choices made by the political leadership in the postcolonial Free State and Republic. It would appear that the poet's work can be divided into competing visions — that of innocence and experience, to borrow William Blake's paradigm. In Robinson's opinion, Ó Direáin's work is weakened by the move away from the inspiration and point of view that rendered the early poetry so luminous. It seems possible to me, though, that Robinson has overstated this dichotomy. To be sure, as he got older, Ó Direáin would have noted the changes in Ireland and Inishmore that displeased him and inserted his attitudes to such changes into his work; however, to suggest that this undermined the quality of his poetry is rash. I would suggest that the change that took place was a result of a desire to move forward, to not remain stuck in one mode of writing and be forced to repeat himself to the detriment of his art. The shift in his later work can be compared to similar shifts that took place in the writings of Austin Clarke, with whom his poetry has much in common, Yeats, and Thomas Kinsella. Ó Direáin, interested in formal innovation and possessed of the impatient mind that often goes with such an attitude to the poetic status quo, was not the sort of writer who would have wished to be locked into one way of representing the world.

Why is Robinson so directed towards Ó Direáin? The "On the Shores Past" chapter from *Pilgrimage* provides a key that might explain this attraction, specifically Robinson's translations of Ó Direáin's poetry and prose — "An tEarrach Thiar" ("The Western Spring") and *Feamainn Bhealtaine* (*Mayweed*), respectively. The former poem celebrates springtime and the sense of communion between space and people that it fosters:

Tollbhuillí fanna	Languid hollow strokes
Ag maidí rámha	Of oars
Currach lán éisc	A currach full of fish
Ag teach chun cladaigh	Coming to shore
Ar órmhuir mháll	On a slow golden sea
I ndeireadh lae;	At the end of the day;
San Earrach thiar.	In the western Spring. (*Pilgrimage* 136)

Robinson is drawn to such a celebration because it gives voice to his own feelings about Inishmore—its beauty, complexity, and mystery. Most important, he examines Ó Direáin's etymology of place:

> "The Western Spring" will have to do as English for this title, but it could also be the late spring, or even, stretching a grammatical point, a spring of the old days, of the Dublin literary figure's Aran origins, for the word *thiar* and its derivatives have two sets of meanings as intimately related as warp and woof: one is connected with "west" and the other with "back," as relative position in space or time. Further, the frictions of Irish history and geography have given the concept of "the West" such a charge that *thiar* is almost as potent a word as *sean*, old, is in Irish. Indeed this whole book, like all possible books on Aran, could be read as a footnote to the full explication of these two simple Irish words. (135)

Ó Direáin's location of the sublime in Sruthán will remind us that the islanders too, and not only the literary visitors, could see their world as beautiful, timeless, and different; and this gave Robinson permission, as it were, to think and write likewise without falsely representing Inishmore. The connection between *thiar* and *sean* in Ó Direáin's case is an interesting one: he did see that the West was changing for the worst and that the old had been trumped by the new. His vision is similar to Goldsmith's and Wordsworth's, two poets who also reacted against the negative and destructive march of progress and modernization. Robinson, though a well-rounded thinker, is steeped in Romantic ideology and cause and, like Wordsworth, is smitten by the past.

At the same time, as *Stones of Aran* clearly demonstrates, the present and past are inextricably entwined in the total landscape — buildings, beliefs, ecologies, and so on — though it is the future and what it might portend that is the most problematic issue. From Ó Direáin, Robinson has inherited these linked paradigms (*thiar, sean*) to guide him forward, to remind him, for example, of the many intersecting points of locals' and visitors' views of Inishmore, and of interfaces between the most remote corners of Europe and the most cosmopolitan state-of-the-art modes of literary representations. Ó Direáin, seen in such a light, is a Picasso-like figure. From the excerpt quoted from *Feamainn Bhealtaine*, describing the harvesting of seaweed, and from a bitter passage from Liam O' Flaherty's short story "Poor People," focusing on hard toil and cold poverty, Robinson learns that the "shore's own indications of its past . . . are meager," but that elements "of the authentic pigments for its restoration" are present in the work of Inishmore's literary artists (*Pilgrimage* 137). Here, he is shown the connection between observation, listening, and writing, and how neither can offer a complete view; instead, he must combine them to find the heart of place.

If Inishmore is for Robinson the exemplary space, connected to the larger world, then Sruthán is the island's microcosm. It is the repository of literature, folklore, history, natural science, and linguistic complexity; it is the role played by the literary artist in his/her community; it is the perception of the artist held by those among whom he has lived. In short, Sruthán contains all that Robinson is interested in. He concludes that "Ó Direáin's version of Aran will be re-worded again and again throughout whatever future we have" (*Labyrinth* 417). Further, he explores the binary world that the poet has left us. The first of these is formed of Ó Direáin's writings; the second is what lies under, but near to, the surface of the space that inspired him. Instead of Robinson's being the one to effect a synthesis between these two related aspects of the poet's work, the two men will walk together on a journey of discovery/recovery like Virgil and Dante or Dedalus and Bloom. To achieve his ends, Robinson must enter not only into the spirit of place but also into the personality of Inishmore's creative genius:

And if he rejects this as mere whistling in the dark, I would take him down the twisty lane to the field below the old house, and set him to search through the grass and the holes in the walls until he had re-assembled those once-impassioned pebbles of his childhood games, which, it occurred to me once in passing the spot, must still be lying there; and together we would contemplate the mysterious essence of stones, which is not their constancy—they were his, they are mine, and will be another's—but their ability to absorb all the words we write on them into the darkness of their cores. (*Labyrinth* 417)

This relationship goes straight to the heart of oral culture where, in traditional music most clearly nowadays, a tune is passed on, and modulated by the player's personality, from one generation to the next. Even though the musician will die, his/her personality, or some part of it, is encoded into the tune and is, thus, made immortal. Also, one suspects that Robinson is drawn toward Ó Direáin's feeling of being rootless in his altered home place, perhaps reflecting his own sense of discomfort in Yorkshire and, likewise, their shared commitment to modern and postmodern modes of artistic expression. Both men have broken away and become solitary wanderers; clearly, Robinson sug-gests, they need each other. An important part of Robinson's endeavor is assemblage—on a small scale, this involves bringing the pebbles of Ó Direáin's childhood in Sruthán back to their original shape while, on a larger one, he wishes to restore some sort of similar shape to the whole of the island. Robinson's "encounters" with Ó Direáin are a good example of the meandering shape of *Stones of Aran*—a book of turn-ings and returnings, where figures continue to reappear. The land-scape is the form, the foot the engine. This life-like methodology is reminiscent of what Boland employs in *Object Lessons: The Life of the Woman and the Poet in Our Time*, another prose work in which the author is the transgressive outsider:

I have put this book together not as prose narrative is usually con-structed but as poem might be: in turnings and returnings. In parts which find and repeat themselves and restate the argument until it loses its reasonable edge and hopefully becomes part of a cadence.

Therefore, the reader will come on the same room more than once: the same tablecloth with red-checked squares; the identical table by an open window. An identical suburb, drenched in winter rain, will show itself, twice, then disappear and come back. The Dublin hills will change color in the distance, and change once more. The same October day will happen, as it never can in real life, over and over again. (xiii)

Nowadays one is loath to think of Tim Robinson as an English writer; in every respect, he appears to belong to Ireland. Arguably, no Irish writer knows his given literary parish, to borrow Patrick Kavanagh's phrase, better than Robinson knows his. His monumental work has enriched Ireland: we understand Inishmore in particular, and Ireland in general, better as a result of what he has written. Also, having been elected a member of *Aosdána*, the Irish academy honoring creative artists, he has been officially recognized by his peers for his contributions to Irish writing and Irish life. It would hardly be an understatement to call him a national treasure and to suppose that his work will be invaluable for generations to come. At the same time, it is equally important to note that when Robinson first arrived in Ireland in 1972, he was neither a writer nor an Irishman. Generally, he was an Englishman abroad; specifically, he was a visual artist in flight from the London art scene in search of a new beginning. In this regard, he was treading a well-worn path: since Elizabethan times, following in, or sometimes leading, the imperial progress, numerous English men and women have left us accounts of places and peoples touched by this worldwide progress, many of which have been at variance with imperial aims. Others, such as Edmund Spenser in his writings on Ireland, dovetail severely with the mission of empire and conquest. A great deal of this work has been distinguished and valuable. However, in keeping with what we have been taught by Edward Said and Chinua Achebe, among many critics of Eurocentric versions of colonized spaces, these accounts can amount to a rather "exotic" body of writing that should be read cautiously. These British representations straddle and criss-cross all of the literary genres, carrying both imaginative and "factual" weight. As the empire waned and died, English

writers continued to travel widely, both to the centers of former influence and farther afield, and this impulse has continued unabated
into the postcolonial period. Writing of Patrick Leigh-Fermor's work,
Colin Thubron has attempted to explain some reasons for, and aspects
of, this phenomenon: "It includes, of course, boarding school, the
affliction that is perhaps one of the reasons the British have taken so
naturally to travel writing. It was an institution ideally suited to the
sons (and sometimes daughters) of parents abroad on colonial business. It imposes self-reliance, confidence, perhaps a dangerous sense of
invulnerability, sometimes harrowing loneliness. Its products are often
well-suited for solitary travel. Even today most British travel-writers
are middle class creatures of the system" (31).

This paradigm only partially fits Robinson, who was a grammar
school product, rather than someone who attended an elite British
public school, such as Thubron, an Eton alumnus. However, as Dominic Sandbrook has pointed out, the grammar schools, the result of
the 1944 Education Act, while set up to democratize British schooling, in fact "were devoted to the ideals of the middle-class, and their
pupils were taught to see themselves as an elite" (423). These schools
prepared their students for university and mimicked the public schools
in many respects. As a writer and traveler, Robinson, born in 1935,
can be compared and contrasted with others of his generation such as
Thubron, born in 1939, and Bruce Chatwin, born in 1940, and also,
like Robinson, a grammar school product. Such an approach will allow
for a better understanding of Robinson's degree of belonging to, and
divergence from, the paths followed by his peers. Of course, compared
to the wide spaces inhabited by Thubron and Chatwin, the area of
Robinson's wanderings must seem modest, restricted, and fixed; however, at the same time, all three men have much in common, not least
their shared desire to recover indigenous worlds, places, and peoples.
What separates them most is that for the first two, many places are
important and explored, whereas Robinson is really interested only in
a few small, discrete, though related, parts of Counties Galway and
Clare. While Thubron and Chatwin moved on, Robinson stayed put.

In his first book, *Mirror to Damascus* (1967), an intimate, detailed, and personal history of the city and its surrounding areas, and the

one of his books that is closest in purpose to *Stones of Aran*, Thubron takes stock:

> To gaze down on Damascus is to view confusion. The streets are artefacts from different ages, contorted and overlapping. Even from a height the city takes pains to conceal her identity; enmeshing the eye with walls, enigmatic trees and alleyways curling in irrational directions; for here it's a custom that beauty be veiled. But the western mind, with its love of order, wishes to know how things have become what they are, and demands a discipline. The wish can only be fulfilled, and the discipline imposed, by history. If the city is engaged in her entirety, she evades and bewilders. Encountered age by age, she may be a little understood. The past may be lured back into sight, figures stand as men of their time instead of staring out of chaos, buildings be explained. (3)

As Robinson does on Inishmore, Thubron traverses the city on foot and on a bicycle to describe both what is on the surface and what is hidden in the layers beneath Damascus, literally and metaphorically. He is drawn to a place that, unlike Inishmore, has been neglected by writers, but which is at the center of Judeo-Christian and Islamic history, in the widest sense. Robinson, on the contrary, sees Inishmore more modestly, though it is for him an "exemplary space" and he hopes that his work there will permit for his reader a particular understanding of a single place. Unlike Robinson on his arrival on Inishmore, Thurbron comes well prepared, having read widely in fields germane to his purpose and learned Arabic, though he is often left nonplussed and confused by the local dialects. Also, like Robinson, he is blessed with patience and desire: "It did not matter how long the walk would be, for in front of me the orchards of paradise were beginning to close in again" (7). He lives among the people in the home of a poor Syrian Christian family, becomes well known on the streets and in the local cafés, and absorbs everything that is available to him. At the same time, his stay is more limited than Robinson's, and thus he is unable to penetrate Damascus to the depth of Robinson's exploration of Inishmore. Robinson is not interested in cities; for him, only a small island, defined by an unchanging boundary, is mappable and "holds out the delusion of a comprehensible totality" (*Setting Foot* 1).

Both writers are thoroughly modern in outlook. They share a post-Enlightenment, rational view of the world, and neither possesses the religious faith of the people whom they live among and write about. Often, they can easily debunk received opinion and folk versions of history to show that events could not have happened at times recorded in oral culture; however, both understand the power and primacy of oral culture as records of truths that are often of wider significance than literal versions, themselves often in dispute. Their rationality, combined with a respect for and interest in views that contend with theirs, allows both writers to give accounts of place that are comprehensive and nuanced. And both Thubron and Robinson allow their own certainties to be undermined, and their perspectives ultimately broadened, by contact with people and views that contend with their own. These writers, like Momaday and Least Heat-Moon, yield to the space at hand rather than impose themselves upon it, as might an old-fashioned empire builder. They accept the primacy of the local account, the one that has absorbed the totality of the lived landscape.

Published in 1988 and set in the Australian Outback, Bruce Chatwin's *The Songlines* is his attempt to explore the meaning of the Aboriginals' ancient, invisible "Dreaming-tracks." These tracks are recorded in oral culture where "a song . . . [is] both a map and direction-finder. Providing you knew the song, you could always find your way across country" (13). Within the Aboriginal belief system, "an unsung land is a dead land; since, if the songs are forgotten, the land itself will die" (74). Literally, "a musical phrase . . . is a map reference . . . and music . . . is a memory bank for finding one's way about the world" (108). For Chatwin, the Outback becomes *his* exemplary space, which allows him to unite all songs and mythologies and view them as moving along together toward identical ends: "And it struck me, from what I now know of the Songlines, that the whole of Classical mythology might represent the relics of a gigantic 'song-map': that all the to-ing and fro-ing of gods and goddesses, the caves and sacred springs, the sphinxes and chimaeras, and all the men and women who became nightingales or ravens, echoes or narcissi, stones or stars—could all be interpreted in terms of totemic geography" (117). Here, the Songlines share their purpose with Ovid's *Metamorphoses*.

The Aboriginal Songlines intersect in various way with Irish practice as it existed before the seventeenth century—the ancient Irish practice of "tracing" and the stories, poems, songs, and music that served as the backbone of oral culture, which, when combined, amount to a concept akin to the Songlines. Neither the Irish nor the Aboriginal Australians drew maps, though both have relied on alternative systems and strategies for mapping their spaces. Also, both indigenous cultures have aided the cartographic enterprises of their conquerors. In seventeenth-century Ireland, as Smyth has pointed out, "the Ulster Irish, then, had their own 'scholars' and 'surveyors' who knew the names, shapes, boundaries and values of a hierarchy of territories. They had a most intimate knowledge of their own dynamic landscapes and could translate this oral knowledge into a language that English cartographers could turn into map form" (73).

In *The Songlines,* the developers of a proposed railway line running from Alice Springs to Darwin have employed Arkady Volchok, possessed of a deep knowledge of Aboriginal languages and Songlines and a man who has earned the respect of the Aborigines, to serve as their go-between. The developers are bound by the Land Rights Act, which gave "Aboriginal 'owners' the title to their country," to respect property rights; therefore, Arkady, as a result of discussions and negotiations with the Aboriginal people, must "interpret 'tribal law' into the language of the Law of the Crown" (3). As was the case in Ireland, the drawing of maps in Australia depended on the cooperation of indigenous peoples who did not draw maps. For both the Irish and the Aborigines, memory was and is more important than lines sketched across a page, and what Smyth has written of Ireland is equally applicable to Australia: "it can be said to have sustained a scholarly geographical imagination, which—through the schematic listing of key landmarks—was able to demarcate and define the boundaries of the provinces and plot Ireland as a whole by tracing the coastal landmarks of the provinces all the way round the island" (83). We might say, therefore, of Robinson's work on Inishmore that his mapping is a series of Aran Songlines. Of course, it would not have been possible for Robinson to have completed his work without the islanders' cooperation.

However, in many respects the authors of *Stones of Aran* and *The Songlines* are very different. Although Chatwin comes well prepared to the Outback, he is never able to fully enter into the Aboriginal world that he is seeking to understand. Always, he serves as Arkady's sidekick, and he hears the stories of the Songlines second-hand and in translation. Robinson arrives without any background and patiently develops one, learns the Irish language, and becomes an expert. Also, as Nicholas Shakespeare has pointed out in his biography, Chatwin's subjects had no idea that they were to become characters and players in a literary drama, and they were surprised to find their lives and work discussed upon the novel's publication. Robinson, on the other hand, made it clear to his collaborators that he was engaged in research that he hoped would be published, and he was encouraged by the islanders in his general and specific aims. We should not assume that *Stones of Aran*, a prose work, and *The Songlines*, a novel, are not comparable. In every respect, as Shakespeare makes clear, Chatwin's book is a prose work and not a novel, albeit one published as a novel at Chatwin's insistence. This is another example of the stranger's need to play fast and loose with the genre.

But these writers also have much in common. Both men benefited from personal acts of renunciation and learned, as Chatwin points out, that "renunciation ... even at this late date, can work" (133). The two of them—Chatwin, raised in the Midlands, and Robinson, in Yorkshire—had renounced their competitive London lives to pursue primarily oral cultures where the connection between past and present had not been sundered. Chatwin learned in the Outback that "the idea of returning to an 'original simplicity' was not naive or unscientific or out of touch with reality" (133). While such a view is certainly subjective, idealistic, and Wordsworthian to an extreme, it is also a testament to the truth of Chatwin's having arrived at a new and elevated state of consciousness. His searchings were more far-flung and his attitude more flamboyant than Robinson's, though, for all of their differences, they remain writers transformed—Chatwin by his flight from his comfortable position at Sotheby's, and Robinson by his rejection of the London art scene. It would not have been possible for either man to have realized themselves as writers without making these life-changing moves.

Writing of *The Songlines'* form, Hans Magnus Enzenberger has declared: "to my mind it's at the interstices of genres where the most interesting things happen. . . . Chatwin's transgression is much more important than any avant-garde fumbling. . . . Once he had decided he wouldn't be restricted by the English, he became rather defenseless" (Shakespeare 513). One can also argue that *Stones of Aran* is a hybrid work that combines the styles and voices of an array of modes—literary, historical, scientific, for example. Also, Chatwin, as Nicholas Shakespeare reminds us, "[u]nlike Colin Thubron, Jonathan Raban, Redmond O'Hanlon, Paul Theroux, Andrew Harvey . . . does not put his traveling self at the centre. His stance is unflappable, detached, discreet—'a pose rather than a subject,' writes Manfred Pfister, the result of a 'brilliant self-stylization rather than the self-reflective depth and emotional richness of subjectivity.' Bruce's lack of introspection is old-fashioned, but his style is contemporary. This unusual blend accounts for his distinctive voice" (568–69). Likewise, Robinson does not put himself at the center of his narrative—*Stones of Aran* is about Inishmore and not about Robinson—and he is unflappable, detached, and discreet. Clearly, though, he is more self-effacing than Chatwin, having almost obliterated the pose from his narrative. For Chatwin, walking was also of great importance:

> He believed that walking "is not simply therapeutic for oneself, but it is a poetic activity that can cure the world of its ills." Plante found a clue to his restlessness in Thoreau's "Walking." To saunter, [Thoreau] thinks, could mean to be *sans terre*, without land or home, but to be equally at home everywhere. . . . Plante believed that Bruce in his wandering "was looking for the Holy Land, looking at least for the small objects that remained of his former habitation as

evidence of something deep in humanity that might be humanity's saving grace." (Shakespeare 471)

Sauntering or walking away, Chatwin believed, was both the method of renouncing one's attachment to one's own given place and destiny and the means of slowly learning the new space that one had chosen to inhabit. As Robinson has described, walking was the vital connector between the old and new lives: "a devotion to footsteps was something I carried with me on that decisive step from city to island" (*Setting Foot* 214). In this regard, Chatwin and Robinson's methodologies are the same. On a visit to Leigh-Fermor, a writer who greatly influenced Chatwin, "Leigh Fermor told him the Latin expression *solvitur ambulado*—it is solved by walking—and immediately [Chatwin] whipped out his notebook" (Shakespeare 472). Certainly, the problem of how to map Inishmore was solved, then framed, for Robinson by walking.

At another level, and one that cannot be separated from Robinson's objectives as an author, *Stones of Aran* is a love story. Meeting up with his Irish-born partner Máiréad in London opened to Robinson the possibility of living in the West of Ireland, and this partnership has sustained him throughout his work. Robinson gives voice in *Labyrinth* to the quality of this relationship: "Remembering such times, I am moved to a declaration: that making love with Máiréad has been the sustaining joy of my life. There's a certainty! And where else but in the secret heart of my book could I dare such simplicity? From where, proclaim it to so wide a world?" (297).

In the years since the publication of his Aran volumes, Robinson has often looked backward to account for the role these books have played in his own life and career. Initially, his departure from London signified a breaking away from convention; however, with the passing of time, he has come to see his life as an organic and artistic whole, centered on his relationship with his life partner. In 1996, for an exhibition held at the Irish Museum of Modern Art in Dublin, Robinson assembled works from the three aspects of his career—as visual artist, cartographer, and writer—and found in the collection a common sense of purpose:

Whereas I used to be dismayed by the breakage and loss caused by that sudden change in habit and habitat, nowadays it is the un-chipped good order in which my little store of imagery accompanied me on the jolting journey from city to island that makes me wonder if it is ever possible to step beyond oneself. The question became sharp for me recently as I approached completion of the body of texts and maps I would have claimed had been inspired by my encounter with the West of Ireland, because in trying to foresee what I might do next I mentally revisited that earlier time of change, unwrapped some artworks stored away from my last year in London before the transition date of November 1972—and discovered in them a concentrated abstract of the suite of images that has controlled my subsequent writing and is implicit in my cartography. (*The View from the Horizon* 9–10)

After the excerpts from his prose works had been "lightly reworked to wean them from their original contexts and confront them with their dependence on the same fund of imagery as the three visual works," Robinson was struck by their reliance on the same creative fund (*The View from the Horizon* 13). Among the prose pieces taken from his published works to complement the three visual installations ("To the Centre," "Autobiography," and "Inchworm") are his account of his encounter with the dolphins, his exploration of the "adequate step" paradigm, and his supposition that, working from a hill above Connemara, he would "arrive at a crude estimate of the size of the Earth in terms of [his] own stride, without recourse to astronomy, the compass, or even a map" (41–42). Influenced by Einstein's relativity theory, at the level of metaphor, Robinson believes that this theory can explain the seemingly random choices that contributed to his removal from London to Aran. What had seemed "incomprehensible and unknowable" was, in fact, no mere accident. For Robinson, even his childhood fascination with moths is seen as a signpost informing the artistic talent that would mature in adulthood. These recountings in *The View from the Horizon* are classic examples of syntheses recalled in tranquility, and, to some extent, one must read them cautiously. The artist, after all, is not always the best evaluator of his/her own creative processes. In this instance, however, Robinson does not make the case for the value of his work; instead, he tries to tease from his own life the mystery of how it all came about, and how he made the transition from Timothy Drever, the pseudonym he used as a visual artist in London, to the cartographer, geographer, and writer he became in Ireland.

It is not easy to pigeonhole Robinson: it is much easier to describe his achievements. He sees himself as a visual artist, cartographer, mapper, and writer with the four in constant negotiation and free play, though such a mode of operation leaves him open to a charge of dilettantism, of which Robinson was reminded when *Pilgrimage* received a negative review on publication. In this review, printed in full in *Labyrinth,* Robinson is taken to task and accused of being merely a dabbler:

> A more fundamental flaw is the work's uncertainty and equivocation about its own purpose. Striding roughshod over the bounds of specialisms and genres, it seems to imply that some overarching meaning of it all is going to be revealed through the juxtaposition or pile-up of viewpoints, but alas this higher truth never quite emerges, and in trying to be "not just" a historian or geologist or botanist or even a poet, Robinson ends up being nothing in particular. (307)

The reviewer, offended by Robinson's presumption, mistakes ends for process, roughshod for step, and fails to understand the nature of his achievement. At no point does Robinson argue or suggest that his work will have an overarching meaning or significance; in fact, even when he is at his most definite—as he is on the Connemara hill when he tries to align his own step with the Earth's size—he never extends his view beyond the bounds of speculation. Also, the juxtapositions and piling-up of viewpoints are read too literally and out of context by this reviewer. These are the literary and artistic tropes forming part of Robinson's gentle carnivalesque vision; they are bricolage elements of the kind that are often found in paintings and in writing that cannot always be counted as if they were numbers on a page moving toward a definite end. The review is an example of the kind of criticism that could equally damn the works of such writers as Borges, Joyce, and Pound, to name only three. Of course, Robinson does not arrive at Inishmore's ultimate truth because no such truth can exist. Ultimately, *Stones of Aran* needs to be read for what it is—a literary text. I am certain that readers and scholars will continue to enjoy it for a long, long time.

Two

WINGS BEATING ON STONE
Richard Murphy's Ecopoetry

Of the new generation of poets who emerged with Dublin's
Dolmen Press in the 1950s, Richard Murphy is the only one to
have been born in the West of Ireland. His 2000 volume of *Collected Poems* is an impressive and varied achievement, essential
reading for all with an interest in Irish writing. In its exploration of the West of Ireland, County Galway in particular, it is
also a prophetic work that represents the beginning, albeit unintentionally, of a contemporary Irish ecological literature. Even
though it is likely that Murphy never sought to underline his poetry with ecotheory, or that he was even schooled in it, his work
can been seen to address, implicitly and explicitly, environmental concerns in Ireland throughout the modern and contemporary periods. His ecological consciousness is the product of a
fine-tuned attentiveness to the communities in which he has
lived and to their interactions with the world they have created
both for themselves and with nature. Murphy's community is the
larger one of all beings and things that define our world. His
work challenges the view of the West of Ireland that has been
handed down from Yeats and other English-language poets of
the Celtic Twilight, who were all inclined to read it symbolically
and to objectify people, places, and living things to suit their

own anthropological, historical, racial, and historical visions. Clearly, younger poets such as Moya Cannon, Mary O'Malley, and Seán Lysaght have followed in Murphy's path.

My purpose will be to examine Murphy's 1974 volume, *High Island* (included in his *Collected Poems,* 2001), and his 2002 memoir, *The Kick,* under the umbrella of ecological literature, a mode of reading that has developed in recent times—especially in the United States—and that sheds important light on Irish writing, contemporary poetry in particular. It seems fair to say that in the Ireland of the future, ecology and literature will probably become more closely intertwined than they are at present. Certainly, as I hope to show, ecological consciousness has long been a somewhat unheralded aspect of Irish poetry, as Seamus Heaney has made clear. For centuries, ecology has been a central aspect of Irish poetry, though it has not been referred to as such; instead, in critical discourse, ecology has passed as absorption with place, itself a central tenet of contemporary ecopoetical theory. In addition to a discussion of Murphy's poetry and prose, I will examine his work alongside Gary Snyder's collection of poetry *Turtle Island,* also published in 1974, and Snyder's prose, to better understand the global reach of ecopoetry and to show that ecology has attracted poets across continents. To conclude, I will suggest the work of other contemporary Irish writers whose works can be considered under this rubric.

In his introduction to *The Greening of Literary Scholarship: Literature, Theory, and the Environment,* Steven Rosendale cites Glen A. Love's 1990 manifesto "Revaluing Nature: Toward an Ecological Criticism" as an "influential declaration of ecocritical purpose [and] an important document in the history of ecocriticism's movement into the academy" (xvi):

> Love's argument begins with a hypothesis that has and must continue to underlie the project of ecocriticism—that human-caused environmental catastrophe is imminent and must be urgently addressed. . . . Arguing that literary scholars have largely "placed self-interest above public interest, even, irrationally enough, in matters of common survival," he decries our profession's "narrowly anthro-

pocentric view of what is consequential in life." . . . Instead, he advocates for an "eco-centric" criticism that radically rejects the anthropocentric concerns that have characterized literary study. For Love, the project of replacing "anthro"- with "eco"-oriented criticism entails three specific shifts: (1) the elevation of western American and nature-writing texts over ostensibly more human-centered canons, (2) the restoration of realism over "poststructuralist nihilism" as the dominant mode for the revaluation of nature, and (3) the supplanting of nationalist with global, ecological perspectives. (Rosendale xvi)

Although, as Rosendale points out, many scholars take issue with some of the more strident aspects of Love's polemic, his position paper remains the text that has framed the current debate. One aspect of this debate is the attempt to reconcile aesthetic and political concerns. In literary studies published since 2000, the year of George W. Bush's election and the putting in place in Washington of an administration that ecocritics considered unsupportive of environmental causes, the political consciousness has come to the fore. Scholars in the field argue that the changed political climate has added a new level of urgency to their ambitions.

Ecocritics in the United States are organized under the umbrella of ASLE, the Association for the Study of Literature and the Environment. Rosendale points out that there is a growing demand in the United States for classes at university level in the field, and that the ASLE Web site provides links to 150 classes in ecological literature. These include university writing classes that are constructed around environmental issues, thus indicating the wide reach of these classes and perhaps confirming, as conservatives are quick to point out, the pinko-liberal-green biases of American academics. Affiliates of ASLE are active in Japan, Korea, India, Australia, New Zealand, the United Kingdom, and elsewhere. Some of the most discussed works in the field include John Elder's *Imagining the Earth: Poetry and the Vision of Nature* (1985), Wendell Berry's *Standing by Words* (1983), Cheryll Glotfelty and Harold Fromm's *Ecocriticism Reader* (1996), Roderick Nash's *Wilderness and the American Mind* (1982),

Bernard W. Quetchenbach's *Back from the Far Field: American Nature Poetry in the Late Twentieth Century* (2000), J. Scott Bryson's edited volume *Ecopoetry: A Critical Introduction* (2002), Leonard M. Scigaj's *Sustainable Poetry: Four American Ecopoets* (1999), and Jonathan Bate's *The Song of the Earth* (2000). Of contemporary American poets considered by these critics, most attention has been focused on Berry, Snyder, Adrienne Rich, A. R. Ammons, Louis Glück, W. S. Merwin, Robert Bly, Linda Hogan, and Mary Oliver. The work of all these poets is available in Ireland, and both Rich and Snyder have had a marked influence on contemporary Irish poets.

Also of note, emerging in response to the contributions made by women poets, has been the advent of an ecofeminist criticism. Given that much of the energy and focus of ecocriticism is Western American in origin, ecofeminism serves as a useful mode of reading the works of women poets from the West of Ireland: Moya Cannon and Mary O'Malley, to mention only two. Among literary critics in the Irish Studies field, Edna Longley and John Wilson Foster are two of the most prominent of the few who have broached the significance of this mode of critical inquiry when reading Irish texts.

However, ecocritics in the United States do not merely chart the currents of contemporary poetry; in fact, an important direction that scholars have taken has been their new readings of poets through the centuries in the light of ecotheory. In this respect, one of the most notable studies is Gyorgi Voros's *Notations of the Wild: Ecology in the Poetry of Wallace Stevens,* which locates Stevens's ideas of the sublime within an ecological context to show, as Guy Rotella has pointed out, that Stevens "attends to the moments of natural change" (100). Stevens has said that "the great poems of heaven and hell have been written and the great poem of the earth remains to be written" (*The Necessary Angel* 142), and Voros notes that his favorite ingredients are "sun, clouds, mountains, and humans being brought into strange relation" (1). While Voros points out the existence of an ecological vision within Stevens's work, she also makes clear that his complex poetry is composed of many other elements. Denis Donoghue has described the many-sidedness of Stevens's work: "The philosophic positions registered in Stevens's poems are severally in contradiction. If we were to list every variant reading in the argument of epistemology, for instance, we could quote a poem by Stevens in favour of each" (Rotella 101).

Ecocritics, as Voros's study makes clear, have no desire to claim sole ownership of the poets they write about, because to do so would result in wrongheaded readings. There is much more to Rich's and Ammons's work, for example, than their ecologies. Similarly, when we move forward to examine Richard Murphy, we will note, in addition to its ecological aspects, his dense explorations of history in *The Battle of Aughrim* and of the Anglo-Irish world of his family, colonial and postcolonial, which are such strong presences in his work. Robinson Jeffers has received much attention from ecocritics, and it is interesting to note, in the Irish context, that he visited Yeats's Thoor Ballylee in 1929, 1937, and 1948. Indeed, it was from Yeats's example that Una Jeffers "conceived the notion of her husband building a tower in imitation of Thoor Ballylee"—what was to become Tor House (Fleming 39). These towers represented their singular views, as Gilbert Allen has pointed out: "Yeats renovates, in order to reaffirm what strikes him as most admirable within the cultural past; Jeffers builds, in order to express in cultural terms a geological history that human beings habitually ignore" (39).

Although "Western-ness" is a central aspect of Yeats's aesthetic and worldview, his articulation of it, in contrast to Jeffers's, is anthropocentric rather than ecological. Houses are central to Murphy's work also: family houses at Milford in County Galway and in Colombo, Sri Lanka (or Ceylon, as it was known to Murphy as a child), the coast guard cottage on Rosroe Quay, New Forge in Cleggan, the room in the miner's hut on High Island, the Hexagon on Omey Island, and Knockbrack in south County Dublin. These homes put Murphy in dialogue with Yeats on their shared Anglo-Irish inheritance, with Eastern culture and Buddhism, with the artisans from the forge and with the world of manual labor on land and sea, with the monk's cell and his poetic glosses, and with the tension between poetic form and wild nature. Even though Murphy's and Yeats's visions differ in many respects, they are united by shared attachments to ancestral Anglo-Irish homes and to the West of Ireland.

Richard Murphy was born in County Mayo in 1927 and spent his first five years in Ceylon before returning to Europe to attend boarding schools in Ireland and England. The poet's father, Sir William Lindsay Murphy, who was born in an Irish rectory, retired from the British Colonial Service as governor of the Bahamas and then took up farming in Southern Rhodesia, which later became the subject of his son's ambivalent celebration in "The God Who Eats Corn" (*Collected Poems* 74–80). Murphy won a scholarship to Oxford, where he was tutored by C. S. Lewis. Between 1951 and 1956, Murphy rented a cottage on Rosroe Quay, a former coast guard station, between the Big and Little Killary harbors in County Galway. Eventually settling in Cleggan, County Galway, he lived there until 1980, when he moved to Dublin. In 1969, he purchased Ardilaun Island, the Irish name for the High Island of his poems. There he renovated one room in an old miner's hut, where many of his High Island poems were written, and which he saw as a sanctuary for birds and wild Atlantic seals. On the day after he purchased the island, Murphy reflected:

> Buying an island, even with the intention of creating a wild life sanctuary, is a predatory act among predators, much easier than writing a book. Once you become the owner, your view of the island alters: you turn possessive and protective . . . . But I know that High Island can never be possessed because it will always remain in the possession of the sea. Its virtue will grow from its contemplation, not its use, from feelings and ideas evoked by its wild life and its end of the world terrain. (*The Kick* 277)

High Island is a celebration and exploration of the island itself. Murphy lived and wrote among the flora, fauna, birds, and seals. Like an ancient Irish monk, he sought clarity in solitude. He got away from the world in order to be drawn into closer communion with it. Whereas William Golding's *Lord of the Flies*, the great desert-island novel of recent times, is concerned with people, *High Island,* an Irish desert island with plenty of rain and bad weather, is concerned with nature, place, and history. Like Snyder's *Turtle Island,* written thousands of miles away from Ireland during the same period, Murphy's *High Island* gains its clear-sightedness from elements of Christian/ Buddhist isolation. Of course, both Murphy and Snyder had spent important parts of their lives in the East (in Sri Lanka and Japan, respectively) and then settled in the western parts of their native countries to write these books. We can say that both works, for all of their diversity, speak to a shared personal, artistic, and historical moment. But, unlike Snyder, Murphy favors the more traditional poetic structures, though at a cost, as he has made clear:

> I stressed the value of mastering metre and rhyme before attempting to write free verse. But my theories that the iamb derives from the heartbeat and the structure of the poem needs a body's or a building's symmetry put me out of key with the time. Metrical rhymed poetry had never come easy to me, nor did I expect it to be easy for students who equated poetry with self-expression. Too often I'd written myself to a standstill going over and over the same lines or stanzas, making no progress. (*The Kick* 295)

Occasionally, as in "Ardilaun" from *High Island,* the beautiful formality that is such a noticeable characteristic of Murphy's work breaks down, though to wonderful effect, to better reflect the conflict between the wild landscape and the soft human body. The privations of island life force Murphy to review his literary aesthetic as well as the relationships that have defined his life and governed his way of seeing the world. Cut off from the larger island of Ireland, he must seek to reshape both his personality and his art by listening carefully to nature rather than to the human voice. High Island, the place, may well be inspirational; however, it is simultaneously a collection of opposing and contrary forces with which the poet must do battle:

Ocean blue light
Breaking through

Four days of mist
And calculated solitude
Is lifting up
White and mauve parasols of angelica
Briefly to celebrate. ("Ardilaun," *Collected Poems* 101)

The magnificent isolation of High Island allows Murphy to confront history, both primal and human-made. Alone in this remote place, though with the gathered hindsight of history, the poet can understand, as Wordsworth, often cited as an early ecopoet, had understood, that the roots of experience and language are to be found in nature:

For I have learned
To look on nature, not as in the hour
Of thoughtless youth; but hearing oftentimes
The still, sad music of humanity. (237)

In more isolated places the poet will most likely develop what Snyder calls "a much larger perspective on the historical human experience" (107). Although Murphy's habitation on High Island can be read in multiple ways, it can certainly be read in a manner that Snyder learned from one of his teachers, Oda Sesso: "In Zen there are only two things: you sit, and you sweep the garden" (111). Seamus Heaney, connecting monasticism and nature poetry, joins ancient poets and monks to contemporary poets and scholars. Examining a poem from a ninth-century manuscript from St. Gall in Switzerland, he notes:

This poem has been called "The Scribe of the Woods" and in it we can see the imagination taking its colouring from two very different elements. On the one hand, there is the *pagus*, the pagan wilderness, green, full-throated, unrestrained; on the other hand there is the lined book, the Christian *disciplina*, the sense of a spiritual principle and a religious calling that transcends the almost carnal lushness of nature itself. The writer is as much hermit as scribe. ("The God in the Tree" 183)

On High Island, the ascetic Murphy serves as a medium between the *pagus* and the *disciplina:* he negotiates a place in this tradition for modern language, for an Enlightenment-influenced worldview, and for modern poetry while he shelters in a miner's hut. Heaney negotiates a way between Gaelic and Japanese poetry, which suggests a reading of *High Island* through the lenses of both the Occidental and Eastern traditions: "In its precision and suggestiveness, this [Gaelic] art has been compared with the art of the Japanese *haiku.* Bashō's frog plopping into its pool in seventeenth-century Japan makes no more durable or exact music than Belfast's blackbird clearing its throat over the lough almost a thousand years earlier" (181).

Just as Yeats and Jeffers shared the vantage points of their Western towers, so too do Murphy and Snyder share their island isolation, though Murphy, of the four, chose the most extreme living conditions. However, Snyder's island concept differs from Murphy's physical island most notably with respect to scale: "What I realistically aspire to do is to keep up with and stimulate what I think is really strong and creative in my own viable region, my actual nation; northern California/southern Oregon, which we might call Kuksu country, subdivision of Turtle Island continent" (*Gary Snyder Reader* 116). Called "Kitkitdizze," Snyder's house on Turtle Island is located north of the South Yube river in the foothills of the Sierra Nevada (613). Among North American writers, Snyder is not alone in reimagining space ecologically rather than politically. Laurie Ricou in *The Arbutus/ Madrone Files/Reading the Pacific Northwest* has reconfigured his region, comprising parts of the United States and Canada, in relation to where the arbutus or madrone tree is dominant:

> The arbutus tree (*Arbutus menziesii*), a native broad-leaved ever-green, often serves as a regional symbol; the boundaries of its distribution offer one way of mapping the Pacific Northwest. . . . What I name *Arbutus*—and my home in Vancouver, British Columbia, is just a few blocks from Arbutus Street, and the Arbutus Shopping Centre—is in Bellingham, Eugene, and Vancouver, Washington, called *Madrone.* One species, one shared regional marker with two names: one Canadian and one American. (1)

When maps are drawn ecologically rather than militarily or politically, our sense of space is altered in relation to nature, in its widest sense. National barriers seem artificial and redundant.

That Murphy's poetry in its design, and a good deal of Heaney's work, too, finds register in ancient Irish and Japanese poetry is further emphasized by what Kuno Meyer has written:

> In Nature poetry the Gaelic muse may vie with that of any other nation. Indeed, these poems occupy a unique position in the literature of the world. To seek out and watch and love Nature, in its tiniest phenomena as in its grandest, was given to no people so early and so fully as to the Celt. . . . It is a characteristic of these poems that in none of them do we get an elaborate or sustained description of any scene or scenery, but rather a succession of pictures and images which the poet, like an impressionist, calls up before us by light and skilful touches. Like the Japanese, the Celts were quick to take an artistic hint; they avoid the obvious and the commonplace; the half-said thing to them is dearest. (xii–xiii)

Writing from their respective islands, Murphy and Snyder are the able inheritors of ancient traditions of seeing and composition. Both poets forge connections with indigenous worlds—Murphy with the Irish-language writers of pagan and Christian Ireland and Snyder with Native American and Asian footprints on the American Northwest—and these vital contacts allow both poets to challenge, and ultimately forego, elements in their own cultural upbringings. For both writers, engagements with their respective, lonely Wests put in motion these revisions of their individual relationships to the world. For Murphy and Snyder, as was the case for Yeats and Jeffers before them, the West is the sacred space where hard questions are posed and great transformations begin. These questions are not posited by humans but by the landscape.

The "tang and clarity" that Heaney admires so much in early Irish nature poetry is found in both the poetry and prose written by Murphy on High Island:

The ballet of birds continues in the sky . . . though it really is dark and this church is a ruin, I feel inexpressibly happy . . . the wind in the doorway is playful . . . all things as well as creatures seem to be rejoicing in summer, the high point of life . . . nothing will stop the music of the masonry until those birds come to the end of their dance and vanish before daybreak. . . . I shall lie down and sleep for a while on cushions of thrift between the abbot's clochán and the lake, while the stormpetrels go on feeding their young, instructing them in flight and in song. (*The Kick* 293)

The absence of the noise made by humans allows for this radical shift in focus from the anthropocentric to the ecocentric; however, the monastic ruins are both a reminder of mutability and mortality and a link to the lined pages on which the monks' poems were composed. Murphy is not getting away from it all; instead, he is linking up with a more ancient mode of living and writing poetry. His High Island language is derived from his observations of the physical present, the literary past, and the influence of place on his work. As Berry has written of the influence of his rural Kentucky environment on his own work, so, too, can we see similar sets of connections underlining the visions and languages of Murphy's and Snyder's work: "The place has become the form of my work, its discipline, in the same way the sonnet has been the form and discipline of the work of other poets; if it doesn't fit, it's not true" (*Standing by Words* 92).

At the same time, both Murphy and Snyder are aware that their knowledge is limited. They have returned to their wild origins in their respective Wests to be reeducated, as Snyder illustrates in "Pine Tree Tops":

> in the blue night
> frost haze, the sky glows
> with the moon
> pine tree tops
> bend-snow blue, fade
> into sky, frost, starlight.

the creak of boots.
rabbit tracks, deer tracks,
what do we know. (*Gary Snyder Reader* 476)

The relationship between action, creativity, and language is also expressed in similar ways by two other American poets whose careers
mirror Murphy's in some important respects. Berry declares that "What
I stand for / is what I stand on" (Scigaj 129); and, at more length, Merwin declaims from Hawaii:

When the woods had all been used
for other things
we saw the first day begin

Out of the calling water
and the black branches
leaves no bigger than your fingertips
were unfolding on the tree of heaven
against the old stained wall
their green sunlight
that had never shone before

waking together we were the first
to see them
and we knew them then

all the languages were foreign and the first
year rose. (Scigaj 40)

No less than a radical return to the beginning of time mediated by nature, a degree of isolation, and effort, is what these poets propose. They
seek, as Stevens sought, those points where the present intersects with
our shared beginnings:

They go to the Cliffs of Moher rising out of the mist,
Above the real,

Rising out of the present time and place, above
The wet, green grass.

This is not landscape, full of the somnambulations
Of poetry

And the sea. This was my father, or, maybe,
It is as he was,

A likeness, one of the race of fathers; earth
And sea and air. ("The Irish Cliffs of Moher," *Collected Poems*
   501–2)

It is important to note that for Murphy, Snyder, Merwin, and Stevens, actions of repair and renewal must begin in the rural western
parts of their nations, those regions that would appear, on first sight, to
be less tainted by industrialization and profit. Only when the ground-
work has been laid here can there be concerted movement toward
reclaiming the cities that lie to the east. Such a view is somewhat short-
sighted, however, because much of the most sustained urban development in recent decades has occurred in the American West (Phoenix and Las Vegas, for example) and in the West of Ireland (Galway).
   In Paula Meehan's *Painting Rain*, we can observe the emergence
of urban Irish ecopoetics:

The field itself is lost the morning it becomes a site
When the Notice goes up: Fingal County Council—44 houses

The memory of the field is lost with the loss of its herbs. ("Death
   of a Field" 13)

For Meehan, the intrinsic value of the field is obliterated by development and replaced by bland commercial products:

The end of dandelion is the start of Flash
The end of dock is the start of Pledge

> The end of teasel is the start of Ariel
> The end of primrose is the start of Brillo
> The end of thistle is the start of Bounce
> The end of sloe is the start of Oxyaction
> The end of herb robert is the start of Brasso
> The end of eyebright is the start of Persil. (13)

As Kathryn Kirkpatrick has pointed out, Snyder is "central to the development of Meehan's eco-poetics and politics," still another indicator of connections forged between American and Irish poets ("A Maturation of Starlings" 196).

Murphy, and likewise Snyder, is clearly a product of Englightenment thinking, with a healthy regard for the natural sciences, as is evident from how he records the natural world. While following in the footsteps of Robert Lloyd Praeger, he is also serving as an influence on Lysaght, the younger poet whose work can most profitably be spoken of as a companion to Murphy's. What is important about *High Island* is its clarity and depth of description: its poems liberate the Irish West from the mist of the Celtic Twilight. Here, we have birds as birds, not as emblems of something else; nature is celebrated without objectification. The world of nature is not separate from the world of people: both are in constant negotiation, as Murphy reveals in "Stormpetrel":

> Gypsy of the sea
> In winter wambling over scurvy whaleroads,
> Jooking in the wake of ships,
> A sailor hooks you
> And carves his girl's name on your beak.
>
> Guest of the storm
> Who sweeps you off to party after party,
> You flit in a sooty gray coat
> Smelling of must
> Barefoot walking across broken glass. (*Collected Poems* 107)

His presence on High Island involves Murphy in what Voros describes as "a web and a text, or, perhaps more accurately, . . . a text that represents a web. A science whose subject is no animal, vegetable, or mineral but rather the complex interrelationships among these things" (79).

Present throughout the language of *High Island* and *The Kick* is a palpable tone of passionate, ecological discovery. Here are two descriptions of seals—the first, a prose excerpt:

> As I was standing in the pookaun, wondering should I wait for the fog to clear, or haul up the anchor and risk being wrecked on a submerged rock, capsized by a breaker, or carried out to sea by a two-knot current in the sound between High Island and Friar, I heard a voice that pierced me. It was very clear, high and beautiful, crying and exulting from the darkness of a cove. I presumed it came from a seal, but it sounded like a solo in a requiem or a clarinet in a concerto of the sea. Combining joy with lamentation in a falling atonal cry, it seemed to emanate from the heart of all creatures and go beyond the utmost human grief to reach the music of the spheres. Mermaid, banshee and siren crossed my mind. It left me shaken, enthralled. (*The Kick* 283)

The second, a poem:

> The calamity of seals begins with jaws.
> Born in caverns that reverberate
> With endless malice of the sea's tongue
> Clacking on shingle, they learn to bark back
> In fear and sadness and celebration.
> The ocean's mouth opens forty feet wide
> And closes on a morsel of their rock. ("Seals at High Island" 83)

In his introduction to *Ecopoetry*, Bryson brings together the varied theories of scholars and poets and concludes that there are three primary characteristics of ecopoetry, all of which are relevant to *High*

Island and Murphy's other work. The first is that "ecopoetry is a subset of nature poetry that, while adhering to certain conventions of romanticism, also advances beyond that tradition. . . . [There is] an emphasis on maintaining an ecocentric perspective that recognizes the interdependent nature of the world: such a perspective leads to a devotion to specific places and to the land itself, along with those creatures who share it with humankind" (5–6). This interconnectedness "leads to the second attribute of ecopoetry: an imperative toward humility in relationships with both human and non-human nature" (6). The third is "an intense skepticism concerning hyperrationality, a skepticism that usually leads to an indictment of an overtechnologized modern world and a warning concerning the very real potential for ecological catastrophe" (6).

At the outset I suggested that Murphy had somewhat unintentionally opened the door to a contemporary Irish ecological literature. It is clear that his work exhibits the first two of Bryson's characteristics; however, except by implication, the third, and more overtly political one, is absent from his work. However, given Murphy's identification with formal poetics and the dictates of the "New Critical" ideology that underline his aesthetic, it is not surprising that this element is missing, though certainly the potential for ecological disaster can be read into *High Island.* Of course, for all poets, it is dangerous to align poetry with political ideology because the likely result of such alignments will be propaganda rather than art. Indeed it is wrong to expect poets to be propagandists: poets serve in their own way, as Seamus Heaney has noted of Osip Mandelstam: "Mandelstam served the people by serving their language" ("Faith, Hope and Poetry" 218). It is because Murphy's poems are so well made that they are so effective on various levels, including the ecopoetic.

Beyond this remarkable volume, comprising a mere twenty-nine pages of *Collected Poems,* Murphy's work is ripe for further discussion in the context of ecoliterature. In his poems and memoir, he depicts his extended Anglo-Irish family as they work their farms, forests, and gardens, and this allows the reader to see in their labor and husbandry, in which women figure prominently, both an ecological consciousness and ecological practices. In this respect, the Anglo-Irish world becomes an even more complex conundrum for scholars. In the received versions of Irish history, we have been trained to view the Anglo-Irish landlord in a mostly negative light as planter, evictor, absentee, and cruel exploiter. Murphy reminds us, however, of the role that the Anglo-Irish played in the maintenance of the Irish ecosystem by their practice of selective rather than intensive agriculture. This was often made possible by the fact that their estates were so large that they did not need to resort to intensive cultivation, a luxury that their tenants could not afford. It is no doubt easy to develop an aesthetic view of one's place when one has great resources at one's disposal. Over time, of course, all planted and transplanted people can come to identify with their new places, a process that is explained by Snyder in regard to the native people and white settlers in America: "Sometime in the mid-seventies at a conference of Native American leaders and activists in Bozeman, Montana, I heard a Crow elder say something similar: 'You know, I think if people stay somewhere long enough—even white people—the spirits will begin to speak to them. It's the power of the spirits coming up from the land. The spirits and the old powers aren't lost, they just need people to be around long enough and the spirits will begin to influence them'" (*Gary Snyder Reader* 193).

Such a process, we should believe, will allow the residents of the Council houses built on the field in Paula Meehan's poem to hear the Earth's voice. In Ireland, the Anglo-Irish have been attentive listeners, and the creative writers from that tradition have been the true inheritors of the bardic, nature-oriented voice. For Murphy, the great atonal cry of the seal is at once individual and fixed in time and place. Nature is not a hierarchy: it is a circle enclosing all of us.

This idea of community is a primary tenet of ecocriticism. But another key term in ecocriticism is wilderness: the wild places, what they represent symbolically in the mythic American West, and the political battles that are continually fought over their exploitation and preservation. Compared to the United States, Ireland possesses no wilderness comparable to Alaska, to choose an extreme example. Despite the devastating effects in the 1840s of the potato famine and emigration, which halved the population, all parts of Ireland are inhabited and all are connected by roads or technology. But for Snyder, wilderness is more cultural than geographic: "It has always been part of basic human experience to live in a culture of wilderness. There has been no wilderness without some kind of human presence for several hundred thousand years. Nature is not a place to visit, it is *home*— and within the home territory there are more familiar and less familiar places. Often there are areas that are difficult and remote, but all are *known* and even named" (*Gary Snyder Reader* 169–70).

Snyder refuses to assign hierarchies of value. Instead, in this instance, he stresses the interconnectedness of the world: rural, urban, remote, internal. Like Snyder, from evidence presented in *Collected Poems* and *The Kick,* Murphy, though he has lived a rather solitary life, has been engaged intensely with the local people—builders, stone workers, fishermen, boat builders, farmers, as well as with various literary communities—and has lived in the type of "revised" wilderness that Snyder describes. Both poets have also been involved in the physical labor of house building, the sort of activity that Snyder sees as a kind of prayer: "Some people don't have to do a hundred thousand prostrations, because they do them day by day in work with their hands and bodies. All over the world there are people who are doing their sitting while they fix the machinery, while they plant the grain, or while they tend the horses. And they *know* it; it's not unconscious. Everybody is equally smart and equally alive" (*Gary Snyder Reader* 125).

It will always be tempting for poets to view time relative to literary tradition. In both Ireland and the United States, these traditions are relatively young when confined to work written in English, and older when enlarged to include the work produced in indigenous languages. However, ecocriticism asks us to go back further than we are accustomed to, or are often comfortable with, to our beginnings as members of communities. Given that Irish poets have been occupied with place and community and that language and literary form in the Irish context have evolved as a collaboration between humans and the natural world, it would seem that ecocriticism is ideally suited as a mode for reading Irish literature. In fact, one could argue that Irish writers, and Irish poets in particular, have exhibited some measure of a collective ecological consciousness from ancient times to the present, notwithstanding ongoing obsessions with religion, politics, and history.

Looking at the work of other writers who are either from the West of Ireland or who have set their work there—Michael Longley, Michael Viney, Colum McCann, Mary O'Malley, Seán Lysaght, Tim Robinson, Moya Cannon, Eamon Grennan, Joan McBreen, John McGahern, to choose a few of the better known—we can see not only that Richard Murphy is not an isolated figure but that ecology has also permeated through from the poem to the short story, the novel, and interlinked the narrative forms found in the fields of science. All seek to "distil ecological processes into aesthetic techniques to restore our lost sense of connectedness to the planet that bore and sustains us," as Scigaj points out, though for most writers—and this is as true of Murphy as it is of Snyder—ecology is merely one aspect of their work. At the same time, their writings serve to remind their readers that any view of the world that is formed on a purely anthropological basis is lacking: it will undermine and misrepresent the complexity of the various interdependent relationships that sustain us. Poetic theory and practice must always embrace the full complexity and wonder of our world.

Three

TRACING THE POETRY
OF MARY O'MALLEY

The poetry of Mary O'Malley is collected in six volumes: *A Consideration of Silk* (1990), *Where the Rocks Float* (1993), *The Knife in the Wave* (1997), *Asylum Road* (2001), *The Boning Hall: New and Selected Poems* (2002), and *A Perfect V* (2006). In a brief and intensely productive sixteen-year period, coinciding with her return to Ireland, after ten years spent in London and Portugal, to live in the Moycullen Gaeltacht in her native County Galway, O'Malley has published work of great originality, well received and widely translated, that has won her a place in *Aosdána,* the Irish academy honoring creative artists. To a degree, her many-sided and variously shaped work can be difficult to describe and even harder to place. While keeping this in mind, I will focus on some of the more clearly defined aspects present in O'Malley's early work, though I will conclude by suggesting other themes and obsessions in her poetry that critics should also consider. My purpose will be to show the degree to which her work, and what drives it, is rooted in the specific literary, historical, gender-related, and linguistic issues central to the history of the West of Ireland. At the same time, because little has been written in the Irish Studies field on women writers from the West, I will bring into the discussion some recent scholarship from the United States that examines several contemporary Western American writers and that sheds light on O'Malley's poetry.

In "Na Beanna Beola/The Twelve Pins, Connemara," O'Malley describes the mountains that dominate the Connemara skyline:

> Twelve guardians watched
> over my child dreams
> sometimes soft as peaked cream
> sometimes gods of stone.
> Always minding, always men. (*Where the Rocks Float* 36)

The key word here is "minding," which suggests the extent to which women felt husbanded and herded by men whose moods might shift between the softness of cream and the hardness of stone. The mountains that watched over and protected them had male attributes ascribed to them over time. The position of rural Irish-speaking women in the West was fatally undermined by the Famine, as Ann Owens Weekes has pointed out: "Gaelic-Irish women had some economic independence before the famine, but they had little independence of any kind after this event" (13).

O'Malley was born in the 1950s in a transitional decade in Ireland: she was raised by women who carried with them some of Irish history's heaviest burdens while, at the same time, they belonged to the first generation of young women and men who would avail themselves of free secondary education, introduced in the mid-1960s, which would open up educational and job opportunities and transform the Republic. Many of O'Malley's most resonant and obsessive themes are contained in "Na Beanna Beola/The Twelve Pins, Connemara." In each succeeding volume, she will explore the Galway landscape; she will return to it the erased lives and bodies of women; and she will celebrate the lives of men, not always ironically, who have appointed themselves the guardians of its physical, economic, sexual, and artistic aspects. This is not to suggest, as O'Malley points out, that the West is necessarily a more hospitable place when its feminine characteristics are restored, as is made clear in "The Countrywoman Remembers":

The West is hard
with a treacherous yielding,
so sometimes in summer
there is softness. . . .

They used to make me wonder
until I learned the cost, before
they taught me to trust
the surer comforts of stone. (*Where the Rocks Float* 30)

It is in "The Boat Poems" sequence from *Where the Rocks Float* that the concerns raised in "Na Beanna Beola/The Twelve Pins, Connemara" are brought into sharpest focus. O'Malley's father was a fisherman, and boats were part of the everyday world of childhood: "I was allowed out on the *currach,* and later the bigger boats, with my father. Those boats were lovely but far from romantic. I learned that early, my stomach heaving as the boat slapped around in the swell while lobster pots were hauled or set" (*My Self, My Muse* 35). As a child, her ambition was "to become the first woman skipper in Ireland" (37). However, as she leaves childhood, she is no longer welcome on board, just as Alice Munro's young women in such stories as "Boys and Girls" are no longer welcome in the fields in rural Canada. Though "something in her belly stirs / and draws her out / to stare at the shiny sea," O'Malley must reach "under her pillow / for a book without a heroine." In "The Vigil," the men have put to sea and left her at home:

She is landbound,
lately kept from the sea
by men that know their lives hang
on such a thing as luck in a boat. (*Where the Rocks Float* 14)

For the fishermen, boats are female, notwithstanding the superstition that women on board will bring bad luck. Indeed, so much time is spent at sea that these boats are seen as rivals by the shore-bound fishermen's wives. From "Jealousy":

> Look at her, the black bitch.
> I see nothing beautiful.
> He spends his day with her,
> his nights thinking about her.
> I only have peace in October
> when he becomes dutiful,
> a full-time husband for a stretch. (*Where the Rocks Float*, 57)

And, to be sure, these wives have much to be wary and jealous about: only on the sea, and in their boats, will the men allow their true passions to surface. As they chase the catch, roll wildly or gently on the waves, and gut fish, the fishermen allow the raw sexuality and dreamy gentleness that is dormant when they are on land to emerge. In "The Maighdean Mhara," we understand that the men at sea are held in thrall by their boats' voices that speak, alternatively, in the tongues of lovers or of mothers. To be on the sea is to be liberated from the constraints that underline life on the land, and to enter the realm of folklore and mythology, both of which are of great interest to O'Malley:

> But I can make them sing out
> a shower of curses and commands.
> I challenge them to win
> against the sea and other men.
> They listen for the slightest whisper
> between me and the wind. They understand
> my lightest sigh and respond.
>
> Here in my belly where men feel safe
> I draw out their soft talk,
> rising, falling, low as breath.
> At ease and sure of their control
> they are, in Irish, eloquent.
> I never let on anything
> but fall and rise and humour them. (*Where the Rocks Float* 63)

In "Tracing," dedicated to O'Malley's father and to the poet Richard Murphy, the two men sit together "tracing the genealogy of pucáns" while a woman sits to one side of their conversation, "thinking of women measuring / the rising skirts of the wind, scanning / the swollen sea for one speck / to lift out of a trough," and recalling that she had always wanted to be among the men at sea and not on shore (*Where the Rocks Float* 52–53). In this poem, alike in its focus on the father's work at sea and the other course taken by his daughter to Seamus Heaney's poem "Digging" from *Death of a Naturalist,* the woman follows her father's path, though indirectly: she will write instead of catching and gutting fish, though the making of poetry also draws on all of the individual's physical, psychic, and sexual strength. For both Heaney and O'Malley, poetry is not only connected to the physical world, but it is also an integral part of it. In "Digging," Heaney writes:

> Between my finger and thumb
> The squat pen rests; snug as a gun.
>
> Under my window, a clean rasping sound
> When the spade sinks into gravelly ground:
> My father, digging. (1)

In "Tracing," O'Malley writes:

> I feel the heft of a satin handled
> fish-knife. The poem forms,
> a lobster pot turning
> on a wooden wheel. (*Where the Rocks Float* 53)

Both metaphors, the spade and the knife, are violent, invasive, and a reminder that poetry is an ancient and essential art. Even though, by its nature, the conversation in "Tracing" excludes the woman who is listening in the background, both her father and Richard Murphy are central figures in O'Malley's development as a writer. In many poems, her father is seen as an inspirational and enabling figure, generous in how he passed on his gifts to his daughter. Here, in "Lullaby":

> Golden nets and silver fish
> Floating in the sky,
> Lift me on your shoulders Daddy,
> Daddy swing me high.
>
> And if the fishes are all tears
> And if the nets are dry,
> We'll chase the moon with blazing spears
> Across the ice-cold sky.
> Carry me on your shoulders Daddy,
> Daddy swing me high. (*The Knife in the Wave* 14)

Richard Murphy is an important literary model for O'Malley: in her boat poems and in her exploration of the West of Ireland, she is following in his path. Murphy is of the generation of poets first published by the Dolmen Press in the 1950s and the only major figure of that generation to come from the West of Ireland. Like O'Malley, Murphy is from County Galway. After attending college in England, he returned to Galway to write, and, for many years, as is pointed out in *The Kick*, his 2002 memoir, he operated a ferry service between the Galway coast and the island of Inishbofin. Murphy's poetry is full of his own boat poems—"The Last Galway Hooker" and "The Cleggan Disaster" are two prominent examples—and O'Malley's use of personification and symbol is borrowed from Murphy's work. In "The Last Galway Hooker," the relationship between the boat owner and the boat is cast as that between husband and wife, with the physical make-up of the boat compared to the body of a woman:

> With her brown sails, and her sleek skin of tar,
> Her forest of oak ribs and larchwood planks,
> Cut limestone ballast, costly fishing gear. (Murphy, *Collected Poems* 19)

O'Malley is the most important new poet to emerge from Galway since Murphy. She is clearly influenced by his work, though she revises it. She belongs to another generation, and her poetry, though highly crafted and equally allusive, is less formalist than his, and the perspective is often different. In Murphy's boat poems, one hears the voice of the sea captain, whereas in O'Malley's, one hears the often ironic voice of the feminized boat, or the voice of the wife or daughter left at the quayside.

A cornerstone of feminist poetics is Adrienne Rich's 1972 poem "Diving into the Wreck," which is physically and symbolically filled with boats and the sea, and which has had a huge influence on Irish women poets. Though elements of wreckage are evident in O'Malley's work, she simultaneously seeks to strike a balance and to suggest, as Eavan Boland does, that the hand that has been dealt to women is a mixed one. An antidote to the oppressed woman is the figure of Grannuaile, the pirate queen, the subject of another of O'Malley's sequences, "Untitled":

> I am Gráinne, Queen of men,
> mistress of a thousand ships,
> Bunowen's chatelaine.
> A working mother,
> I keep my maiden name. (*Where the Rocks Float* 69)

O'Malley, like Boland, is the kind of poetic messenger whom Rich imagines in "North American Time":

> I have felt like some messenger
> called to enter, called to engage
> this field of light and darkness. ("North American Time" 117)

O'Malley's work has much in common with Boland's, Paula Meehan's, and that of other contemporary Irish women poets. Patricia Boyle Haberstroh has summarized the achievements of this generation: "In much of the poetry by Irish women published since 1980, a growing consciousness of the importance of self has led not only to the proliferation of female personae but also to a more confident female voice expressing the value of women's experience and perception" (*Women Creating Women* 197). O'Malley's work emerges from a received and many-sided landscape and seeks to leave a singular mark. Like Cannon, Rita Ann Higgins, and Joan McBreen, O'Malley is a woman living in Galway and the West and involved in the process of literary reinvention, though, as a result of the range of her subject matter and her literary influence, her work is arguably more diverse and complex than that of her contemporaries. In terms of literary influence, for example, even though Boland seems the most important, strong echoes of Fernando Pessoa, particularly in the use of personae, Derek Walcott, John Montague, Pablo Neruda, Ted Hughes, Federico García Lorca, Paul Celan, and Anna Akhmatova are also notable. O'Malley's deft and extensive use of personae and points of view are reminders to her fans of the many dangers inherent in reading her poetry as sets of autobiographical statements. As in traditional music, another of O'Malley's artistic métiers, nothing is firmly fixed. Montague's *The Rough Field* is a major influence; it is a volume, O'Malley notes, that "released and inspired me, and it inspires me still. The right lines can cut through darkness like a comet" (*My Self, My Muse* 39).

O'Malley has noted that "she was raised between languages. . . . We spoke English, but almost the entire specialized vocabulary of the sea, the names of fish, rocks, birds, and plants was in Irish," and, in such Montague poems as "The Severed Head," she was able to find, for the first time in poetry, an articulation of the world she had been born into (37). This dualism also appears in the bilingualism of her work, where often, when most appropriate, the Irish word takes precedence over the English one. In no respect is the use of Irish instead of English a mere *blas* designed to convey the merry flavor of place; instead, its use is a means of describing and representing the language she was taught, the language of experience and place. Today, as a poet writing in English who lives in an Irish-speaking area of County Galway, she continues to give voice to this dual universe, often with comic effect. In "The Second Plantation of Connaught,"

The locals, sure of what they are
do the opposite. They listen to country music,
speak Irish on the mobile, misbehave
linguistically.
"Connemara Rock, a deir sé. No hassle." (*Asylum Road* 40)

In regard to her contemporaries, Boland points out that "in the poem written by women at the moment the authority of the poet is offset and challenged by the necessity of dailyness and the awareness of a language which needs to be reclaimed and re-possessed"; and, in O'Malley's case, this involves multiple recoveries ("New Wave 2" 144). Although he does not cite O'Malley's work, David Wheatley shows that what she seeks to recover is also sought by some, though by no means all, of her contemporaries:

> While many older Irish poets have been deeply marked by the Irish language, the same cannot be said in truth of Quinn, Groarke, and O'Callaghan. Applied to them, Thomas Kinsella's claim for "a divided Tradition" scarred by the loss of the Irish language seems almost nostalgic. Irish language influences have far from disappeared from the work of younger writers, however, as the examples of Moya Cannon, Peter Sirr, James McCabe, Tom French and Frankie Sewell all show. (253)

Although the importance of Boland as an influence on O'Malley cannot be overestimated — her work is frequently referenced, alluded to, and her themes and obsessions are expanded upon — it must also be said that O'Malley provides a counterargument to Boland's own view of the West of Ireland. For Boland, the West of Ireland is a silent wreck from which its most muted voices, those of its women, must be recovered, and this is achieved with great success is such poems as "The Achill Woman" and "That the Science of Cartography Is Limited." It is clear that O'Malley, too, wishes to recover the voices of lost women; however, as a poet who, unlike Boland, lives in the West, O'Malley does not separate the historical West from its present condition. For Boland, the West is synonymous with the Famine, and thus she views it as the point where time begins and ends. However, for O'Malley, the West continues into the present and even has a future, albeit an uncertain one.

Boland's position is in keeping with the view that Declan Kiberd has expressed of John McGahern's attitude to the West when he notes that "whenever a word is about to disappear, a poet emerges to utter it, and through the poet it achieves a comprehensive articulation" (195). Boland provides an elegy for the West that perished in the 1840s just as McGahern's *Amongst Women* elegizes a West that will die with the last hero of the War of Independence. Other writers, as various as J. M. Synge and Heinrich Böll, see in the fading Irish West the sunset of ancient Europe. However, for most people currently residing in the West of Ireland, and for a majority of its living writers—all well aware of the torment endured over the centuries—it will come as a surprise and be seen as an insult to be told, either from Brussels, Dublin, or from within, that their region is dying. Clearly, the rural West is struggling with depopulation, though it is also vigorously seeking its own survival. At the same time, the West's cities and towns, Galway in particular, have grown enormously in recent decades. In her own work, O'Malley is very much engaged with battles for survival and with efforts to define the shape of the West of the future. She is willing to remember the past, record the present, and imagine the future: all are equally vivid in her poetry. She is concerned with the negative efforts of overdevelopment on Galway City and with the crass exploitation of the environmentally sensitive coastal areas. One aspect of her battle is the coming of second-home owners from the East of Ireland, for whom the West is not a real place but rather a kind of Bainín Disneyland, fashioned by the Celtic Revival, the Hinde postcard company, and *Father Ted*. In "The Second Plantation of Connaught," it all amounts to a kind of faux Celtic sublime:

> "We love Connemara. Bought a little place there.
> It's paradise," the woman brays, adjusting
> her children like accessories.
> Even Cromwell knew better.

Failed the first time. Scraggy blackthorn
not covering the rock's shame, the soil
taken to Aran as a joke. To hell
was the alternative, a hell without golf,
decent restaurants or friends from Blackrock.
Now they come to play, copper-fingered
as that old snob Yeats predicted. (*Asylum Road* 40)

In this poem, Connaught ironically is spelled in the British rather than
in the Irish manner, and it suggests that the newly arrived holiday-
makers may be disappointed to find Connacht surprisingly resilient
and shockingly raw. In "Dublinia," not only does O'Malley parody the
bourgeoisie who have decamped from the capital to vacation in the
West, but she also wickedly dismisses Dublin's claims to prominence
and superiority:

Even those of us that never liked it,
whose capitals were Lisbon and New York,
didn't want it to come to this, the sidewalks
littered with discarded people and a spike
driven through its pot-holed heart. (*A Perfect V* 67)

Little critical attention has been devoted to the role that O'Malley and
other women writers have played in the recent reimagining of the
West of Ireland in contemporary letters; however, a good deal has been
said in recent times about the role played by American women writers
in reimagining the American West, and much of what has emerged
from their work seems applicable to the Irish situation. Of particular relevance is Elizabeth Cook-Lynn's polemic *Why I Can't Read Wallace Stegner and Other Essays,* in which she refutes claims made from
outside the region that Western History ended in the late nineteenth
century and that her own people, the Plains Indians, were even then
vanishing. Through Cook-Lynn's work, one might begin to answer
Kiberd, McGahern, Synge, Boland, and the legislators in Dublin and
Brussels who are often inclined to read the West in the past tense.

Kathleen Norris is another Dakota writer whose literary and moral vision is similar to O'Malley's. In *Dakota: A Spiritual Geography* (1993), she attests to the resilience of the West:

> When I look at the losses we've sustained in western Dakota since 1980 (about one fifth of the population in Perkins County, where I live, and a full third in neighboring Corson County) and at the human cost in terms of anger, distrust, and grief, it is the prairie descendants of the ancient desert monastics, the monks and nuns of Benedictine communities in the Dakotas, who inspire me to hope. One of the vows a Benedictine makes is *stability:* commitment to a particular community, a particular place. If this view is countercultural by contemporary American standards, it is countercultural in the way that life on the Plains often calls us to be. Benedictines represent continuity in the boom-and-bust cycles of the Plains; they incarnate, and can articulate, the reasons people want to stay. (8)

As young women, both Norris and O'Malley had left their respective Wests only to return to become anchors of collective stability. In both the United States and Ireland, women writers have played prominent roles in Western writing and have, with some frequency, explored similar themes.

Every discussion of the work of O'Malley and other women writers will involve an examination of their relationship with Literary Revival writers who, it might be argued, invented the West. Another productive source from America will be Susan J. Rosowski's *Birthing a Nation: Gender, Creativity, and the West in American Literature*. Her approach is oppositional to show how different the male-created American West is, in many respects, from the one imagined by the women: "In 1902 Owen Wister published *The Virginian* announcing what [Margaret] Mitchell refers to as the obsessive concern over 'the problem of what it means to be a man.' That same year, Willa Cather published her first story, 'Peter,' and with it announced her own commitment to freeing women from the alterity of the Western's script" (11). Rosowski goes on to note that "Cather's early fiction tells of seeking ways to save the West from the literary speculators" (64).

Clearly, given the vital role that Lady Augusta Gregory played in the Revival, it would be foolish to see all of its writers as sinister male literary speculators bent on profit; however, in Irish discourse—both literary and political—the actual West has been dwarfed by its nationalist myth, and its inhabitants rendered invisible, and its women perhaps doubly so. It is easy, when an area is designated as being dead and unviable, to turn it into a landscape of golf courses, holiday homes, and visitor centers—a landscape awaiting the carving of the poet's face onto Ben Bulben, and an essay by Umberto Eco. At the same time, we should not place the contemporary women poets from the West of Ireland in permanent opposition to the writers from the Revival period. It is true that these older writers tended to create a particular and rather soft-centered vision; however, as Kiberd attests, their representations are also much more complex than they have often been given credit for, and full of "revolutionary reversals" (*Inventing Ireland* 288). Thankfully, the Revival writers lacked the dangerous machismo of their American counterparts. The Irish Western myth owes more to Eamon De Valera than it does to Yeats. Rosowski uses "script" rather than "myth," and certainly O'Malley in Galway, like Cather in Nebraska, is committed to freeing women from silent alterity.

Krista Comer's *Landscapes of the New West: Gender and Geography in Contemporary Women's Writing* is a study of the work of a variety of writers—Joan Didion, Wanda Coleman, Sandra Cisneros, Louise Erdrich, and others—who have sought to revise readers' views of the American West in the present day. She notes that these writers "serve to recast the spatial field in terms that do not render 'openness' synonymous with male-gendered specialities or 'containment' necessarily synonymous with female gendered roles," a good way of explaining the many transformations of self registered in O'Malley's work that Bernard McKenna has unearthed (28). O'Malley's childhood ambition to be the first Irishwoman to skipper a trawler was an expression of a desire to break free from the constraints of the long-established, preordained role that had been identified as hers. Of course, given Irish literary politics and practices, as Boland has pointed out in *Object Lessons,* choosing a career in poetry was to enter a world as clearly delineated as the sea and the land of the West: "in the old situation which existed in Dublin, it was possible to be a poet, permissible to be a woman and difficult to be both without flouting the damaged and incomplete permissions on which Irish poetry had been constructed" (xii).

At the outset, I pointed out that O'Malley's poetry is complex and many-sided. Let me briefly point toward some other directions that an examination of her work might take. Both classical and Irish mythology are frequently referenced and are often the subject of her poems: in this respect, she has much in common with Kavanagh, Boland, and Nuala Ní Dhomhnaill, who have all sought to describe, subvert, and reexamine these nuggets of their shared literary and psychological heritage. She explores with great sympathy and originality the marks made on the landscape of Connemara by the pre-Christian and Christian belief systems, particularly the sites and iconographies of holy wells. Each volume contains work written to describe the universal suffering of women—this recurring theme was the subject of a vicious and inaccurate review by Patrick Ramsey in *The Irish Review*— to show the degree to which Connemara is, simultaneously, both separate from and belonging to a wider world. The West of Ireland is indeed a popular destination; however, historically, as a result of the diaspora, it is also a region from which many have departed and this phenomenon has served to connect the Westerner to the outside. As O'Malley attests, the people of Connemara are closer to New York than they are to Dublin, in many respects.

In no respect, however, despite its relative distance from the centers of national and European power, is the West of Ireland provincial or disconnected. In fact, even the most cursory glance at O'Malley's and Martin McDonagh's work will convince readers of just how tuned-in is the West of Ireland to worldwide developments. Also found in O'Malley's work are poems of personal suffering, both physical and emotional, often conceived in a magic-realist mode. Although she has written poems of domestic life, her chosen realm of interest is the world beyond her front door and the world of the interior self. In this regard, her poetry is very different from Boland's. Moreover, music and musicians are present throughout her work, and singers as various as Joe Heaney and Billie Holiday are celebrated. Her poems can be sassy and wicked in their humor, for example, "The Poetry Harlots" (loosely translated from the Irish):

> They're the neo-classical can-can girls
> who do not terribly matter,
> but boys must accessorise
> and off-duty they wear pearls. The girls.
> They open their vowels
> and sharpen their smiles
> and converse in iambic pentameter. (*The Boning Hall* 41)

As I have already mentioned, one of the great phenomena of today's West of Ireland is the rapid growth of some of its urban centers, and this growth in Galway has attracted O'Malley's ambivalent gaze. Galway's location on the West Coast of Ireland and its reputation as a mecca for the arts have meant that it has often been compared to San Francisco; however, given how the city has sprawled in recent times and how this explosive growth has resulted in the degradation of its landscape and water supply, it might be more accurate to compare it to Los Angeles or Phoenix.

Writing of poetry in the Republic, John Goodby has noted that "the situation . . . while interestingly fluid, still suffers from a lack of focus which continues to bind together and give cohesion to the work of the best Northern Irish poets. . . . No single historical moment has galvanized poetry in the Republic" (319). Goodby's assumption is that the quality of poetry written in the Republic would improve if a big historical event were to occur. For him, the Republic's *Zeitgeist* is running on empty. The lack of focus that Goodby notices might be lauded by another reader as positive evidence of diversity. Similarly, cohesion could easily be viewed as a recipe for weak, formulaic verse. In effect, because of the infinite variety of directions and turns that poetry has taken in recent decades, there is no such thing as a definable "Poetry of the Republic," though this is not to say that what is written is weak: the work is diffuse, layered, and complex. Goodby devalues the historical moments that have taken place, the most important being the introduction of free secondary education in the 1960s (a Great Reform Bill of the Republic), which brought new voices into Irish poetry, particularly those of women, and transformed it. Furthermore, he fails to understand the extent to which loyalties in the Republic are local and regional rather than national. Evidence of this is to be found in the poetry currently being written in the West of Ireland, where the frames of reference and the poetics are local, regional, and international rather than national. At the center of this endeavor is Mary O'Malley, a gifted and original voice.

Four

HIGH GROUND
John McGahern's Western World

As the author of acclaimed novels and short-story collections, John McGahern has been called by many critics the greatest Irish fiction writer since Joyce and Beckett. Within a small world geographically—comprising the West counties of Sligo, Roscommon, and Leitrim, and the city of Dublin to a lesser degree—McGahern has explored the tangled and complex relationships that exist between people, institutions, and often bitterly opposed ideologies. His work can be both searing and painful; however, I would argue that it has always managed to resonate with emotional truth and is in tune with experience.

Here, I will examine McGahern's third collection of short stories *High Ground* (1985), an important work that has been rather neglected in recent times as a result of the spotlights, both critical and popular, that have been shone on the three works that followed it—*Amongst Women* (1990), *That They May Face the Rising Sun* (2002), and *Memoir* (2005). After the publication of *High Ground,* four more McGahern short stories would appear in print—"The Creamery Manager" and "The Country Funeral" in *Collected Stories* (1992), and "Creatures of the Earth" and "Love of the World" in *Creatures of the Earth: New and Selected Stories* (2006). Given where these new stories are placed in the collected and selected volumes, and how they expand on *High Ground* in regard to time and theme, the point can be made for including them as part of a discussion of that book, as well as for being examples of the late style that is apparent in McGahern's work throughout his final four books. As Denis Sampson has noted, *High Ground* marks "a major departure in narrative style" for McGahern (192). In fact, it is clear that a great deal of the concerns, both thematic and aesthetic, that are central to *Amongst Women* and *That They May Face the Rising Sun* were initially bred in *High Ground*. My particular interest will be to explore how and why the stories are orchestrated, and to address the variety of themes in particular stories that look forward to the novels and stories that follow them, as well as McGahern's view of the West of Ireland and its relationship to the wider world. For the latter, I will seek to indicate aspects of a wider "Westernness" that McGahern shares with such American and Canadian writers as Owen Wister, Wallace Stegner, and Alice Munro. A particular focus will be on the light shed on McGahern's work by the way in which these writers deal with the fate of the individual in violent frontier societies.

Sampson argues that *High Ground* is framed by two Dublin stories: "Parachutes," the first, and "Bank Holiday," the tenth and final one. The timeline is roughly twenty years, from the 1940s to the 1960s, though the Kirkwood stories, "Eddie Mac" and "The Conversion of William Kirkwood," stretch somewhat further back. Sampson notes that "the collection offers a broad and detailed picture of town and country in the forties and fifties, with some flashes forward to later decades, but the social context is embedded in a natural order" (191). In his analysis of *Collected Stories,* Eamon Maher takes this reading a step further by pointing to strong thematic and formal linkages between its opening story "Wheels," originally published in *Nightlines* (1970), and its closing one "The Country Funeral" (1992): "the last story . . . takes many of the ideas found in 'Wheels' but develops them in a more leisurely manner that gives the writer scope for character development and plot elaboration" (63). Both Sampson's and Maher's studies are highly individual and compelling critical works that complement each other nicely, with the former more focused on aesthetic matters and the latter more concerned with cultural, historical, and thematic issues.

As readers, we are accustomed to thinking of McGahern as a writer of rural Ireland—of farms, country kitchens, harvest rituals, visits to Boyle for shopping, and excursions to Strandhill for holidays. We think of such ubiquitous families as the Reegans and Morans as people rooted in the life of the countryside. Of course, the reappearance of characters from one story to the next, or from one volume to another, is not unusual in modern and contemporary writing, and we can see this in the work of Hemingway, Stegner, and others; however, McGahern's process is singular to the extent that he is manipulating names rather than reintroducing characters. One Reegan may not be the same as the next—the first in *The Barracks* is a Garda (police) sergeant while a second in *High Ground* is a senator, and the Moran of "Gold Watch" may or may not be the Moran who reappears in *Amongst Women*. McGahern's purpose here is to narrow the examination to a time and to a society that will be highly concentrated and where characters can be read as individuals, as parts of place, and as rural, Western archetypes.

Even the author himself, as evidenced from Pat Collins's 2005 documentary, is a man who seems tethered to the lanes and fields of Leitrim and Roscommon. Here, ironically, given the detachment that McGahern believed to be the necessary ingredient of good fiction, the author is morphed, uncomfortably, into the milieu of his own work. In the midst of writing *High Ground*, the first book in his late style, McGahern rewrote parts of his 1974 novel *The Leavetaking*, because he felt that the original lacked "that inner formality or calm, that all writing, no matter what it is attempting, must possess" (*The Leavetaking* 6). Collins's splendid documentary challenges the distance that underlines this inner formality. It is simultaneously a reminder of the inseparability of the author from the personal background that underlines the work and a pointer toward McGahern's need, as a literary artist, to adopt the pose of the outsider so that his material will assume its required formal and moral frame.

McGahern's appearance in Collins's documentary and the publication of his *Memoir* in 2005 are indications to his readers of the distinct provinces occupied by the various literary and film genres. To be sure, there are frequent crossovers of places, events, and people; however, each operates under its own set of rules, which McGahern seeks to follow faithfully, so that, for example, we must believe that the fictional barracks is not actually the barracks of the author's childhood and that the fictional character is not actually the person on whom he/she is based. This "inner formality or calm" is the foundation stone of McGahern's late style.

Even though we have been primed to view him as a Western writer, we should not forget that Dublin has always occupied an important place in McGahern's work and particularly so in *High Ground.* In addition to "Parachutes" and "Bank Holiday," "Like All Other Men," considered by Sampson to be the collection's centerpiece, is also a Dublin story, while the setting of "Gold Watch" shifts back and forth between Dublin and the West. McGahern's desire to paint a broad and detailed picture of town, city, and country necessitated this conceit. Dublin is described in its own right and also as the city where rural people settle to pursue careers. And it is, further, the place they flee from to return to the West by train for haymaking, and to recuperate, or to suffer, during holidays spent on family farms. What is different in *High Ground* is McGahern's purpose. Here, he shows us that the city and country, though opposites, are connected and mutually reliant, and that, thematically and spatially, underlying the collection, is what Sampson calls "a drama of opposites" (188). However, following William Blake's notion in his *Songs of Innocence and Experience,* these are two sides of the same coin. Not only do the rural young people of the West go to Dublin to find work as teachers, nurses, and civil servants, but also their parents, who have remained behind, live vicariously in the city through the adventures reported by their children. This degree of connectedness is brought home in "Parachutes" by the drifting thistledown that the drinkers observe through the opened door of a city-center pub:

> "Do you see the thistles?" I said. "It's strange to see them in the middle of Grafton Street."

"There are backyards and dumps around Grafton Street too. You only see the fronts," Mulvey said. "Just old boring rural Ireland strikes again. Even its principal city has one foot in a manure heap." (*High Ground* 22–23)

In this respect, the positioning of these stories points to the growth of Dublin and the unintentional role that it has played in the depopulation of the West. The old people, who must remain on their farms, such as the parents in "Gold Watch" and "Bank Holiday," watch as the young men whom they had hoped would return and take over from them remain rooted in Dublin. McGahern reminds us that time moves at a rapid pace and that the rural world of these characters' childhood passes quickly from sight. The explosion of Dublin's population has occurred at the expense of the rural areas, particularly those in the more remote parts of Ireland, while the distinctiveness of rural life, which McGahern has always shown to be a mixed blessing, has been undermined by the spread of the city through its attitudes and the technologies that it has promoted. For example, in "Oldfashioned," a grown man who goes back to his home place to film a documentary discovers that the people whom he would most like to meet from his childhood are no longer alive. He himself has been unable to gauge the changes that have taken place in his absence:

> In every house across the countryside there glows at night the strange living light of television sets, more widespread than the little red lamps before the pictures of the Sacred Heart years before.
>
> The Sergeant's son came with a television crew to make a film for a series called *My Own Place*. He was older than when his father first came to the barracks. The crew put up in the Royal, and the priest was invited to dinner the first night to counter any hostility they might have run into while filming. It showed how out of touch the producer was with the place. He should have invited the politician. . . . It would be a dull film. There would be no people in it. The people that interested him were all dead. (57)

Among other elements present in the privileging of the Dublin stories are literary ones, specifically McGahern's engagement with Joyce's *Dubliners* and his estrangement from the city's literary and bohemian life, which is held up to ridicule. To better explain the triumph of *Dubliners,* McGahern, in a 1990 essay, proposes a comparison between Joyce and George Moore's *The Untilled Field*: "The authority and plain sense suggest that Joyce was well aware that he was working within a clearly defined tradition. To look towards Moore for any tradition is not useful. All of Moore is self-expression: he constantly substitutes candour for truth. In *Dubliners* there is no self-expression; its truth is in every phrase" ("Dubliners" 65). And lurking behind this desire to follow Joyce's example is a debt to Flaubert's methodology, quoted by McGahern in this same essay. Replying to George Sand, Flaubert offers a defense for his philosophy of composition: "You [Sand] start from the *a priori* from theory, from the ideal. Hence your forbearing attitude toward life, your serenity, your — to use the only word for it — your greatness. I, poor wretch, remain glued to the earth, as though the soles of my shoes were made of lead: everything moves me, everything lacerates and ravages me, and I make every effort to soar" (67).

For McGahern, the Irish short story (with the exception of *Dubliners*), because it is not rooted in the earth and its language, because it seeks to run before it can walk, is a "dubious enterprise" (63). Like *Dubliners, High Ground* seeks to be a "moral history," though one from a later period encompassing both rural and urban Ireland. In the Dublin stories, McGahern consciously treads warily in the master's shadow in homage to Joyce's style. When he describes Joyce's structure, he also points to his own in *High Ground*: "I do not see *Dubliners* as a book of separate stories. The whole book has more the unity and completeness of a novel. Only in the great passages of *Ulysses* was Joyce able to surpass the art of *Dubliners*. In many of these, like the 'Hades' episode, his imagination returns again and again to his first characters, his original material" (71). Still another influence that underlines McGahern's strategies to best represent "our perception of time and existence" is the work of Proust, identified by Maher as "one of McGahern's favourite writers" (90).

Like Joyce before him, McGahern found himself at odds with the literary capital. The characters in the framing stories, of whom Patrick Kavanagh is the most notable and the most viciously satirized in "Bank Holiday," are little more than a crew of alcoholic buffoons who gossip rather than write. In *High Ground,* as Sampson reminds us, gossip, whether it is found in the city or the country, is a form of pornography (204). For McGahern, rather bitterly, the Irish writers of his own time have sought to be personalities rather than artists, to seek, like George Sand, to fly headlong toward the sun rather than to pay attention to what emerges from the earth. This criticism is harsh and certainly unjustified, given the accomplishments of the writers with whom McGahern crossed paths during his Dublin years; however, it does serve his artistic purpose of opening up the space to be occupied by his own unique vision. One might read this as being an assertion of things as they are, part of the natural order, or, conversely, view them as examples of a savage determinism that undercuts Mc-Gahern's lofty aesthetic—where the "self-expression" he decries in Moore is allowed to blur his own vision. But McGahern's attitude to Kavanagh is complex and inconsistent. Even though he holds the writer-as-public-figure up to Swiftian ridicule, he is also able to conclude that Kavanagh "was also a true poet, and I believe his violent energy, like his belief that people in the street steered by his star, raised the important poems to permanence" (*Love of the World* 333).

But personalities are not peculiar only to Dublin. The conflict between two flamboyant, larger-than-life figures is at the root of the drama in *High Ground*'s title story, where Senator Reegan conspires to have Master Leddy removed from his teaching position at the local school. Reegan is crafty, ambitious, and owns little regard for tradition, while Leddy is drunk and irresponsible. Here, a battle is being waged between progress and folklore, two forces that should be reconciled rather than be pitted in conflict. The politician carries with him the weight of the present and the future—the desire that the local children receive a first-rate education so that they will be employable in the new Ireland—whereas, on the other hand, the master is a figure from folklore more at home in the hedge-school or on the pages of Goldsmith than in the modern classroom. Neither man can change

his ways to accommodate the other: the politician insists that everyone must step in line with progress, while the master is too set in his
ways to change. Moran, the young man whom Reegan is trying to
recruit to take Master Leddy's place, is a former star student of the
teacher's and, in a neat postcolonial twist, is asked to occupy the position of the *shoneen*. This story echoes themes explored by Brian Friel
in *Translations* and indicates that the Irish are much more intransi-
gent when dealing with one another than they were when dealing with
the British—a further example of a dramatic clash between reliant
opposites. Clearly, there are many good reasons why Senator Reegan,
and the parents of the local children, would want Leddy to be replaced; and, with the power of the clergy having faded, it would seem
that the rising politician now occupies the moral high ground.

Ironically, the drunken teacher in "High Ground" is a sympathetic figure, whereas the drunken poet in "Bank Holiday" is not—
McGahern's moral vision is hardly consistent. However, this is not
merely a complaint about McGahern's narrow vision but a suggestion
of his art's closeness to Frank O'Connor's, who noted that "the short
story, like the novel, is a modern art form; that is to say, it represents,
better than poetry or drama, our own attitude to life" (13). Consis-
tency is difficult to reach in both spheres. In McGahern's rural West,
the ugly vigor of Senator Reegan, the politician, is contrasted with
the entropy of Catholic clergymen, as exemplified in this collection
by the elderly Archdeacon, who, in "Crossing the Line," is fixated
on the obituary page of the *Irish Independent* where he hopes to read
of the death of the oldest priest in Ireland—"a Father Michael Kelly
from the Diocese of Achonry"—so that he can assume this post (*High
Ground* 84). The elderly priest in "The Conversion of William Kirkwood" has ceded the traditional authority in local affairs that was once
the province of men in his position to Reegan, the public represen-
tative of the new order: "Canon Glynn, the old priest, was perfectly
suited to the place. He had grown up on a farm, was fond of cards
and whiskey, but his real passion in life was for the purebred short-
horns he grazed on the church grounds. In public he was given to em-
phasizing the mercy rather than the wrath of God and in private be-

lieved that the affairs of the earth ran more happily the less God was brought into them altogether" (*High Ground* 129). In keeping with McGahern's overall purpose, the rural stories explore both village and farm life, though, as in the Dublin stories, all parts of modern Ireland are now interdependent and in constant negotiation. "A Ballad" and "Crossing the Line" are the town-based stories—towns that are coarse and undistinguished, that exist as little more than narrow way stations between the farm and the city.

In "Oldfashioned," "Eddie Mac," and "The Conversion of William Kirkwood," McGahern explores the worlds of the Western Protestant, specifically of a retired colonel and his wife, and of a farming family. As will be clear from a reading of his nonfiction, McGahern's own interactions with Protestants aided his own development as an intellectual, helped to refine his moral view, and served as blueprints for his characters ("The Solitary Reader"). The stories in *High Ground* that feature Protestant characters—the Sinclairs of "Oldfashioned" and the Kirkwoods of "Eddie Mac" and "The Conversion of William Kirkwood"—are in the Joycean vein. Explaining how he conceived of *Dubliners*, Joyce noted, "I have tried to present it to the indifferent public under four of its aspects: childhood, adolescence, maturity, and public life," a format that McGahern has followed, often ironically, in these three stories. His exploration of and deep interest in the Protestant world of the West is a new departure for McGahern, allowing him, in the contrasts he creates between the views and behaviors of Catholics and Protestants, to more fully enumerate the failings of both. In these wise and artful stories—McGahern's greatest, I would argue—the chronology of Joyce's four aspects is movable. Childhood is represented by Johnny in "Oldfashioned" and Lucy in "The Conversion of William Kirkwood"; adolescence is defined by attitude rather than by age with Eddie Mac and the two William Kirkwoods suspended in this state well into adulthood, and with disastrous consequences for those who depend on them; maturity seems unreachable, except for Colonel and Mrs. Sinclair in "Oldfashioned," so that McGahern explores maturity by its lack rather than by its presence; and public life, as seen through the representation of the Local Defense

Force during the "Emergency," is little more than a comic interlude for the locals.

McGahern is interested in the vacuums in the moral life of the West, and the nation, and how these affect the well-being of individuals. Postcolonial Ireland, at ground level and beneath the radar of ideology, is a largely dysfunctional space. The rural West, long idealized by Nationalists and writers for the purity of thought and action of its inhabitants, is doubly so. It is, in many instances in these stories, paralyzed and cut adrift from human kindness. In addition, as McGahern slyly points out in "The Church and Its Spire," the rural West is a pagan rather than a Catholic space:

> When I came back to Ireland to live as a small farmer in the countryside I discovered that most of the people there had no belief, and they looked cynically on both Church and State.
>
> "Oh, sure," I was told as if it explained everything and how nothing under the sun is new, "we had the auld Druids once and now we have this crowd on our backs."
>
> "Why don't you go to Mass, John?" I was asked by a dear friend and neighbour once.
>
> "I'd like to but I'd feel a hypocrite."
>
> "Why would you feel that?"
>
> "Because I don't believe."
>
> "But, sure, none of us believe."
>
> "Why do *you* go then?"
>
> "We go for the old performance. To see the girls, to see the whole show." (*Love of the World* 147)

In the Dublin stories, there is a progression from the disharmony caused by lost love and immersion in a toxic pub culture to the harmonious image at the end of "Parachutes" of the drifting thistledown that links the country with the city and the past to the present, while in "Bank Holiday" harmony is found through love and immersion in the civilized life. The first story represents, primarily, the public life; the second, primarily, the personal. In the rural stories, harmony, whether public, personal, or a mixture of both, appears to be unattainable. At the close of "The Conversion of William Kirkwood," William is left to ponder his future and his responsibilities:

> His own house was in darkness when he got home. He knew the back door was unlocked, but rather than go through the empty kitchen he let himself in by the front door with his key. There he sat for a long time in the cold of the library. He had many things to think about, and not least among them was this: whether there was any way his marriage could take place without bringing suffering on two people who had been a great part of his life, who had done nothing themselves to deserve being driven out into a world they were hardly prepared for. (*High Ground* 139)

William has transformed himself from being a remote, Prospero-like figure who favored astronomy over farming into a useful member of the community. To arrive at this point in his life, he has led the local LDF battalion during the "Emergency," converted to Catholicism, and become engaged to Mary Kennedy. However, if he is to retain his newly earned social position and become a full member of the new order by his marriage into the Kennedy family, he must turn his back on his maid Annie May and her young daughter Lucy, who will not be welcome in any household presided over by his future bride. Explicit here is a clash between an ancient Anglo-Irish world that values loyalty, paternalism, and the aesthetic, and the values of a modern Ireland where the pragmatic, for McGahern, will eternally trump the just and the beautiful. Mary Kennedy, already disappointed in love once, will, like Rose Moran in *Amongst Women*, favor a necessary accommodation over a supreme fiction.

In his analysis of this story and its prologue, "Eddie Mac," Sampson makes the following astute observation:

> Most striking of all in this collection is the emergence of a broad sympathy for the women who are trapped in this largely patriarchal and exploitative community; beginning with the portrait of Elizabeth Reegan in *The Barracks*, McGahern's writing shows a remarkable tact in the presentation of women under duress and in

pain, and a remarkable clarity in depicting the sullen violence of male characters, but the two Kirkwood stories seem to be designed to cut across distinctions of class, creed, or ethnic affiliation to show a dependent woman victimized by men. (190–91)

In general, McGahern's female characters are defined and believable, though in *High Ground* these portraits are more nuanced and the women are drawn from the broad spectrum of Irish society and, as Sampson indicates, from across religions and social classes. At the same time, in a savage indictment of the cruelty engendered by the patriarchy that was at the heart of Irish society from the 1920s to the 1960s, McGahern shows that most women of this period had to exist in constrained circumstances, with the poorest (Annie May in the Kirkwood stories being the prime example) being the most vulnerable. In "The Conversion of William Kirkwood," when she sees Mary Kennedy in the house for the first time, Annie May realizes that she and her daughter will soon be forced to depart: "there was no one to blame; that it was the natural order of things only made it more painful. She couldn't even be angry" (*High Ground* 137). Taking a long view of Annie May's and Lucy's displacement, one can make the point that the social status, financial well-being, and job security of the family servant remained the same as it had been during the darkest decades of the previous century. One cannot blame William for wanting to marry, though he is guilty of being railroaded into marriage by the local schoolteacher and others, and of not thinking through the consequences for his dependents. Foresight, as Eddie Mac makes clear, has never been a quality that the two William Kirkwoods, father and son, favoring bee-keeping and astronomy over farming, have been imbued with: "they're both fools. . . . The only thing you could be certain of is that no matter what he turned to it was bound to be something perfectly useless. . . . If I owned their fields, I'd be rolling in money in a few years, and they can't even make ends meet. The whole thing would make a cat laugh" (73). Mary Kennedy, though she appears dominant, cold-hearted, and ready to take control of both William and his property, is a somewhat pathetic character who, having had a failed relationship with a doctor while she worked as a nurse in Dublin's Mater

Hospital, has decided to marry Kirkwood in part because "she had suffered and was close to the age of reconcilement" (136).

In McGahern's fiction it is a given, as Sampson points out, that a household will disintegrate after the mother/wife dies, and this was the case in the Kirkwood home after the death of William's mother. Father and son closed up many of the rooms, gave up entertaining, retreated to the kitchen for their meals, and took little notice of their farming chores. In this context the imminent arrival of Mary Kennedy in "The Conversion of William Kirkwood" is full of irony. Certainly, as an energetic woman who seeks to arrest the house's decay, her arrival will seem timely; however, she will also displace Annie May, who, as its unsung caretaker for years, has lacked the legal status to effect large-scale changes. This is a good example of one of McGahern's contraries at play—one woman about to replace another, though these opposites, and the two women also, are as related as the heads and tails of a coin. Mary Kennedy's return to the West looks forward to Rose Moran's return, in somewhat similar circumstances, in *Amongst Women.*

While the fate of Annie May in "The Conversion of William Kirkland" points to the weak position of vulnerable women in Western society during the decades from the 1940s to the 1960s, the fate of her only daughter Lucy does not hold out much hope for young women in the decades to follow. After her father had absconded to England, the Kirkwoods raised Lucy as their own daughter, giving her old Mrs. Kirkwood's Christian name, allowing her mother to continue in service in the house, and, most important, raising her against type: "the old man and child were inseparable. Every good day they could be seen together going down to the orchard to look at the bees, she, clattering away like an alarmed bird, trying to hold his hand and hop on one foot at the same time, he, slow by her side, inscrutable behind the beekeeper's veil" (*High Ground* 122). When old Kirkwood died, Lucy transferred her allegiance to his son and "started to go with him everywhere, about the sheds and out into the fields. She was as good as any boy at driving sheep and cattle. Annie May tried to put some curb on these travels, but Lucy was headstrong and hated housework" (122). From the Kirkwoods, Lucy learned to be unconventional and independent, to shun the drudgery of housekeeping for the excitement

that the outside world promised. It is almost certain that the marriage
of William and her banishment from the farm will end Lucy's idyll
and force her to inhabit a more narrow space. Of course, her independence was always an illusion: she is always subject to the whims and
desires of men—like the great majority of the women of McGahern's West, the great exception being Kate Ruttledge in *That They May
Face the Rising Son*. The events that shaped Kate's character took place
outside the West: she has chosen to live there rather than tie herself
to it out of necessity.

No doubt Lucy, possessed of foresight and intelligence, had
understood for a long time—ever since William decided to begin
the process of converting to Catholicism—that her way of life was
threatened. The whole force of the impending upheaval is brought
home to her when everyone is gathered for a celebratory breakfast:

> The only flaw in the perfect morning was that Lucy looked pale and
> tense throughout and on the very verge of tears when having to re-
> spond to polite questions during the breakfast. She had been strange
> with William ever since he began instruction, as if she somehow
> sensed that this change threatened the whole secure world of her
> girlhood with him. As soon as they got home from the breakfast, she
> burst into an uncontrollable fit of weeping and ran to her room. By
> evening she was better but would not explain her weeping, and that
> night was the first night in years that she did not come to him to be
> kissed on her way to bed. (131)

The marriage of Protestantism and Catholicism is symbolized by the
festive breakfast, the meal that, until recently, followed the traditional
early morning wedding. However, such a union of faiths is not a true
marriage because one excludes the other. In the sense that William's
identity as a Protestant has died upon his conversion, he is certainly
the last of the Kirkwoods. Ironically, the locals, given their tribal view
of the world, would have been happier had he remained a Protestant.
As William is brought more fully into the local community, Lucy's
position in it is undermined. His conversion has upset the apple cart,
or natural law, of West of Ireland society, and only trouble can ensue.

In "Oldfashioned," Sergeant Casey notes that "You don't ever find robins feeding with the sparrows," a nugget of "wisdom" that is reprised throughout the volume. Society is locked into destructive views and outmoded ideologies (*High Ground* 49).

Alice Munro's short story "Boys and Girls" similarly explores a girl's coming-of-age in a tradition-bound society, in this instance on a fox farm in rural Canada. Unlike the broad canvas that McGahern paints in "The Conversion of William Kirkwood," Munro's eyes are fixed on the few transformative moments in childhood and adolescence during which a free-spirited outdoor girl is molded into a docile young woman. Here, the narrator, now grown up, is looking back on her childhood and recalling how, like Lucy, she thrived on working out of doors with her father:

> Nevertheless, I worked willingly under his eyes, and with a feeling of pride. One time a feed salesman came down into the pens to talk to him and my father said, "Like you to meet my new hired man." I turned away and raked furiously, red in the face with pleasure.
>
> "Could of fooled me," said the salesman. "I thought it was only a girl." (115–16)

The narrator recalls that "it was an odd thing to see my mother down at the barn," but she herself disdains indoor tasks: "It seemed to me that work in the house was endless, dreary and particularly depressing; work done out of doors, and in my father's service, was ritualistically important" (116–17). She considers her mother to be her enemy; however, she also comes to understand, as time passes, that "the word *girl* had formerly seemed to me innocent and unburdened, like the word *child*; now it appeared that it was no such thing. A girl was not, as I had supposed, simply what I was; it was what I had to become" (119). At various points from this time onward, the narrator traces her progress toward an indoor girl confirmed in her assigned role. That she grows into such a role, rather than is forced into it, like Lucy, does not render it any less cruel. It is clear that both McGahern's and Munro's rural societies (Irish and Canadian, respectively) are founded on strict, traditional, paternalistic ideologies and patterns—partly

cultural, partly religious—and that these are underlined by strict gender roles. In *High Ground,* and throughout McGahern's fiction, women
rarely flourish.

High Ground is dominated by brutal, if memorable, males: the
Dublin literary men ("Parachutes" and "Bank Holiday"), O'Reilly the
engineer in "A Ballad," the Sergeant in "Oldfashioned," Eddie Mac in
"Eddie Mac," Senator Reegan in "High Ground," and Moran in "Gold
Watch." The latter is one of McGahern's finest stories and the work-
shop for *Amongst Women,* the novel that would follow in 1990. "Gold
Watch" is a profound and harrowing version of the theme of time
passing, as Eamon Maher points out (80), in which Moran places the
new watch his son has bought him, as a replacement for an old one
that no longer worked, in a barrel of poison:

> I went idly toward the orchard, and as I passed the tar barrel
> I saw a thin fishing line hanging from a part of the low yew branch
> down into the barrel. I heard the ticking even before the wrist watch
> came up tied to the end of the line. What shocked me was that I
> felt neither surprise nor shock
> I felt the bag that we'd left to steep earlier in the water. The
> blue stone had all melted down. It was a barrel of pure poison, ready
> for spraying. (*High Ground* 118)

His violent, rage-filled purpose is twofold—to test the watch's in-
destructibility and, both literally and metaphorically, to stop time. As
the father has aged, he has seen his grip on life loosen, and the future
that he imagined—one in which his son will return to the farm—
will never happen, because his son prefers to remain in Dublin. The
placing of the watch in the barrel is the story's climax and points
backward to the poison spread by Moran throughout his lifetime.
Moreover, his act is not only a violent one directed toward his son but
also a futile gesture of revenge against the inexorable force of time
passing. Male violence, in general directed toward women, children,
and grown-up sons and daughters, plays an important role in Mc-
Gahern's West throughout his work, from *The Barracks* (1963) to
Memoir (2005).

In his 1923 volume *Studies in Classic American Literature,* D. H. Lawrence observed: "But you have there the myth of the essential white America. All the other stuff, the love, the democracy, the floundering into lust, is a sort of by-play. The essential American soul is hard, isolate, stoic, and a killer. It has never yet melted" (2). Moran, and many of McGahern's fictional males, fit into this construct and link two Wests—the American and the Irish. *High Ground* is a violent work teeming with hard, isolate, and stoic men. In McGahern's West, individuals are not killed by gunfire until the appearance of "Love of the World" in *Creatures of the Earth* in 2006; rather, men and women are rendered insensible by the effects of hatred and greed. The Irish Western male has failed to think of himself as part of a community or, to put it another way, as one who belongs to polite society. For McGahern, according to James Whyte, "the closest thing we have to a society in Ireland is the family. . . . Society was, in fact, made up of thousands of little republics called families" (136). Within these Irish families, or little republics, the father rules tyrannically. Fathers in "Gold Watch," *The Barracks, The Dark,* and *Amongst Women* cannot control the world beyond the hearth and the farm, but they *will* control their families and their home ground. In the long run, because what they seek is against nature, they fail. But it is these attempts at control, and how control is dramatized, that is at the core of McGahern's fictional enterprise. It is that same predicament of trying to live in a place separate from the intrusions of the outside world that was also explored by Joseph Conrad, most notably in *Victory.* Both McGahern and Conrad remind us that time cannot be halted and that, no matter where you hide, the world will invent a stratagem to find you.

McGahern's Western males are rugged individuals, frustrated in their need to be in charge of their destinies, who view themselves as being morally and intellectually superior to others. Moran in *Amongst Women* and the Sergeant in "Oldfashioned," two typical examples of the McGahern male, are unable to prosper in a world where compromise must trump ideology and, at times, what is right and just. The former, a hero of the War of Independence, has been set adrift after the Treaty, while the latter is "given notice of transfer to Donegal" when he persists with his investigation into the fire that destroyed Rockingham

House long after his superiors have lost enthusiasm for determining its cause (51). Both men retreat bitterly to farms. In many respects such characters have much in common with the American Westerners described by Wister in his preface to *The Virginian* (1902). Wister asks:

> What has become of the horseman, the cowpuncher, the last romantic figure upon our soil? The bread that he earned was earned hard, the wages that he squandered were squandered hard. . . . His wild kind has been among us always, since the beginning: a young man with his temptations, a hero without wings. . . . He and his brief epoch make a complete picture, for in themselves they were as complete as the pioneers of the land or the explorers of the sea. A transition has followed the horseman of the plains; a shapeless state, a condition of men and manners unlovely as that bald moment in the year when winter is gone and spring not come, and the face of Nature is ugly. (x)

Reading *The Virginian* in the light of *Amongst Women* is most instructive. Both heroes—Moran and the Virginian—are aristocrats by reason of their abilities rather than by birth; they have come into maturity after periods of wildness; they are both excellent letter writers—an indication of intelligence—and sure with firearms; they are disdainful of pomp and have little regard for such professionals as lawyers, whom they see as being weak and parasitic; they insist on sticking to principles and are intent on performing tasks properly and honestly; their standards—what they expect of themselves and of others—are exacting. Though both men are iconic, archetypical heroes of their respective Wests, their trajectories are quite different: the Virginian, the hero of the more romantic text, remains forever in the ascendant; he gets what he wants and is rewarded for his actions and intelligence, while Moran, on the other hand, feels cast aside when his service is no longer required. As Max Westbrook has written, "The Virginian's heroism is not a matter of social class or narrow realism. He is a hero, and he represents the belief that class should be a matter of performance, the biology of excellence: and this is why sanctimonious religion, Popular Opinion, snobbish barriers, and the destructive ambitions of

Trampas all melt before the Virginian's willingness to work and fight for what he believes" (331).

McGahern's purpose is the opposite of Wister's because he seeks to demystify and de-idealize his West, to strip it of its covering of Celtic Revival gauze, and to represent it as he has observed it. Moran is not rewarded for his heroism during the War of Independence and is a man in bitter retreat. Unlike Wister's American West, where it is possible for adventurous men to create a new society, McGahern's West is one in which, after the struggle for independence has ended, the conservative new leaders embrace the class and social systems of the old order. Moran learns that the natural man must play second fiddle to the professional man: "What did we get for it? A country, if you'd believe them. Some of our own johnnies in the top jobs instead of an Englishman. More than half of my own family works in England. What was it all for? The whole thing was a cod" (*Amongst Women* 5).

Certainly, McGahern would agree with Larry McMurtry's remark that "the romance of the West was always more potent than the truth" (Benson 304). Moreover, Richard White has noted that "the nationally imagined West has been far more powerful than the locally imagined West" (619–20). Just as Wallace Stegner, born and raised in the West, seeks to present it realistically as a buffer against mythology, so, too, does McGahern—as much of a true Westerner in his world as Stegner was in his—seek to demythologize his home place. Both Wests, as colorfully imagined by outsiders, were imbued with elements of the sublime, and, even when dealing with its violence, as in Synge's *The Playboy of the Western World,* these writers felt impelled to do so softly and comically. McGahern, using a hard realism, as had Kavanagh before him, has sought to explore a darker West that would resonate more with lived experience. His West, imagined from its often violent inside, is a revision of Yeats' gentle West.

For Wister, "the brief epoch" of the heroic male West and Westerner was over by the time that *The Virginian* appeared in 1902 and had become an unrecognizable "vanished world" (ix–x). *High Ground* is McGahern's own exploration of a male Irish West that he sees as vanishing, one in which the complex and often corrosive idealist is replaced by the confident and compromised opportunist. Moran, the Sergeant, Master Leddy, and the parish priest represent the old with the Senator and Kennedy, the school principal in "Crossing the Line," standing for the new order. What all of these men lack is any sense of the aesthetic. They are busy, but graceless. To find what is elegant in life McGahern looks to the inhabitants of another vanishing world—the Anglo-Irish. It is among the Sinclairs and Kirkwoods where resonant aspects of the civil and aesthetic will be found, though, in the complexities of *High Ground,* both families have some severe shortcomings. Unlike their Catholic neighbors, the Sinclairs and Kirkwoods are quiet and reflective, as exemplified by the scene in "Oldfashioned," in which Johnny, the Sergeant's son, who helps the Sinclairs with their gardening, recounts what he appreciates most about their world:

> Beyond the order and luxury, what he liked best about the house was the silence. There was no idle speech. What words were spoken were direct and towards some definite point. At the barracks, the movement of a fly across the windowpane, Jimmy Farry pushing towards the bridge with his head down, and the cattle cane strapped to the bar of the bicycle, were enough to start an endless flow of conjecture and criticism, especially if Casey was around. "If you could get close enough to the 'huar' you'd hear him counting, counting his cattle and money, counting, counting, counting." (*High Ground* 43)

Eamon Maher has summarized the gulf that exists between the Sinclairs' house and the barracks: "the humdrum nature of life in the barracks, devoid of any intellectual or cultural stimulation, is a far cry from the sophistication of the Sinclair house" (83). Yet, for all of their culture and grace, the Protestant Sinclairs in "Oldfashioned" are undermined by a narrow vision: they cannot anticipate the Sergeant's objections to their proposal to have his son educated at Sandhurst. And, the newly empowered Catholic postcolonials, for all their energy, are a group without culture or grace, as William notices when he goes to the McLoughlins' for dinner: "Before this got under way, William Kirkwood came to the McLoughlins' bungalow to dinner for the first time. He felt ill at ease in the low rooms, the general cosiness, the sweet wine in cut glasses, and Mrs. McLoughlin's attempts at polite conversation. Not in all the years of his Protestantism had he ever felt his difference so keenly, and what struck him most was the absence of books in a schoolmaster's house" (*High Ground* 133–34). For a writer, there can hardly be a space more hostile to his calling than one without books, a world where both beauty and reflection hold no weight.

The Virginian resorts to violence when it is called for, to restore a semblance of order to a frontier community; however, outside of dire necessity, he is not a violent man. Instinctively, he is concerned with fostering respect for others, with fairness in dealings between people regardless of social class or gender. It is his desire to belong to a workable and egalitarian community. In this regard, he is a more complex character than he is given credit for, and one who escapes from under Wister's utopian cloud. He fits nicely into Stegner's definition of the Westerner:

> For Stegner, the West was not settled and built by the lone adventurer on horseback; social maturity involved cooperation and required the individual's assumption of responsibility to others. Following the "frontier tradition" and "code of the West," they learn to exclude girls from their play as incompetent, and they are taught by their culture — usually regardless of how pacifistic their parents might be — that violence is an essential part of the masculine role. Our love of guns also runs very deep since it defines who we, as males, are (and what we are as Americans). (Benson 18–19)

Stegner also believed in "the benefits of community versus the futility of individual efforts" (Fradkin 33). A great many of McGahern's Western males are burdened with the negative characteristics that Stegner exposes: generally misogynists, they are "lone adventurers" who are prone to violence. At a primal level, many do not see themselves as belonging to a community. Instead, they are patriarchs of families whom they rule with iron fists. Like the American West, the Irish West, in its postcolonial epoch, can be seen as a frontier area where democracy must be tested. In Wister's novel, democratic ideals are promoted by and personified in the figure of the Virginian. On both the community and personal levels, McGahern's males, with the exception of Colonel Sinclair and the Kirkwoods, show little interest in or tolerance for democracy. Clearly, they have not yet learned how to live in a country that, after a long period of foreign rule, is now their own.

Writing of the American West and the Western novel, Jim Kitses has noted that what gave the American West its "particular thrust and centrality" is that it is placed "at exactly that moment when options are still open, [when] the dream of a primitivist individualism, the ambivalence at once beneficent and threatening horizons, [is] still tenable" (14). In post-Treaty Ireland a related dynamic was at play that McGahern dramatizes through such characters as the Sergeant ("Old-fashioned") and Moran (*Amongst Women*), men who had hoped to have had their bravery rewarded. However, as McGahern shows, particularly in his dramatization of Moran's anger and disenchantment in *Amongst Women,* the "moment" did not make it beyond the Treaty; independence, though of great value, did not result in a new order that would promote egalitarianism but, instead, allowed for the continued dominance of a professional middle class. Kitses also observes that "the western has posited the sadder truth that the establishment of democratic order required the cowboy or gunman to subordinate his personal freedom to the greater good. The cowboy could ride the open ranges and heroically battle the outlaw with his six-gun, but only until the social order was made secure" (15). The Sergeant and Moran confront a landscape similar to that of the American cowboys. Just as the cowboy had to be reined in when democratic order had been established in the American West, so, too, had the Irish revolutionary to put aside his wild ways and his guns when the Treaty had been signed and the Civil War settled. What rendered them bitter was a combination of their own intractable personalities and the failure of the new nation to suitably reward them for their service. As a result, men such as Moran and the Sergeant have never adapted to the democratic order. Their brief moment of influence has passed, and they know it. The Virginian, much like McQuaid in *Amongst Women,* is able to fashion a smooth transition from cowboy to land and mine owner.

Even though many parallels can be drawn between Wister's and McGahern's Wests, they are quite different in important respects. Writing in a volume of essays that revisits *The Virginian* on the centenary of its publication, Zeese Papanikolas notes how the Native Americans of Wyoming "exist only at the margins" in Wister's novel (188). No such erasures are found in McGahern's *High Ground*: it is a fictional work written by an indigenous author whose vision is inclusive. Moreover, the relationships of these authors to their respective Wests are also dissimilar. What Papanikolas has noted of Wister is not true of McGahern: "the West that he came back with was a territory of the imagination formed out of what he had seen and experienced in a few months in Wyoming, but more important, it was the theatre for the working out of his own psychological and political drama" (176). McGahern proceeded in the opposite direction: he had left the West of Ireland, where he had grown up, after finishing secondary school only to return as an adult. Unlike Wister's, McGahern's work is the fruit of long observation.

The four stories that follow those that appeared in *High Ground*—"The Creamery Manager" and "The Country Funeral" from *Collected Stories* (1992), and "Creatures of the Earth" and "Love of the World" from *Creatures of the Earth* (2006)—are explorations of a contemporary West that has taken the place of the one that has vanished. Here, McGahern has pushed his marker beyond the 1960s into the present. In "Creatures of the Earth," Mrs. Waldron, a widow who has left her large house in Castlebar to live in her summer home on Achill, looks back on her time on earth and concludes that "authority could not be questioned then, especially when vested in a priest or doctor. How rapidly all that had changed. Sometimes she could hardly believe it had all taken place in the brief space of a lifetime" (*Creatures of the Earth* 324). Notwithstanding the great changes that she has witnessed, this story is underlined for two scenes of gratuitous violence to animals: the stealing of, and subsequent drowning of, Mrs. Waldron's cat by two drunken holiday-makers; and Tommy McHugh's killing of his dog by tossing it from a cliff into the ocean. Violence against women is reprised in "Love of the World" when Kate Ruttledge is murdered by her coarse and violent husband. As in "Creatures of the Earth," McGahern reads cruelty to animals as an offense that foreshadows not only cruelty to men and women but also to the ecology.

Late in his career his vision is enlarged to shift animals, in their own right, into central and equal positions in his Western world. In this respect, his fiction comes under the influence of Alistair Mac-Leod, an author whom McGahern admired and wrote about (*Love of the World* 208–12). In "Love of the World," the retired guard who will murder his wife has a lucrative business as a guide to German tourists: "While Tracy had managed the properties only, Harkin threw himself into the whole lives of the tourists. Soon he was meeting them at Dublin airport and taking them back. He organized shooting expeditions. He took them on fishing trips all over. These tourists did not return their catch to the water. The sport was in the kill. As well as pheasant, duck, woodcock, pigeon, snipe, they shot songbirds, thrushes, blackbirds, even larks" (*Love of the World* 345). In these four stories set in the present day, people work in the Middle East and return home flush with cash on holidays, while others come back from New York to attend weddings. Yet, despite the changes that Mrs. Waldron has seen, many aspects of the old life have been retained: men remain violent and unpredictable, teaching continues to be a lousy job, and life in a small house with a tiny garden in suburban Dublin is not an effective antidote to the misery of an upbringing in the West. While the contemporary West may be different, it is hardly more enlightened. To grow up there, McGahern reminds us, is to be poorly prepared for life.

Though he continued to probe the West's darkness and dysfunctionality in the works that followed *High Ground* and in the stories that reprise that volume, these stories point toward another track in McGahern's work that would reach its greatest point in *That They May Face the Rising Sun,* and this is his sense of its splendor. The narrator in "Love of the World," in surveying the country scene—the lake, wildfowl, stars, and fields—wonders "who would want change since change will come without warning? Who this night would not want to live?" (*Love of the World* 368). These lines are reworked, and the vision reinforced, by Moran at the end of his life in *Amongst Women* when he concludes: "to die was never to look on all this again. It would live in others' eyes but not in his. He had never realized when he was in the midst of confident life what an amazing glory he was part of" (179). The lake would reappear in the opening of *That They May Face the Rising Sun*: "The morning was clear. There was no wind on the lake. There was also a great stillness. When the bells rang out for Mass, the strokes trembling on the water, they had the entire world to themselves" (1). His last novel, his most expansive work, would bring into free play the sublime and the brutal West, the Blakean two-sided coin that is the central tenet of McGahern's moral vision and literary aesthetic.

Five

A WILD WEST SHOW
The Plays of Martin McDonagh

Five of the Martin McDonagh plays that have been produced for the stage share West of Ireland settings: *The Beauty Queen of Leenane, A Skull in Connemara, The Lonesome West,* the three plays that comprise the Leenane trilogy; and *The Cripple of Inishmaan* and *The Lieutenant of Inishmore,* two parts of an Aran Islands trilogy. These works have been extraordinarily popular and, in equal measure, have brought renown, wealth, and controversy to their author, a young Londoner of West of Ireland background. It is perhaps ironic that the most widely disseminated contemporary representation of the West has been written by an outsider; however, such contradictions are not unusual in literary history, either in Ireland or elsewhere. Also, given McDonagh's nihilist vision, negative portrait of West of Ireland life, and showboating of his own talents, it is hardly surprising that the critical reaction to his work has been mixed.

How these plays came into being has proven to be as interesting, and as unlikely, as the plays themselves. As McDonagh pointed out to Fintan O'Toole, in a profile that appeared in *The New Yorker* in 2006, the drafts of his seven plays—his complete oeuvre as a dramatist to this point—were written in a nine-month period in 1994–95 when he was in his mid-twenties and living alone in his parents' house in Camberwell, London (44). Except for *The Pillowman,* set in a nameless and generic East European Soviet-type state, all of McDonagh's plays are located in County Galway: the Leenane trilogy in the eponymous village near Killary Harbour, also the location of Jim Sheridan's movie *The Field*; and the second trilogy on Inishmore and Inishmaan, the largest and the middle of the Aran Islands. *The Banshees of Inisheer,* a third play in the Aran Islands trilogy, has not been produced for the stage. After the fashion of David Bowie and Prince, McDonagh, at the height of his fame, announced his retirement from the theatre. Instead of writing plays, he would devote his time and talents to film. To date, he has written and directed *Six Shooter,* an Oscar-winning short; and a well-received feature, *In Bruges,* co-starring Colm Meaney and Colin Farrell. The absence of new plays has served to increase his audience's hunger for more work and is a reminder of McDonagh's shrewd business acumen. His retirement, like Bowie's and Prince's, was a brief one: in early 2010, *A Behanding in Spokane* opened on Broadway.

McDonagh's West of Ireland plays are dramatic representations of highly dysfunctional and hyperviolent rural societies. Even though Irish writing has traditionally been a consistent purveyor of bad news, audiences will still be shocked by the over-the-top violence in these plays—murder, mayhem, dismemberment of people and animals, as well as the hatred and cruelty that flies so easily off the tongues of old and young alike. Even audiences trained by such prominent contemporary works as John Banville's *The Book of Evidence,* Patrick McCabe's *The Butcher Boy,* and John McGahern's *Amongst Women,* all of which include various examples of physical and psychological brutality, will be challenged by the seemingly unrelenting and gratuitous violence present in McDonagh's work:

> **Mairead:** One of ye's chop up Padraic, the other be chopping the fella there with the cross in his gob. And don't be countermanding me orders, cos it's a fecking lieutenant ye're talking to now. (*The Lieutenant of Inishmore* 66)

However, given what the contemporary theatre has inherited from the ancients of Greece, who certainly knew a thing or two about murder, mayhem, and blood-curdling revenge, it has proven impossible to dismiss McDonagh's work on the grounds of bad taste. His plays also fit nicely into the "in-yer-face" movement that has been a feature of contemporary British theatre. Furthermore, for all of their bleakness, McDonagh's plays can be hilarious, with the result that audiences are constantly kept off guard by being forced to laugh at what is truly horrible. It is clear that McDonagh is a spell-binding author, a Pied Piper of the gross, a Marlow-like figure presenting the material of a Galway version of Conrad's *Heart of Darkness* as a comedy of manners. Every audience member must join, shamefully perhaps, in the raucous laughter. Cruelty, murder, dismemberment, vengeance: it's a hoot. A purpose of this essay will be to search for the genesis of McDonagh's vision of the West of Ireland, which is as rooted in his immersion in popular culture as it is in his own experience as a product of the Irish diaspora.

As O'Toole points out, McDonagh grew up in an immigrant neighborhood where his "parents coped with their dislocation by trying to re-create the world of home, living among other Irish families," and where Irish culture was favored over British (41). So eager were his parents to embrace various captivity narratives, it must have seemed to McDonagh as a child that independence had yet to come to any part of Ireland. His family sought to exclude British cultural influences from the home. By choosing, of necessity, to live in Great Britain, the McDonaghs were returning, economically and psychologically, to a world of colonial servitude. Theirs was a complex and painful narrative of dispossession; however, it seemed more honorable and loyal for them to accept this dispossession than to embrace what England had to offer. As a result, McDonagh and his brother grew up in a home where Irish music was privileged, were educated at Catholic schools where most of their teachers were Irish priests, and were encouraged to participate in Irish sports such as hurling and Gaelic football. To reinforce this at-home immersion, the boys spent six weeks of each summer in Connemara among their father's extended family, many of whom were Irish speakers. We might call their upbringing a cultural home schooling whose aim was to curb assimilation and to burn everything English including its coal.

It is clear that this immersion in Irish culture was pivotal in McDonagh's journey to find his voice as an author: "writing in an Irish idiom freed me up as a writer. Until then, my dialogue was a poor imitation of Pinter and Mamet. I used to try and write stories set in London, but it was too close to home. Now I've shaken off these influences, I can move back" (Russell 2). McDonagh's summers in Galway recall Yeats's equally pivotal holidays spent with his West of Ireland relatives, the Pollexfens of Sligo. McDonagh's experience is echoed by Michael Stephens, a writer who grew up in an Irish-American neighborhood in Brooklyn and whose attitude to language and literary form is not unlike McDonagh's:

> Even being American, and raised more in the ways of American culture, the residues of that Irish past seem to imbue one's life and writings, and there is still an attitude, cultivated, no doubt, from those early myths of James Joyce, that suggests that English is a foreign language, and that coming from an Irish background one has an obligation to use this language in two ways. The first is to write it better than any native speaker—which could as easily be construed as Polish and Conradian as Irish and Joycean—and, second, to subvert that language at every chance, knowing that the tradition you have inherited is one of experimentation. The tradition is to be original, un-English, and never bend in the pursuit of these ideals, no matter how impossible they may seem, and probably are. (*Green Dreams* 77–78)

For both writers, Irish connections are central to the emergence of distinctive literary voices. In McDonagh's case, the whole idiom is Irish—both setting and language—whereas Stephens's work is Irish only in the nuances of its speech. Though both men are masters of English, they are keen to subvert what they have mastered, and it is this sparkling and toxic dualism that is at the center of their enterprise.

While McDonagh's family was promoting all things Irish to him, London, a great capital drawing all manner of talent to its streets, was holding out to him exciting alternatives to home truths. Like many second-generation immigrants, McDonagh was inexorably drawn toward what the city offered—the anger and profanity of punk rock, and the worlds of the cinema, television, and theatre, all proffering generous helpings of cosmopolitanism to counter the Irish parochialism preached by his parents. From his home he received language. From London, he received form. But it is clear—and this is crucial to his artistic identity—that McDonagh belongs to neither England nor Ireland. As Catherine Rees has pointed out, "Born in London of Irish parentage, McDonagh is in the perfect position to interrogate the mythology of Irish drama, while simultaneously able to claim this heritage as his own. As Graham Whybrow, literary manager at the Royal Court [Theatre in London], puts it, 'McDonagh writes both within a tradition and against a mythology'" (Chambers 130). Lilian Chambers and Eamonn Jordan have noted that "McDonagh is the man from nowhere, elsewhere, anywhere and everywhere, displaced without the longing for a place or a position either within a single nationality or canon" (10–11).

McDonagh's ambivalent view of his cultural inheritance allows him to borrow and steal from everywhere without finding it necessary to owe allegiance to anyone. His outlook is local and global rather than national, and his ability to recreate a world from many fragments and strains is a key aspect of his work. Ironically, for McDonagh to succeed in his desire to create a hip, contemporary New Wave/punk theatre required him to use, for the most part, Irish idioms and locales. Whereas he could easily reject his parents' worldview, he needed to embrace the places where they came from as well as their idiom in order to find his literary voice. By fastening himself to punk, McDonagh set himself in opposition to the Irish world that his parents valued and to the polite British world that they rejected. This pose is similar to Joyce's in his rejection of both the Gaelic League and the Literary Revival, and its purpose was for McDonagh to scratch out his own artistic space. He was also the product of a bitterly divided political and social climate in England—strikes, the Thatcher Revolution, the Brixton Riots, the IRA bombings—and the discord he absorbed from this aspect of his childhood has found a way into his work.

At the heart of all discussions of McDonagh's oeuvre must be the issue of violence. Helpful will be two books that explore the representation of violence in American film and culture: Richard White's *"It's Your Misfortune and None of my Own": A New History of the American West* and Richard Slotkin's *Gunfighter Nation: The Myth of the Frontier in Twentieth-Century America*. Both works are particularly useful for the exploration of the roots of violence in the history and representation of the American West and provide ways of reading the violence in McDonagh's Irish West. As we shall see, a play such as *The Lieutenant of Inishmore* follows the blueprint of the classic Hollywood Western movie. Indeed, as has been pointed out by many critics, American culture—film and drama in particular—underlines McDonagh's vision. He owes much to Quentin Tarantino and Sam Peckinpah, writer-directors whose work in film carries on and updates classic Western themes and commonplaces.

As Slotkin makes clear, violence is at the savage heart of the American West. Is the Irish West as wild as its American counterpart, and to what extent are McDonagh's representations of the West of Ireland tied to Hollywood's representations of the American West? Are the people who inhabit the West of Ireland inherently violent? In addition to answering these questions, I hope to trace McDonagh's debts to punk rock, a genre of rock music that emphasized the shocking and the violent, and the connections between his revenge plays and the Elizabethan and Jacobean versions. I will suggest, for the latter, that comparisons between Shakespeare and McDonagh are not as far-fetched as they might appear. Even though we think of punk as being an English phenomenon, many writers such as Tricia Henry have pointed out that it had its origins in the United States (59).

The critical work that has been published to date on McDonagh's plays is engaged, engaging, and even quite breathless. The most notable contributions are two edited volumes of essays: Lilian Chambers's and Eamonn Jordan's *The Theatre of Martin McDonagh: A World of Savage Stories*, primarily the work of Irish and British scholars; and

Richard Rankin Russell's *Martin McDonagh: A Casebook,* writings by U.S.-based scholars, though there is some overlap with Patrick Lonergan, for example, who contributed to both. The former also reprints some of the original reviews of the plays. Both younger and senior scholars are found in these collections, all seeking to make sense of the McDonagh phenomenon, to alternately praise and decry his representation of Ireland and the Irish, and to place his work within the pantheon of Irish drama. Nicholas Grene notes that "the cult of Connemara, the culture of weepy Irish nostalgia, is treated to a savagely sardonic iconoclasm" (45), while Werner Huber declares that "the comparison has frequently been made [that] McDonagh is doing to contemporary playwriting what the Pogues did to traditional music in the 1980s" (13). Christopher Morash thinks of the Leenane trilogy as "copies that have forgotten their originals" (269), while Dominic Dromgoole argues that McDonagh's "greatest talent is as a pasticheur, he is able to produce perfect forgeries" (quoted in Jordan 174).

In the midst of much praise for his work, some dissenting views emerge, the strongest being from Mary Luckhurst:

> Here I argue that McDonagh is a thoroughly establishment figure who relies on monolithic, prejudicial constructs of rural Ireland to generate himself an income. I wish to counter the disturbingly widespread notion amongst English commentators that McDonagh's excess is of itself radical, and to challenge arguments that his use of stereotypes undermines received ideas of "Ireland." Stereotyping is as much a feature of McDonagh's person as it is of his plays: a typical example of the dominant construction of him by the English press is an article by Liz Hoggard in which he is presented as "One of London's Angriest Young Men," "a punk playwright," and a man with a "rock'n'roll reputation." All are constructions that McDonagh consciously seeks to sustain, as the same article demonstrates. (118)

Luckhurst in unable to find "a single intelligent Irish character in any of McDonagh's plays," and she is aghast at the notion put forward by critics that he is a "brave" writer (120–23). For Luckhurst, English audiences delight "in the sheer stupidity of McDonagh's characters" (119). As far as she is concerned, McDonagh is nothing more than a phony. A challenge to this point of view comes from José Lanters, who sees McDonagh's work as being wildly ambiguous, full of displacements, and the sort of postmodern work that should be read with caution. For Lanters, to ascribe too much meaning to McDonagh's plays is to miss the point altogether (16–23).

Many commentators, such as Maria Doyle, align the violence present in *The Lieutenant of Inishmore* with that found in contemporary movies: "Martin McDonagh's approach to theatre hinges on violence—violence recalled, violence threatened, violence narrated, and violence enacted" (92). His objective is to "get as much John Woo and Sam Peckinpah into the theatre as possible" (93). Despite the truth of this comparison, Luckhurst's objections to the stereotyping present in the plays are well taken and as valid as Spike Lee's complaints about how African Americans are portrayed in Tarantino's movies, as Lonergan has pointed out (166). So many commentators explore the connections between McDonagh's and Tarantino's works that one might think of *The Lieutenant of Inishmore* as the *Pulp Fiction* of the Aran Islands.

Interestingly enough, as Joan FitzPatrick Dean states, "McDonagh's commercial success rests on his uncanny skills as a playwright, especially his deft manipulation of multiple and shifting dramatic illusions within a largely conventional, representational dramaturgy" (27). According to Dean, McDonagh is fond of such dramatic clichés as mistaken identity, hidden truths, running gags, mysterious secrets, misdirected letters, sudden reversals, lost lockets, undying revenge. And, quoting Clare Wallace, she reminds us that "while McDonagh's plays continually draw attention to the genres, themes and stereotypes they quote, formally they are highly conservative dramas" (27). Thus, formally and technically, this is traditional theatre.

McDonagh has claimed that he came "to theatre with a disrespect for it. I'm coming from a film fan's perspective" (Chambers and Jordan 114). He learned how to write, he has claimed, from watching films and television programs—media in which both traditional and postmodern narrative structures are deeply embedded. Similarly, according to Jerome Charyn, Tarantino had said of his own autodidactic education: "the video store was like my tenure at college . . . when your four years are up, you have to actually start your life, but you end up hanging on to that free zone" (xii). And, Charyn continues, "the five years he spent behind the counter at Video Archives in the Los Angeles suburb of Manhattan Beach have been mythologized into the most successful crash course in the history of filmmaking"(xii). Charyn notes of Tarantino that he is "like a brilliant anteater who's sucked in all the debris around him and hurls it back at us, as Donald Barthelme did in story after story" (105). It is likely that McDonagh's "education" has been equally mythologized, both by the press and by the author, though it is undeniable that he is as brilliant an anteater as Tarantino.

One of the illustrations included by Robert S. Miola in *Shakespeare's Reading* is "The Reading Wheel" from the work of Agostino Ramelli. He points out that this "machine, enabling the consultation of many books simultaneously, suggests the kind of associative and eclectic reading the Elizabethans regularly enjoyed," and he goes on to show how writers such as Shakespeare assembled their plays from a wide variety of sources (5). Thus, both Renaissance reader and present-day television viewer become anteaters. MacDonagh and Tarantino read as Shakespeare had read, spewing out their art like crazed, postmodern Jacobeans.

Much has also been made of McDonagh's ill-mannered behavior, most famously his showing up drunk to receive the Most Promising Playwright Prize at the London *Evening Standard* Theatre Awards ceremony for *The Beauty Queen of Leenane,* where he told Sean Connery to "fuck off" (O'Toole 45). Such boorishness is reminiscent of the excesses of Brendan Behan and Richard Harris, two figures from a bygone age when the Irish artist was nothing if not an entertaining clown. Most commentators warn their readers to take what McDonagh has said about himself as an author with a grain of salt, while, simultaneously, such is their degree of infatuation with the man, whether positive or negative, that they privilege what he says at every turn. Other critics, somewhat dyspeptically, point out that he does not qualify as an Irish writer at all, though this will hardly displease McDonagh, who has sought to resist being labeled: "I always felt somewhere kind of in-between. . . . I felt half-and-half and neither, which is good . . . . I'm happy having a foot in both camps. I'm not into any kind of definition, any kind of -ism, politically, socially, religiously, all that stuff. It's not that I don't think about those things, but I've come to a place where the ambiguities are more interesting than choosing a strict path and following it" (Russell 151). This resistance goes to the truth of his upbringing (raised in a diasporic gray area somewhere between the West of Ireland and Greater London), but it is also a defense mechanism: he could hardly get away with claiming to be Irish, and if he claimed to be Anglo-Irish, he risked having his work pigeon-holed and pushed to the margins. To a large degree he is global man belonging, in an unattached way, to global culture.

Arguing in this vein, Lonergan writes that we should see McDonagh's work as part of a "'world' literary tradition": "I want to suggest, then, that the problems created by critics' attempts to categorize McDonagh in terms of Irish drama arise because of a clash between the assumptions underlying literary criticism on the one hand and the globalized quality of much contemporary cultural production on the other; that is, we are attempting to use a nationalized discourse to critique work that has transcended national boundaries" (Russell 155). Lonergan goes on to detail, for example, what McDonagh has learned of plotting from soap operas and to propose reading his plays in relation to contemporary films such as *The Crying Game, Trainspotting, In the Name of the Father,* and Tarantino's work in particular. Crucially, he shows that McDonagh's manipulation of Irish speech is similar to what Tarantino does with African-American speech (162–68).

Among contemporary dramatists, McDonagh is not alone in having received an unconventional training as a writer, as we learn from an account of August Wilson:

> Wilson was not much influenced or inhibited by the canon of western theatre, for the simple reason that he had not read or seen any of it. (With the exception of his own plays, and a few by his friends, when we spoke in 2001 Wilson claimed to have seen only about a

dozen plays.) "I consider it a blessing," he said, "that I had not read Chekhov. I hadn't read Ibsen. I hadn't read Tennessee Williams, Arthur Miller, or O'Neill." It had taken him eight years of reading and writing to find his voice in poetry. "I didn't want to take eight years to find my voice as a playwright," he said. (Lahr 23)

Also, when we consider McDonagh's debts to contemporary television, we should not underestimate the quality of good programming available in England while he was growing up, in addition to the soap operas he favored. In *Glued to the Box,* a gathering of the television criticism written for the *Observer* from 1979 to 1982, Clive James noted that "British television provides enough worthwhile programming, week in and week out, to convince even the most demanding viewer that he is not necessarily committing mental suicide by tuning in regularly. Those demanding viewers who say otherwise are usually doing more demanding than viewing" (19). He goes on to describe the range of shows available during his ten-year stint as a critic— from the most artful drama and opera to *Brideshead Revisited, Dallas, Hill Street Blues,* Wimbledon tennis matches, football, game shows, and so on. One could see a dramatization of Muriel Spark's *The Girls of Slender Means* or Arthur Miller's *Playing for Time* (24–27).

James also found that the coverage of the Troubles in Northern Ireland became more extensive and grew more sophisticated as the 1970s faded and the 1980s began, and this must have been a valuable resource for McDonagh (21–22). Perhaps, with the growth of other media and with the availability of good programming, particularly in the United Kingdom, a bookish education was no longer the prerequisite it had been for a career as a playwright.

To write of a sophisticated oral culture, McDonagh delved into another, mostly oral medium—television. Literary scholars expect those men and women who write books to have learned their craft from them. Nowadays, these same scholars must defend the text vigorously against the push of other media that, they feel, are driving civilization toward illiteracy. To such academicians, McDonagh must appear to be the barbarian at the gates proudly trumpeting his ignorance; however, we should be aware that today's "Reading Wheel" includes more than traditional written texts. Nevertheless, McDonagh's criticism of theatre is derivative and specious and the kind of sentiment we had heard from Antonin Artaud decades before: "The contemporary theatre is decadent because it has lost the feeling on the one hand for seriousness and on the other for laughter; because it has broken away from gravity, from effects that are immediate and painful—in a word, from Danger" (*Theatre and Its Double* 42).

Implicit in McDonagh's artistic pose is the punk/New Wave revolt against the stylized music of the 1970s. He has frequently described The Clash, for example, as an enabling force that helped form his own voice. Jeremy Black has defined punk in this way: "the punk style set out to shock and transform popular culture in reaction to the commercialized world of popular music. Punk was a conscious reaction against the technical wizardry and excessiveness of 'Glam rock'" (*Britain since the Seventies* 47). Like McDonagh, the punk performer traded his/her lack of musical training for high-energy and shocking material. A punk performance, like a McDonagh play, could be both violent and provocative, with the former highlighting "behaviour such as vomiting on stage, spitting at the audience, and displaying wounds which were the result of self-mutilation—[the musicians] having cut and bruised themselves with objects such as broken bottles, fish hooks, and knives" (Henry 4).

It is only a short step from the violence of a punk performance to the violence of a McDonagh play. On a particular level, punk rock was also known for its emphasis on masculinity and, simultaneously, for what Henry calls the "sexually ambiguous appearance," as personified by the New York Dolls (38). Henry also reminds us that "punk rock has been a significant factor in shaping Western aesthetic trends since the mid-1970s. It has influenced not only the evolution of performing arts but also fashion, graphic arts, literature, film, and popular entertainment" (6). In McDonagh's West of Ireland plays, particularly in *The Lieutenant of Inishmore,* issues of masculinity and sexual ambiguity are important. Mairead, as the result of how she dresses and has her hair cut, is frequently mistaken for a man; and when Padraic declares that "there's no boy-preferers involved in Irish terrorism, I'll tell you that! They stipulate when you join," he is indicating the macho, heterosexual nature of his organization (33). Such juxtapositions contribute to the humor in the plays. At the center of "punk philosophy was the anthem 'No Future' (taken from the lyrics of 'God Save the Queen,' 1976, a song by the Sex Pistols . . .), a nihilist vision of the future that McDonagh has clearly absorbed" (Henry vii). The lyrics to this song were written by another child of the Irish diaspora, John Lydon, aka Johnny Rotten.

Many of the scenes we witness in the plays are gross and disturbing—the skull and bones bashing in *A Skull in Connemara*, the mutilation of the bodies in *The Lieutenant of Inishmore*, and Maureen's pouring oil on Mag in *The Beauty Queen of Leenane*, not to mention the constant verbal assaults; however, this material would not have been alien to contemporary English audiences. Jeremy Black reminds us of some of the controversies that arose at that time in the visual arts:

> The presentation of parts of animals, fixed in formaldehyde, by Damien Hirst, including "The Physical Impossibility of Death in the Mind of Someone Living" (a dead tiger shark), "Away from the Flock" (a dead sheep) and "A Thousand Years" (the head of a slaughtered cow being assailed by flies), and the display of the cast of a house by Rachel Whiteread did not strike everyone as art. This reached a height with the "Sensation" show at the Royal Academy [in London] in 1997, which led to unprecedented media attention on British art. Although Hirst's animals were on display, much of the controversy related to Marcus Harvey's large portrait of the sadistic murderess of children, Myra Hindley, a portrait painted in 1995 with the template of a child's hand. (*Britain since the Seventies* 61)

Animals are also exploited by McDonagh—killings, blindings—and the use of this violence for comic effect is one of the most disturbing aspects of his work. It seems clear that McDonagh, like Hirst, understands that the killing of humans, after the terrible wars of the twentieth century, will not shock his audiences, but violating the innocence of animals will, to audiences newly tuned in to notions of fair treatment of animals.

Such abuse of animals in Irish drama is hardly confined to Mc-Donagh, as Patrick Burke makes clear: "In stark contrast, a manifest hostility towards, or cold indifference to animals may, within the *corpus* of Irish drama, betoken cruelty or even savagery in a maimed or diminished community" (156). Of course, theatre audiences have already seen the blinding of animals (Peter Schaffer's *Equus*) and of people (Shakespeare's *King Lear*). As Burke suggests, there is a larger purpose at work here, beyond mere shock value, and that is to remind us of just how maimed society has become. In this regard, a maimed West of Ireland points toward the larger world, itself maimed on a larger scale.

Violence directed toward children also has a role in McDonagh's work, though hardly to the same degree as it does in Edward Bond's *Saved*, a savage contemporary play in which a child in a pram is stoned to death, and a play that is often read alongside McDonagh's work. Even at the level of bad language, we can argue that none of Mc-Donagh's plays is quite the "feck"-fest that James Kelman's *How Late It Was, How Late* is, the controversial Booker Prize winner for 1994. It is clear that McDonagh, the talented anteater, is the product of a specific time and place, 1970s and 1980s England, and of a not-unusual family dynamic, the immigrant family who resisted integration.

What makes McDonagh's plays work is juxtaposition: everything becomes strange when his nihilistic, avant-garde, postmodern, and often weird aesthetic visions are transported to County Galway, a bastion, if only on the surface, of traditional values. Clearly, the combination of traditional setting and punk attitude, allied with a wicked linguistic talent, is what makes for such compelling theatre. He also interjects references to popular culture, as Rees explains in regard to *The Lieutenant of Inishmore*:

> The play thus articulates the widening and hybridizing of Ireland into the "Global Village," and is punctuated by references to media influence. The characters understand and articulate their experiences through television programmes, for instance, the local policeman glamorizing his job "just like *Hill Street Blues*," while Catholic doctrine is reduced to, "so that fella from *Alias Smith and Jones*, he'd

be in hell?", and Padraic's view of women is limited to idealizing "Evie off *The House of Elliott.*" (137)

Thus, it is clear that the residents of Leenane and the Aran Islands are very up to date, and that traditional values are being eroded by the popular media. McDonagh's leadership figures such as Father Welch are emblems of civilizing traditions that have been undermined by a mixture of entropy and corruption. It would appear likely, however, that the lifting of such customary restraints on behavior has allowed the local inhabitants to revert to savagery. In this regard, McDonagh's vision of County Galway is as uncompromising as V. S. Naipaul's is of Zaire in *A Bend in the River.* Both writers feed artistically on post-colonial civilizations set adrift in the contemporary world, which, as they see it, seesaw back and forth between the savage and the sophisticated. In the literary background is Conrad's *Heart of Darkness,* with Kurtz's shout, "The horror! The horror!" (154). As theatre audiences, sitting uncomfortably in our seats, we get to play the role of Kurtz during the performance of a McDonagh play. Interestingly enough, Conrad, Naipaul, and McDonagh cast their glances to peripheral places—the Belgian Congo, Zaire, the West of Ireland, respectively—from London, a center of civilization to which each is ambiguously attached. And present in Padraic is the trickster figure of Native American literature that sets up a comparison between McDonagh's work and Sherman Alexie's. "Footloose, irresponsible and callous, but somehow always sympathetic if not lovable," Alexie's tricksters are not unlike the sort of characters that McDonagh might create (Russell 11).

For McDonagh, County Galway is a space suspended between two worlds, the ancient and the modern, and this reflects the two worlds of his own childhood, the ancient Ireland of his parents and the modern England where he was brought up and where he continues to live. Situating the plays in Galway allowed McDonagh the space to explore what was his mind. And Galway was what he has called, referring to the theatre, "a box to tell a story in, basically" (Russell 2). Absent from McDonagh's work is warmth in general and affection for the West of Ireland in particular, and this is what makes him an exception among nonnative writers who have located their work there.

We can think of McDonagh as the Sam Peckinpah of our time and read his West of Ireland plays as American Westerns. As already noted, many McDonagh scholars have compared his work with Peckinpah's; therefore, a comparative analysis of *The Lieutenant of Inishmore* and *The Wild Bunch* can be instructive (Luckhurst 122). *Six Shooter,* McDonagh's first film, is a typical Western—gunplay, murder, mayhem, an outlaw, a train—though, in typical McDonagh fashion, it is laden with inversions of these commonplaces. Even though the age of the classic Western is over, their themes and settings, updated to meet contemporary tastes, have been retained by filmmakers as various as Tarantino and George Lucas. As Slotkin points out, many of Peckinpah's hyperviolent films belong to the genre of the Mexico Western, in which American gunfighters venture across the border into Mexico, which parallels the movement of the action in *The Lieutenant of Inishmore* from the North of Ireland to the Aran Islands. It is interesting to note that both Peckinpah and McDonagh situate violent work not at home but in neighboring countries. In Peckinpah's case, the often pointless and extreme violence reflects back to the United States and describes his dark vision of America during the Vietnam War. McDonagh's vision is not so specific to Great Britain, indicating his detachment both from it and from Ireland, so the violence of his plays and films can be read as reflecting a wider vision of a violent, whole world.

The thirst for revenge is a driving factor in Peckinpah's work, and it is achieved by violent means, the modus operandi of the Wild West. This is also the case in McDonagh's Irish Wild West, one conceived under Hollywood's influence. In Westerns, as Jenni Calder has pointed out, "the hero is allowed to kill," and this is certainly the case for Tarantino and McDonagh (128). Such violence, however unpalatable and shocking, transfers easily from Peckinpah's Mexico to Tarantino's Los Angeles to McDonagh's Leenane and Inishmore because, as Peckinpah has said, "You can't really escape it anywhere" (Calder 129). Human beings are united by the desire to hurt one another. Both Padraic and Mairead in *The Lieutenant of Inishmore* are old-fashioned gunslingers. In the pantheon of Western heroes, Padraic is an Irish Billy the Kid and Mairead is Annie Oakley, the "Little Sure

Shot" of Buffalo Bill's Wild West Show (Slotkin, *Gunfighter Nation* 68). In the Wild West Show were "spectacular feats of marksmanship" (68), and these rituals, though subject to parody, also appear in *The Lieutenant of Inishmore*:

> **Mairead (pacing angrily):** Everybody slings me cow blinding at me, no matter how many years go by! What nobody ever mentions is it was from sixty yards I hit them cows' eyes, which is bloody good shooting in anybody's books. If I'd walked bang up to them I could understand it, but I didn't, I gave them every chance.
> **Padraic:** Ah, hold your horses, Mairead, I was only fooling with you. I meself once shot a fella in the eye with a crossbow, but that was from right next to him. Sixty yards is marvelous going. (34)

Instead of fixing her sights on bottles or cans, Mairead aims at the eyes of cows. Like any good cowgirl or cowboy, she adheres to the Wild West ethic where the rival or target is given a fair chance. To shoot someone in the back is a transgression of Wild West rules, but Mairead contends that the unarmed and unaware cows were given "every chance." McDonagh's cynical version of valor and fair play is reprised in Scene Nine:

> **Donny:** I'd say this about Mairead. She's fecking accurate. Knock your eye out from a mile.
> **Davey:** I always knew that cow practicing would pay off some day.
> **Donny:** Padraic has an entirely different style.
> **Davey:** Padraic goes all the way up to ya.
> **Donny:** Padraic goes all the way up to ya, and then uses two guns from only an inch away.
> **Davey:** Sure, there's no skill in that.
> **Donny:** I think the two guns is overdoing it. From that range, like.
> **Davey:** It's just showing off, really.
> **Donny:** Mairead sees more of the sport. (55–56)

It is a reminder to us as audience that killing, on stage or on screen, is governed by rules and underlined by style. In fact, in all gunfighter movies, which Tarantino and McDonagh seek to emulate, there is a strong focus on the theatrics of gunplay.

As for Billy the Kid, he was first known as Henry McCarty, born in New York in 1859 to Irish parents who had fled the Famine. His first skirmish occurred during the Lincoln County Wars in the late 1870s, in which a "motley crew of Irish, English, and Scottish settlers [fought] among themselves for supremacy" (Utley 48). The dynamics of this war have much in common with the one being fought in *The Lieutenant of Inishmore* between republicans of various shades and with the colonial history of Ireland in general. According to Robert M. Utley, Billy the Kid and his friends "were willing to take human life in circumstances that violated even the lax ethical code of the time and place," a statement just as easily applicable to Padraic (68). Also, Padraic's many methods of torture and murder, from the small scale of individual encounters to the larger one of bombings, are not unlike those of Billy the Kid, who "had also grown callous toward human life and stood ready to kill, without hesitation and by any means fair or foul, when the cause seemed to require it" (88). Billy's devotion to his horses is inverted by Padraic's devotion to Wee Thomas, his cat—the unwitting cause of the mayhem in the play—while his devotion to marksmanship is transferred to the behavior of Mairead. Frank Coe, a fellow outlaw, said of Billy: "He was a fine horseman, quick and always in the lead, at the same time he was kind to his horses and could save them and have them ready and fresh when he needed to make a dash. . . . He would practice shooting at every thing he saw and from every conceivable angle, on and off his horse" (Utley 88–89). Like Billy the Kid, Padraic has remained a rebel in a constant state of revolution. Such characters cannot expect to survive. Even more benign Westerners—Shane is a good example—are forced to leave the polite society to which they are unsuited. In the world of the Western, the gunman must be alert to change and be ready to adapt.

In *Showdown: Confronting Modern America in the Western Film*, John H. Lenihan provides us with some examples of the qualities that the Western should embody:

The Western translated a relatively brief segment of American history into an idealization of socially responsible individualism, of a transitional social order both needing and permitting personal freedom and the exercise of individual power. . . . The western hero was a democratic Oedipus and Hamlet who acted on behalf of, but apart from, the larger society to correct some injustice or moral imbalance in the universal schema. Because of his unique relationship with nature, the Westerner, like his ancient counterparts who similarly transcended the mundane, was able to counter extraordinary dangers that defied ordinary people. He often did so to his own personal detriment, since the mundane social order he salvaged did not always accommodate, let alone reward, his kind of self-determination and stature. (15–16)

In Irish drama, such values are held up to ridicule by both Synge in *The Playboy of the Western World* and by McDonagh in *The Lieutenant of Inishmore*. At the same time, both Christy Mahon and Padraic transcend the norm and would seem to be above the petty concerns that occupy ordinary people. They are independent, but they are also misfits whose idealism is questionable and whose methods are savage. They are both reminders of the marginal status occupied by men of violence in our world: they are of some use in time of violent conflict but are quickly cast aside in peacetime. It would appear that society knows that the gunman can never disavow his/her calling and is by nature unstable. A character such as Padraic is inherently violent and untamable.

Another version of this kind of hero in Irish writing is Moran, the patriarch of John McGahern's *Amongst Women,* a violent, old IRA veteran who, because he cannot fully belong to polite society, founds his own republic on his farm, Great Meadow. Moran knows that a man with his views can only survive in his own private nation situated within, though on the edge of, the larger one. Moran is like the Virginian of Owen Wister's classic novel. Both men had started out as outlaws but, in order to survive, the Virginian "had the genius to recognize that the Wild West [was] changing, that civilization and law

[were] arriving in the territory, and that the imperative to be equal to the situation therefore [required] him to change his way of acting and thinking" (Slotkin, *Gunfighter Nation* 176). But Padraic, like Steve and Trampas in *The Virginian,* is inflexible, and because he is unable to reinvent himself, he will move from one violent conflict to the next before being eventually destroyed. Characters such as the Virginian and Moran, as Slotkin points out, are aristocratic and autocratic rather than democratic (175–76). What distinguishes them the most, however, is their virility: "in Wister's novel the primary sign of social and moral superiority is not nobility but *virility;* and on this score the Virginian is pre-eminent" (176). In *The Lieutenant of Inishmore,* Padraic's virility is mocked by his demented attachment to his cat.

From the outset of "his career as a director, Peckinpah was disposed to develop new movies as implicit commentaries on the canonical films of the genre tradition," and such "commentaries" have also had a major part in McDonagh's work (Slotkin, *Gunfighter Nation* 593). McDonagh's plays point toward the work of Peckinpah and Tarantino, as has been noted by many critics, in the same way that Peckinpah's work comments on John Ford's (Luckhurst 116–27). For both Ford and McDonagh, Galway is the primary Irish place of connection; it is where both men spent time among relatives. In 1921, at the height of the War of Independence, Ford arrived in Galway with the intention of joining in the armed struggle on the Irish side:

> Jack Ford ignored the fact that his wife was nursing his baby son. Trusting to his neighbors to feed his family in his absence, he took the train to Maine to see his parents. He told them he must go to Galway and help in Ireland's struggle for independence. His father and mother supported his decision. He took the boat to Galway and tried to contact his cousins, the Thorntons. Their family house had been burned down by the Black and Tans as a reprisal while one of their boys was fighting for independence in the hills. (Sinclair 31)

However, it is highly unlikely that Ford picked up a gun in Ireland. Eventually, he returned to Hollywood "to find a pile of debts, a career in a state of suspense, and an angry wife, tired of being deserted"

(32). Nevertheless, he remained a lifelong supporter and fundraiser for the IRA. In contrast, McDonagh's attitude to the violent Irish republicanism of his time is the opposite of Ford's: Irish republicans are the object of heavy and often hilarious satire. One might argue that when Ford went to Ireland in 1921, he was really seeking to fight in a "real" West located in Galway because it was no longer possible to engage in battle in its American equivalent, except in his imagination— by writing and directing movies. He saw the West of Ireland, as Yeats and others had done, as a premodern and mythic space. White has explained the dynamic (to a large degree it is psychological) present in this mythology in regard to the American West, and it also fits the Irish context well:

> Late-nineteenth-century Americans imagined the West—that most modern of American sections—as the premodern world that they had lost. In it life was primitive but also simple, real, and basic. Every action in this world mattered, and the fundamental decisions of everyday life supposedly involved clear moral choices. Life in the West could restore authenticity, moral order, and masculinity. Life in the premodern [world] could, ironically, justify the very core of modern values that had come under question. For in this imagined primitive West, as it turned out, autonomy and self-discipline were the qualities that mattered most. In the end, the imaginative journey to the primitive West rehabilitated modern values and reoriented Americans toward a version of progress that supposedly avoided "overcivilization" and decadence. (621)

Whereas the "authentic" American West could only be imagined, the Irish one, for Ford, could be experienced firsthand: he could become a "real life" gunfighter. For McDonagh, on the other hand, who had witnessed the atrocities committed in the name of Irish freedom in London, republicanism was synonymous with savagery. In his West of Ireland, McDonagh has exploited and undercut the rampant masculinity that is a central element in the Wild West genre, and also gender role ambiguity. He has discovered a violent and anarchic place wholly lacking in a moral order—Dante's Dodge City.

For an author such as McDonagh, looking to explore a morally bankrupt society and to shock his audience, *The Wild Bunch* is a perfect model:

> Sam Peckinpah's *The Wild Bunch* is the most complex, controversial, and arguably the most popular of these films. Its critical reception was remarkable for the intense partisanship it aroused. Some saw it as a masterpiece of one kind or another, serious in its ambitions and innovative in its form, a critical allegorization of American political culture; others saw it as a symptom of the American "madness," an exploitative exercise in excessive, inadequately motivated, technologically augmented and estheticized violence. (Slotkin, *Gunfighter Nation* 593)

Like McDonagh's and Tarantino's work, *The Wild Bunch* has been controversial, and it has divided critics as to its value or lack thereof. All three artists share a desire to cast aside the notion of the heroic outlaw and instead to present figures who are compromised either by money or by their own insanity (595). Some of the republicans in *The Lieutenant of Inishmore,* like the Wild Bunch, are as much involved "in a business enterprise" as they are part of a political movement (598). Also, in the face of the rampant violence that is taking place around them, as Slotkin points out in regard to *The Wild Bunch,* "the citizens are pathetic, but their utter haplessness suggests that theirs is not a moral order that can thrive in a ruthless world" (598). With some justification, the point can be made that all of the characters in McDonagh's plays who are not men and women of action are pathetic. In such weak societies, dysfunction, hatred, murder, violence against animals—the bread and butter of his plays—will rule.

At the outset I mentioned the specious comparisons made by the media between McDonagh and Shakespeare to put the former's success in perspective. However, a grasp of the role that violence plays in Shakespeare's works, and in those of his contemporaries, does help us to understand McDonagh's plays, and why audiences have been able to stomach their excesses. In *Shakespeare & Violence,* R. A. Foakes examines violence in general and then in relation to Shakespeare. On the macro level:

> Our world is deeply troubled by the problem of violence, as manifested, for instance, in violent crime, in terrorism, in war, in prolonged feuds between neighbouring groups (as in Northern Ireland), and in territorial battles such as those between street-gangs in inner cities. The horrific acts of terrorism on 11 September 2001 that demolished the World Trade Center in New York provoked, understandably, an instant response in the American bombing of Afghanistan, with calls for the extirpation of terrorism throughout the world. The aim is laudable, but history suggests that it is also impracticable. Human beings, especially males, have been addicted to violence since myths and legends first circulated and recorded history began. (1)

Indeed, as Foakes reminds us, "our history begins, so to speak, with Cain's killing of Abel, and we are all descendants of Cain" (215). In his own time, Shakespeare "was not alone in being fascinated by acts of violence that seem to have no cause, to be unmotivated or inadequately motivated," and violence of various sorts is featured in many of his plays (Foakes 9). Aaron the Moor, from *Titus Andronicus*, can certainly be compared to Padraic when he says, in two distinct speeches:

> Vengeance is in my heart, death in my hand,
> Blood and revenge are hammering in my head. (2.3.38–39)

> Ten thousand worse than ever yet I did
> Would I perform if I might have my will. (5.3.186–87)

The Lieutenant of Inishmore is a revenge play of a long tradition: "Revenge tragedy goes further back, of course, at least to Aeschylus' powerful trilogy, the *Oresteia* (fifth century B.C.). And never really out of fashion, it forms the basis today of any number of Hollywood action films, especially those starring Sylvester Stallone, Mel Gibson, Charles Bronson, and Clint Eastwood. For later writers and filmmakers Seneca's plays, especially *Thyestes,* shaped revenge tragedy into a three-phased action consisting of 1. atrocity; 2. the creation of the revenger; and 3. atrocity" (Miola 116). As Miola explains, this type of play conforms to a formula that has been carried forward from Seneca to Shakespeare to Peckinpah, Tarantino, and McDonagh. Even if the sets and costumes have changed, the basic dramatic structure has remained intact from the fifth century B.C. to the present. Writers and filmmakers continue to be absorbed by violence, and the violence found in McDonagh's plays can frequently be seen as "being unmotivated or inadequately motivated" (Foakes 9). For his audiences in Galway, London, New York, and elsewhere, the shock registered by his plays was only superficially extreme. The experienced theatregoer, the avid movie fan, and even the casual television viewer had seen it all before. This is further confirmation of Dean's contention that McDonagh's work is traditional in nature.

White has explored the several ways in which the American West has been mythologized by writers and has noted some consequences. Also important in this regard are connections between myth and history, and those persons who are "doing the imagining":

> What is, then, the relationship between the variety of publicly imagined Wests—the mythic Wests—and the historic West? Even the question is misleading, for it implies that the two can be easily separated. To understand this relationship, we must make some necessary distinctions. We must, first of all, distinguish among the people doing the imagining. Residents of the West itself have constructed various local versions of a collective past. Such imaginings have often been folkloric—that is, they are songs and stories (originally oral, later often written down) produced by people belonging to groups narrowly defined by occupation, place, or ethnicity. The second version of the imagined West is the work of professional writers, journalists, and filmmakers who are often located outside the West itself or in that peculiar corner of it, Hollywood. They dis-

seminate their versions of the West through mass media: books, magazines, and movies. In terms of audience, this second imagined West appeals to national audiences, although it may also have strong appeal among local groups of westerners, who also produce their own folklore. (613–14)

McDonagh belongs to the second group of writers, and it is as true in Ireland as it is in America that "the nationally imagined West has been far more powerful than the locally imagined West" (White 620). And this national view has spread internationally. In Ireland, this dynamic has worked at various levels and in various ways—the versions of the West spread by English-language writers have gone further afield than those by their counterparts writing in Irish; and, to a large extent, the view of the West of Ireland that has been most widely disseminated globally has been primarily the work of artists who did not grow up there—W. B. Yeats, J. M. Synge, John Ford, Paul Henry, Heinrich Böll, and Martin McDonagh, for example—though they all spent holidays there. What these artists have shared, or been able to develop, have been strong connections to large-scale international businesses: publishers, theatres, galleries, film companies. Homegrown artists, particularly those working in the Irish language and often lacking such connections, have found it more difficult to have their voices heard. Except for the work of Lady Augusta Gregory, the one major female and Western writer of the Anglo-Irish Revival, the imagined Revival West was the creation of male writers. Even today, despite the numbers of published Western women, this dynamic remains unaltered. (However, at a time of waning interest in poetry, it is as poets that women have primarily excelled.) As a result, the picture of the West presented by the outsider can often be fixed, unchanging, and unchangeable. White tells us:

> Myth refuses to see the past as fundamentally different from the present. Again, as Richard Slotkin explains, in myth "the past is made metaphorically equivalent to the present; and the present appears simply as a repetition of persistently recurring structures

identified with the past. Both past and present are reduced to single instances displaying a single 'law' or principle of nature, which is seen as timeless in its relevance, and as transcending all historical contingencies." (616)

Plays such as *The Lieutenant of Inishmore* set out to perpetuate myths rather than interrogate them, and, ultimately, they do little more than dress them up in new clothes. We are left with the impression that the West from Synge to McDonagh remains unchanged. Like the American West imagined by Hollywood, it is simultaneously savage and beautiful.

Six

ACROSS A BLUE SOUND

Seán Lysaght's *Clare Island Survey*

Published in 1991, *The Clare Island Survey* is the second of Seán Lysaght's five collections of poetry. It follows *Noah's Irish Ark* (1989) and precedes *Scarecrow* (1998), *Erris* (2002), and *The Mouth of a River* (2007). Lysaght, born and raised in Limerick and educated at University College, Dublin, lived in Switzerland and Germany for a number of years before returning to Ireland. Presently, he lives in Westport, County Mayo. Lysaght also has written a biography of Robert Lloyd Praeger, the guiding spirit behind the first Clare Island Survey issued by the Royal Irish Academy between 1911 and 1915. For the purposes of this essay, though the primary focus will be on Lysaght's poetry and on his *Clare Island Survey* in particular, three Clare Island Surveys will be discussed to shed light on Lysaght's work: Praeger's RIA survey of 1909–1911, which I have just mentioned; Lysaght's *Clare Island Survey*, for which the starting point is Praeger's autobiography, *The Way That I Went: An Irishman in Ireland*, published in 1937; and the RIA's *New Survey of Clare Island*, of which the first four volumes appeared between 1999 and 2005. In addition, I will explore Lysaght's work in relation to the work of other contemporary Irish writers who have made the West of Ireland a central presence. Also of interest here, given the influence of

Praeger on Lysaght, are the connections that both authors have forged between literature and science.

Lysaght's *Clare Island Survey* is a brief book. The title poem is forty lines long and divided into four sections. It is followed by twenty-nine short lyrics, of which twenty-eight are explorations of sightings of native Irish birds. The first of these poems is "Manx Shearwater," the last is "Yellowhammer," though the collection closes with "Coda," which serves as a concluding aesthetic statement. The collection's title is somewhat misleading because the sightings of birds do not necessarily take place on Clare Island: "a singing yellowhammer among hooped briars" was observed in Kerry, a herring gull in County Wexford, while some others, though they are all cited in Kennedy, Rutledge, and Scrope's *Birds of Ireland*, were seen outside of Ireland (42). Also, in regard to length and scale, the title poem is dwarfed by the poems that explore bird life, with the result that the connection between the two parts of the book can seem tenuous. However, to separate them would be to deny the connection between Praeger's and Lysaght's shared methodologies. Both men are writer/scientists adept at integrating literary and scientific modes of inquiry and representation. The scientific methods used by Praeger and his researchers on their groundbreaking survey have had a marked influence on Lysaght's literary methodology and aesthetic. Both the scientist and poet attend, observe, and describe, and, for Lysaght, his own achievement will be "measured against" Praeger's rather than against that of any literary ancestor (12).

As David Attis has pointed out, a disconnect has long existed between science and literature in Ireland:

> What can science possibly have to do with Irish identity? Science is supposed to be universal, disinterested and objective, practiced by an international community, while national identity is particular, local and subjective. The scientist, claims Desmond Clarke in his survey of Irish science, "unlike the writer, artist or patriot, is rarely a mere nationalist but always has been and always will be an internationalist. . . . There is really no such thing as an Irish, English or French scientist, save by accident of birth, and the genius of the sci-

entific universe is not like that of the writer and artist, redolent of his native soil." (133)

The works of Lysaght and Praeger are both formidable and original because they cannot be discretely placed within these traditional structures: Lysaght is a writer/scientist, while Praeger is a scientist/writer, and for both men the parts are inseparable from the whole. When it is called for, Lysaght can bring to his poetry the power of scientific detachment, while Praeger's work, sensitive to literary models and practice, is a series of celebrations of local places. For both men, the local and the international are in free play, and the barriers between science and literature can be easily set to one side. Desmond Clarke's contention that the place where the scientist was born is not important to his work is correctly challenged by Attis: "I will argue, however, that in fact science in Ireland has faced (and continues to face) the same tension between the provincial and the cosmopolitan as Irish literature, and that the development of science in Ireland must be understood in relation to specifically Irish issues" (133). Moreover, both Lysaght and Praeger are nationalists, though not in a strictly political sense. Their nationalism takes the form of a shared celebration of place in all of its complexity with particular attention paid to nature, in the widest sense of this word. Like Patrick Kavanagh, they are not interested in the provincial.

Nevertheless, the two parts of Lysaght's *Clare Island Survey,* for all of their interrelations, proceed from two separate sources: the title poem from Praeger's memoir; and the bird poems from the "List of Irish Names for Birds" compiled by Seán Mac Giollarnáth, which appears near the end of *Birds of Ireland* and which Lysaght cites as his primary source. Praeger's volume brought the poet to Clare Island, while, as Lysaght notes, "the species treated in my survey were originally suggested by Mac Giollarnáth" (45). The order of species follows the convention established by K. H. Voous.

Lysaght begins with the Manx shearwater from the *Procellariiformes* species and ends with the yellowhammer from the *Emberizidae* species. Voous's objective is to provide comprehensive lists and orders of species in "the whole of the Holarctic Region, that is, the cold and temperate regions of the northern hemisphere" (1). What Lysaght contributes in his exploration of the physical and poetic world of holartic birds is lyricism, imagination, and a sensibility finely attuned to the essences of science, flight, and fancy:

> Show me the lichen I have bruised.
> I'll show you the goldcrest.
> You can't hear its high pitch anymore,
> but when you were young you found its nest. (*The Clare Island Survey* 36)

In poetry, we watch the birds soar and hear their songs.

Timothy Collins has described the importance of Praeger's 1909–1911 biological survey of Clare Island: "Since then virtually every researcher in the areas of Irish botany, zoology, geology, history, folklore, and archeology has consulted these published results. Many subsequent research projects have been modeled on the original survey, which was one of the largest and most comprehensive ever undertaken in Britain or Ireland" (1). The published RIA survey consists of sixty-seven papers grouped in three sections of volume 31 of the *Proceedings of the Royal Irish Academy*, the results of fieldwork conducted both on Clare Island and throughout surrounding areas of Mayo and Galway. Although the land- and ocean-based survey included some academic specialists from their respective fields, it was for the most part comprised of amateur enthusiasts; it was the culmination of endeavors begun by the Belfast Naturalists' Field Club, a group that had traveled outside "Belfast at weekends noting the flora, fauna, and antiquities" present in the countryside (Collins 3).

Praeger himself, though he made his name as a geologist and botanist, had been trained as an engineer and had worked as a librarian. It was his view that the standards and methodologies of the Belfast Naturalists' Field Club were superior to those employed by faculty members in Irish universities at that time. Therefore, the fact that the Clare Ireland survey team was not drawn primarily from the Irish academic community served as a strength rather than as a weakness (Praeger, *The Way that I Went* 7–9). Lysaght, in a note at the end of his *Clare Island Survey*, in which he registers his debt to his guides on Clare Island, indicates that he, too, is more gifted amateur than professional scientist; and, given the composition of Praeger's field outfit, this in no way diminishes his status as an ornithologist (45). On the contrary, it places Lysaght in the lively rearguard of a grand tradition. Like Tim Robinson, both Lysaght and Praeger can be seen as gifted interlopers.

The combination of professional and enthusiast, from Ireland, Britain, mainland Europe, and the United States, allied with Praeger's great skills as organizer and motivator, ensured that the original survey was a remarkable success:

> It came as a remarkable revelation to the world of science that so many species could even inhabit such a small area. In all, some 3219 species of plants were listed, of which 585 were new to Ireland, 55 were previously unrecorded in Britain and Ireland and 11 were new to science — mostly algae and fungi. The total fauna listed comprised 5269 species, of which 1253 were new to Ireland, 343 were previously unrecorded in Britain and Ireland and 109 were new to science. (Collins 30)

One objective of Praeger's was to prove the existence of some degree of species variation between Clare Island and the mainland, such as Darwin had found with his Galapagos finches:

> Islands and their animal and plant inhabitants have a special interest for the naturalist. The study of their fauna and flora raises at once questions of fundamental biological importance, especially with regard to the sources from which their population has been derived, the means by which that population reached its present habitat, and the effects of isolation upon the flora and fauna in their island home. Thus it comes about that the problem of insular populations has attracted the attention of the most eminent biologists, many of whom have given close attention to this study — for instance, Alphonse de Candolle, Edward Forbes, Charles Darwin,

Alfred Russel Wallace, Sir J. D. Hooker. Thus, also, we find that in recent years many notable works on the flora and fauna of islands have been published, narrating, in most cases, the results of special expeditions sent out for the purpose of studying the animals and plants of selected insular areas, and inquiring into their relationships and origin. Places so far apart as Christmas Island, Anticosti, Krakatau, Funafuti, the Faroes, and the subantarctic islands of New Zealand, have been monographed thus in recent years. (Praeger, *Proceedings of Royal Irish Academy*, part 1, p. 1)

Praeger reports in his summary of the survey's findings that it was impossible to find much in the way of species variation:

On the other hand, the proximity of Clare Island to the mainland proved a factor which much lessened its value for the investigation of insular problems. A geological study of an area showed that it was not only probable, but almost certain, that a land-connection between the island and the mainland existed long after the Glacial Period, which would have permitted of the immigration of much of the present fauna and flora after normal climatic conditions were resumed. (part 68, p. 2)

However, Praeger's interest in establishing evolutionary variation does provide a historical and scientific context for the hundred or more workers who took part in the survey (Collins 30).

In the second and third parts of Lysaght's title poem, the focus is primarily on Praeger. He is about to depart the mainland for the island to begin his groundbreaking work, and he needs to hire an interpreter to translate his requests into Irish so that his helpers will understand him. His sense of being an outsider is further emphasized when he is greeted warily by the islanders, who see in him another in a long line of invaders and colonists, though this is not how Praeger views himself:

So I turn to Clare Island, and approach,
as they line up on the pier

and jostle for place, the forefathers
ready to construe my coming,
unwilling to believe that I am strange
to the old score of grant and annexation. (*The Clare Island Survey* 12)

It is tempting to view the work with place names of the Clare Island surveyors as similar to that done by the Ordnance Surveys in other parts of Ireland, so famously dramatized in Brian Friel's *Translations*, where "every hill, stream, rock, even every patch of ground" is Anglicized, and to find in the survey elements of annexation and colonization (34). As Attis reminds us, surveyors and scientists had for a long time been viewed with suspicion by the indigenous Irish:

> Many of the earliest scientists in Ireland came with Cromwell's army. They were surveyors, botanists, and political economists—experts at quantifying and classifying Ireland's natural and human resources for control and exploitation. . . . Science arrived in Ireland primarily as a foreign import in the hands of the colonizer. It also provided a justification for this colonial activity. The English saw their science as evidence of their superiority over the native Irish, and science itself came to be imbued with the language of conquest. (135)

Given these Cromwellian associations, it is easy to see why the surveyors were not welcomed and why science was often held in low esteem in Ireland well into the mid-decades of the twentieth century.

Praeger's surveyors, however, were hardly invaders. Even though their reports were written in English and their labeling was primarily in Latin and English, Irish terms were not shunted aside, though Praeger admitted that the lists of Gaelic plant and animal names were "confessedly incomplete" (*Royal Irish Academy* vii). Clearly, despite the roles played by John (Eoin) MacNeill and N. Colgan in the survey, expertise was available to Praeger on the island, where almost every resident would have been either an Irish speaker or bilingual (Whelan 89). In fact, a purpose of the *New Survey of Clare Island*, in addition to continuing the work begun by Praeger, is to provide a greater sense of the island's cultural and linguistic contexts than was available to the reader of the first survey. Praeger was certainly aware of the importance of such contexts, and they are addressed in the third and fourth parts of his survey; however, they are seen as being minor issues relative to its greater scientific agenda. For purely practical reasons, it is probably just as well that too much interest was not taken in such matters because, by limiting the scope of an already major undertaking, Praeger was able to have all of the reports in print by 1915. At the same time, as he admits, lack of knowledge of the Irish language was an obvious hindrance: "I have always reproached myself for the mental laziness that prevented my getting a working knowledge of that distressful language (for it certainly *is* difficult, and I have no gift for tongues), even if for the sake of place-names alone" (*The Way that I Went* 168).

Nevertheless, Praeger displays a lively interest in the Irish names. One memorable example is rendered in Latin, Irish, and English: "*Gibbula Umbilicata,* called in Irish Faochán Mhuire (the Virgin Mary's Fweecawn)" (159). A reason why *The Way that I Went* remains so engaging, both for natural scientists and ordinary readers, results from Praeger's range of interests, wide reading, and command of the English language. He was a true Renaissance man who was as important to the natural sciences in Ireland as was his contemporary, Yeats, to literature. Because Irish writing has been so widely celebrated and disseminated internationally, and because writing and Ireland can be used interchangeably, Irish science has been ignored, with the result that Praeger's contribution is not generally celebrated. However, as time passes and as the Irish landscape continues to be degraded by development, Praeger's voice will carry profound prophetic power.

For Lysaght, Praeger is a father figure against whose achievement his own work will be measured, though the poet's desires are more subjective and, perhaps, less ambitious. Even though Lysaght's wanderings on Clare Island will not have the weight of Praeger's, they will, nevertheless, allow him to walk the ground that Praeger walked, to return from that journey with a fund of knowledge, an excited countenance and a new language, all of which, when combined, will become the building blocks from which his poem will be assembled:

> I would be measured against you,
> and will lose face, pacing out
> in the footsteps of the early workers
> to where fatigue compels the heart,
> and return then, my face aglow
> with the booty of old words, and new echoes. (*The Clare Island Survey* 12)

The volume is dedicated to the poet's father, with whom he made the journey to Clare Island. At the start of the first section, Lysaght invokes the sketch made by his father:

> I have the sketch of Clare Island,
> in your hand. You drew the great brow
> in silhouette from the mainland,
> and scribbled gulls over a blue sound,
> then etched a furze bush
> with pencilled spikes in the foreground
> and, in between, some trees, a slate roof
> and a red gable huddling together. (11)

Throughout his work, Lysaght's father is alluded to and celebrated as the man from whom the poet derived his interest in the outdoors and ornithology. The son's *Clare Island Survey* is both a companion piece to, and gloss on, his father's as well as Praeger's work, though in shape and genre, given its brevity, it is closer to his father's quick sketch than to Praeger's mammoth undertaking. Nevertheless, the poem's four sections are of equal length—each contains ten lines—indicating the weight that Lysaght gives to the lyrical, the orderly, and the personal. In his biography of Praeger, which would appear seven years later, Lysaght was able to expand on Praeger's achievement at a length that the lyric poem would not allow. The lyric poem is both primary and primal, though modulated by its tightness of form, its carefully chosen diction, and its general lightness of touch achieved by Lysaght's apt use of metaphor and symbol. Above all, true to his father's sketch and in its attempts to see what Praeger saw, the poem is visual.

Language, the "booty of old words" introduced in the title poem, is an important concern in Lysaght's enumeration of Irish birds that comprises the majority of *The Clare Island Survey* (12). Kennedy, Rutledge, and Scrope's *Birds of Ireland,* his source book, was published in 1954 and is a remarkable volume of 437 pages; Mac Giollarnáth's section on the Irish names of birds, which suggested to Lysaght the particular species that he would write about, is included as an appendix and numbers a mere four pages. The entries on the birds themselves are in English and Latin and make no reference to their names in Irish. Their Irish identities are obliterated, and there is the stark assumption in this omission that Irish is not the language of scientific inquiry. In this respect, even the birds are colonized, and Lysaght sets for himself the task of recovery and decolonization. For Lysaght, the Irish names are important because these are often the ones that he heard as a child. He begins "Meadow Pipit" as follows:

> Or *reafóg,* as my father said,
> when the small bird on the sward
> ran away with its splayed
> wing twitching (*The Clare Island Survey* 31)

He indicates the extent to which the older words still exist in the vernacular, and the vernacular can be Irish, not English. This point is further reinforced in the poem when Lysaght is flying into Ireland from Germany and notes the German word for meadow pipit:

> Now my plane flies in
> from where they call them
> *Wiesenpieper,*
> and splays both wings to stop. (31)

Reafóg and *Wiesenpieper* are emblems of identity, and, in the Irish situation, emblems of loss. Whereas in *Birds of Ireland,* the Irish language is the lingua franca of the appendix, in Lysaght's poem it is at the heart of the narrative and at the source of poetic inspiration. Here, the vernacular is complex: it is English, Irish, German. As Attis reminds us, "scientific activity is not only bound up with culture but also helps to create the general cultural context" (134).

In "Yellowhammer," Lysaght explores this issue further with some stunning linguistic and poetic dexterity of his own:

> A singing yellowhammer among hooped briars,
> between the fuchsia
>
> Of a West Kerry hedge, was *siobháinín bhuí*
> *ag briseadh a croí ag gáirí*
>
> while a squall misted in the distance,
> then rose in the near leaves
>
> that tossed, and were glazed, and wept.
> We stared out past them at chilly acres,
>
> flush with memories of golden birds
> and lost domains—until it was all over
>
> and he was the gleaming bunting
> that sang to the steaming pool. (*The Clare Island Survey* 42)

The fuchsia at the end of line two in Irish is *Deora Dé*, literally translated as "God's tears," and this provides a clever counterpoint to the second line in the second stanza, "*ag briseadh a croí ag gáirí*," which translates as "breaking its heart laughing." Therefore, stanza one ends in tears, stanza two in laughter. In Irish the yellowhammer is *siobháinín bhuí*. However, as Lysaght points out in the final stanza, this is not to devalue the complexity of English, where the yellowhammer is called a "gleaming bunting," a reference to its other English name, the yellow bunting (*Birds in Ireland* 413–14). In Irish, *siob-* begins many words that embrace the sense of drift, something that is finely reflected in the rhythms of Lysaght's poem. In "The Fuchsia Blaze," also set in County Kerry, Greg Delanty stresses its tropical origins. Delanty also observes the flower's lively movement, which connects it to music, song, dance, the yellowhammer, and the language of poetry:

> The purple petticoated
> & crimson frocks
> of the open flowers
> are known as Dancers,
> blown by the fast & slow
> airs of the wind;
> one minute *sean-nós* melancholy,
> the next jigging & reeling
> like Irish character itself
> & like these, my fuchsia verse,
> struggling to escape
> the English garden
> & flourish
> in a wilder landscape (viii).

Delanty's wilder landscape is both the Kerry locale of the poem and the point where the English language joins forces with Irish, and with other languages borne from afar, like the fuchsia, by wind and ocean. It is from this collision of imagination and language, in Delanty's view, that poetry emerges. But for Lysaght, as he makes clear in "Declensions," the Irish language is resourceful in its own right:

> Like a currach being hauled
> by craftsmen over a rough sea,
> language sinks into a trough
> and peaks again miraculously,
>
> a tiny black boat diminishing
> on the wide sea of story,
> with words for weather,
> for seaweeds, for stonechat, for flotsam. ("Scarecrow" 50)

This poem finds an echo in Nuala Ní Dhomhnaill's "Ceist na Teangan" in its use of the boat as a rhetorical device:

Cuirim mo dhóchas ar snámh
i mbáidín teangan (*Pharoah's Daughter* 154)

I place my hope on the water
in this little boat
of the language (155)

Lysaght understands, as Declan Kiberd has said of Friel's *Translations*, that "the struggle for the power to name oneself and one's state is enacted fundamentally within words, most especially in colonial situations . . . so a concern for language . . . may be an investigation into the depths of the political unconscious" (*Inventing Ireland* 615). It is common in Irish discourse to seek the literary and political unconscious roots of feeling in the Irish language; however, Lysaght, in addition, locates therein the scientific unconscious, for him very much a part of his calling as a poet. In this respect, his work is notable, prophetic, and corrective. Lysaght points to a dissociation of sensibility in the Irish psyche: *The Clare Island Survey* unifies the literary and the scientific into one coherent whole.

Despite such heady issues as the implications of the language shift and colonization, one should not assume that these ornithological and linguistic matters have been of great interest to ordinary people in Ireland. The editors of *Birds of Ireland* note that "comparatively few of the population are interested in birds and still fewer are capable observers" (vi). Praeger has given a plausible and unintentionally hilarious explanation for this:

The question of early rising is mostly a difficult one, especially in Ireland. To the lover of nature the earliest hours of the day are perhaps the most entrancing: but so few of us can enjoy them. The only dawns that are familiar to the majority are the late, grey, chilly half-lights of winter, as different from the triumphant dawns of May as night is from day. . . . And the number of people whose minds refuse to work at four o'clock in the morning with the alertness which they command at nine is considerable. . . . Knock them up before summer sunrise, or let them make a bed of the heather for a night, and they will not have the mental energy to see and hear as they would during orthodox hours. The loss is theirs, for those first hours have an enchantment about them. And this magic begins early:

> At two o'clock in the morning, if you open your window
> and listen,
> You will hear the feet of the wind that is going to call
> the sun,
> And the trees in the shadow rustle and the trees in the
> moonlight glisten,
> And though it is deep, dark night, you will feel that the
> night is done.

So says Rudyard Kipling. And that first stirring of the sleeping Earth, before the earliest bird ventures on a tentative chirrup, is a thing that is felt rather than heard or seen. (*The Way that I Went,* 303–5)

Of course, it would be equally possible to wrap this antipathy to early rising in a colonial or postcolonial trope, one such being Seamus Deane's reading of *Translations,* in which he points out that there remains "a discrepancy in our language; words are askew, they are out of line with fact" (171). The lack of interest in ornithology and aversion to science that Praeger noticed in his travels can be seen as a byproduct of colonialism.

In "Chough," Lysaght enters into a debate with the figure of Yeats, the Anglo-Irish world he sought to embody, and the great poet's sense of the immortality of beautiful things as revealed in such later poems as "Sailing to Byzantium." For Lysaght, great buildings will revert to nature and to the wild birds of the air:

> With the tower-builders gone from the promontories
> I can inspect the fallen stairs,

the chimneys clogged with mortar and twigs,
no gyre there for my late ascendant. (*The Clare Island Survey* 37)

Also, birds, by the nature of how they live and of the wild energies that drive them, will resist being rendered as emblematic figures in art: "Their bright lobster bills / are a beacon only for themselves" (37). Therefore, to objectify a bird is to record it falsely, which is Yeats's design in the final stanza of "Sailing to Byzantium," when he wishes to be "set upon a golden bough to sing / To lords and ladies of Byzantium / Of what is past, or passing, or to come" (73). For Lysaght, as for another Westerner, the American poet Robinson Jeffers, "the / prehuman dignity of night / Stands, as it was before and will be again," and is what must be celebrated for its unchanging beauty and permanence (Jeffers, "Pearl Harbor," *Selected Poetry* 578). Another issue of which Lysaght is aware in *The Clare Island Survey* is the dangers that birds face as a result of human progress. This point is nowhere more evident than in "Woodcock":

Last year they held
a Geiger counter
to one in Wicklow—
Chernobyl crackled in the box. (24)

In *Noah's Irish Ark*, which precedes *The Clare Island Survey* by two years, Lysaght lays down a firm philosophical and aesthetic foundation. "The Village Tailor" is a magic-realist fable of evolution in reverse, in which a tailor on the run goes to live among the wild creatures of a marsh until "They found him crawling on all fours, / almost crab, mad from swampy nature" (41). If buildings can revert to nature, so, too, can people. In "In the Burren," the speaker notes that "I can only become the thing I look for" (18), a statement that serves as an appropriate lead-in to "Naturalist":

When everything's been said,
the pulse of speculation dead,
I can walk again in a frosty moon,

among shady trees,
and find ghosts of nothing in the gloom. (*Noah's Irish Ark* 19)

Again, this points to the importance of observing without turning
what is seen into a decorative or symbolic object. Frequently in his
work, as in "The Ballinspittle Banshee," Lysaght evokes the positive
condition of darkness:

Since the poled wire led
the light to these parts,
I have keened the loss of darkness,

Holding out in pools of night. (37)

One of Lysaght's great gifts is his ability to bring complex scientific,
literary, and philosophical viewpoints, even when they seem to be working at cross purposes, into free play in his work. Lysaght's vision is
rooted in each, and his work exhibits great unity because all are in constant dialogue. For example, in "Before Anthropology":

Before the first words in Ireland
there were sparse, post-glacial trees,
And northern birds.

Before the hunched primates
of the Bann and their caravan
of history

there were sub-arctic vistas:
herring grounds,
and tundra hills unnamed.

I take palaeo-paths
after Praeger and de Buitléar
into rugged interiors. (29)

In contemporary Irish poetry, Lysaght's work can be placed alongside that of Richard Murphy, who has found new ways of looking at the natural world, and that of Michael Longley and Eamon Grennan. In today's Irish poetry, and not just in work associated with the West, nature is in the process of being demythologized: it requires no term of reference beyond itself. In "Coda," which closes *The Clare Island Survey*, Lysaght introduces the scarecrow, one of his most pointed poetic devices and one he shares with Yeats, to illustrate the degree to which the poet's ego must be set aside:

> My coat flaps and shudders on the wearer,
> knocking to know if I am any more
> than trail, convergence, go-between. (43)

Whereas Yeats's trope requires that the "tattered coat upon a stick" be transformed into a solid shape of "hammered gold and gold enamelling," Lysaght's contends that no such artificial shape is necessary (72–73). For Lysaght, the scarecrow is an instrument of observation and feeling through whose scant clothing wind carries nature's essence. Then, the scarecrow/poet, denuded of ego and historical myth, can take flight:

> Creatures that were seen are now flying
> out of range, so I must be fledged, in turn,
> into convictions that no bird can help
> as I take to the empty air, and dare myself. (43)

Yeats's bird "set upon a golden bough to sing" is a made object/emblem attached to a court, whereas Lysaght's birds are wild, unfixed creatures flying out to sea in search of food (73). Lysaght suggests in "Erris" that whereas human beings are dependent on nature to close gaps in their psyches, nature has no need for humans:

> The eel was finally free of folklore to cross
> the shorn meadow on its way to the sea. The stoat
> hid from the haymakers. The one-eyed deity

abandoned the mountains and came down their aerials
more reliably than when, in the high places,
the hilltop fires lit their stoops and flickering faces. (*Erris* 13)

At the same time, Lysaght is able to juxtapose animals, objects, and ideas drawn from ancient and modern Ireland, classical literature, and the popular culture of the day to illustrate his own belief that the poet's obligations range across time and should be honored democratically. That humans should be sensitive to displaced echoes is made clear in "Lines for a New House," the proem to *Erris*:

> *Man and woman took this place*
> *from the lark's song and the worm's peace*
> *that in their time the heart would know*
> *the lark above and the worm below.* (9)

Though humans have violated the natural world, they still may respect it. For Lysaght, the bird will outlast the castle and outsing the poet.

As readers, we need to pay close attention to the work of Seán Lysaght, a poet who, by bringing lyric poetry and natural science into free play, leads Irish poetry in a new direction. He writes verses devoid of shallow romanticism and Celtic Revival mythology. Because he has peeled away these inherited, smoky layers, we experience Lysaght's vision of a living, lively, natural, and deeply resonant Irish place. In his biography of Praeger, Lysaght proffers a quotation from his mentor's final published work, which summarizes both his own and his subject's driving preoccupation: the scientist and artist must observe and describe "the flexible surface with its amazing variety of aspect and its teeming life, providing us with an infinite field for study and for wonderment" (*The Life of a Naturalist* 162).

Seven

CARRYING THE SONGS
The Poetry of Moya Cannon

Moya Cannon's *Carrying the Songs* (2007), in addition to including two sections of new work, gathers together almost all of the poems that appeared in her earlier collections: *Oar* (1990 and 2000) and *The Parchment Boat* (1997). Two poems are omitted from the latter and five from the former. Cannon was born in Dunfanaghy, County Donegal, and now lives in Galway. During her career, long intervals have elapsed between collections—three slim volumes published in a seventeen-year span—a phenomenon that has had the double effect of heightening interest in her work and ensuring a lively sense of anticipation for each new volume. Cannon's is also an interesting publishing history, with each new collection emerging from a different press. *Carrying the Songs* allows us to see her work as a whole and to understand why her poetry has been widely anthologized and much admired by writers and critics.

    Patricia Boyle Haberstroh has written that "Cannon might be described as a sparse poet; of thirty short lyrics in *The Parchment Boat*, only three run more than a page (none more than a page and a half), and several have fewer than fifteen lines. But the forms of these poems embody an austere elegance appropriate for the feelings and themes they carry" ("Women Poets of the West" 181). Furthermore, "as was demonstrated in *Oar,* Cannon is drawn to the landscape of the West as a repository of the past and a source of renewal for the present. But the renewal comes neither easily nor without pain, and is balanced by loss. Cannon's images are elemental: water, light, stones, birds, sea life, mountains, seasons: she is at heart a nature poet whose probing of this landscape reveals both her own attachment to it and a continuing fascination with the illumination it provides" (182). The new work in *Carrying the Songs* represents a continuation and broadening of Cannon's interests and is, like all of her poetry, notable for a probing intelligence and passionate attachments to people and nature. Because her art is complex and elusive and runs against the contemporary Irish grain, she offers critics multiple interpretative paths. To give this essay a degree of focus, I will concentrate on the following aspects: the *ars poetica* that is revealed in her poetry and prose; and her singular ecological vision, and how this relates to and differs from such contemporary theoretical concepts as ecofeminism and Deep Ecology. In tandem with these discussions, I will explore those constants in Cannon's work that cut through and across all of her endeavors and thematic directions: her relationship to the West of Ireland—its living and the dead; its landscapes, languages, emigrants, animals, and geology—and her ongoing dialogues with poets as diverse as Yeats, Pound, Kathleen Raine, Seamus Heaney, and Eavan Boland.

As Haberstroh has asserted, landscape is a key term in the world of Cannon's poetry. As the poet herself noted in "The Poetry of What Happens," an essay published in 2001, "it is hard to know whether any writer chooses her or his subject or whether the subject does the choosing. Almost from the start the metaphors available to me related to landscape, language, and place names, that most tangible of etymologies, the interface between language and landscape" (127–28). Cannon's landscape is neither purely decorative, isolated on its poetic canvas from other parts of the world, nor fixed in time. Each poem contains discrete decorative elements that will thrive on being examined separately in much the same way as the "gold lunulae or collars" that Cannon so admires in Dublin's National Museum can be appreciated separately or as part of the entire collection to which each belongs (125). And the reader will be aware, while reading Cannon's work, of both the lyric moment that gives the individual poem its energy and the larger history—literary, historical, ecological—that the work embraces.

Her Western landscapes proceed from an anti-hierarchical consciousness with the result that places and people share equal billing, as do humans and non-humans, the living and the dead, and those who live in the West and those who have been forced to leave it to prosper elsewhere. Seeing it in this way, Cannon challenges the literary version of the West that was handed down by the Celtic Revival writers. As Christine Cusick has pointed out, "Cannon's poetic encounter with place offers an incisive contribution to Irish place studies that brings the land down from the early twentieth-century Revivalists' pedestal as mythic repository of the past to the natural history and process of its material and spiritual reality" (63).

At the same time, Cannon places herself firmly within the Irish literary tradition as a writer and woman whose voice heralds change. Her observation that she is working at "the interface between landscape and language" leads her to interrogate language to better understand the handed-down, and highly compromised, English that she must wrestle with. On one level, this engagement with language involves Cannon with philosophical and political issues that are common to all writers in postcolonial societies; however, her interest in language is also primal, as is revealed in her intense absorption in words as living presences in themselves and not merely as bit-players ("The Poetry of What Happens" 128). Cannon finds comfort in English in a way that Stephen Dedalus in *A Portrait of the Artist as a Young Man* could not, and, with quiet insistence, she puts in "Our Worlds" an end to the long-drawn-out funnel/tundish debate:

> But time does forgive them,
> almost forgives them conquest—
> Hard slangs of the market-place
> are ground down to pillow-talk
> and, as the language of conquest

grows cold in statute books,
elsewhere, its words are subsumed
into the grammars of the conquered. (*Carrying the Songs* 16)

Throughout her work, two binary markers constantly appear: one reads word/language, the other life/landscape. In Cannon's world, everything is in constant motion. However, the poet must begin by paying close attention to minutiae, which must be isolated and examined before proceeding onward to such larger issues as language and place. At all times, in Cannon's mind, the poet must be aware that the landscape is not only a space that she is observing but also something vital and dynamic, with a voice of its own. The poet must listen to this voice. And, in Cannon's view, she has been chosen as its medium.

Digging is a familiar trope in Cannon's poetry; for example, in "To Colmcille Returning":

It's time now to dig down
through the shingle of Port a' Churaich,
to bring up the skeleton of ash and oak,
to stretch new skins over the ribs
and to turn the beak of your boat to the south-west. (*Carrying the Songs* 37)

At other times, in such poems as "Scríob" and "Shells," respectively, Cannon will also employ "scraping" and "sifting." These tropes bring Cannon's work in dialogue with Heaney's, with both poets, passionately drawn toward landscape, seeking what Heaney has called the "*omphalos,* meaning the navel, and hence the stone that marked the centre of the world" ("Mossbawn" 17). We are tempted to imagine the two poets, from two generations, digging side by side on a shared ecological journey. As Irish poets finely tuned to literary tradition, both Heaney and Cannon will understand that the use of such tropes connects them to Joyce, particularly to the first episode of *Ulysses,* where *omphalos* heralds a "new paganism" (7).

Some of Cannon's recurring themes are present in "Timbre," a short poem from *Carrying the Songs:*

A word does not head out alone.
It is carried about the way something essential,
a blade, say, or a bowl,
is brought from here to there when there is work to be done.
Sometimes, after a long journey,
it is pressed into service.

A tree keeps its record
of the temper of years
well hidden.

After the timber has been sawn
rough rings release the song of the place—
droughts, good summers, long frosts—
the way pain and joy unlock in a voice. (15)

The poem begins with an almost biblical assertion of the primacy of the word in its own right and then asserts its connectedness to what it seeks to describe, to its own history, and to the history of language from which it has been extracted. The third stanza provides a dialectical moment in which the timbre and timber combine in the song that the felled tree sings to tell the story of its life in a manner unmediated by woman or man.

Throughout Cannon's work, traditional music is an important element. She likes to imagine the parts played by instruments in the transmission of music, and she reminds us in "Timbre" to pay close attention to the song of the sawn wood. Perhaps, as Yeats declared in "Among School Children," it is impossible to "know the dancer from the dance"; however, it is Cannon's belief that things need to be stripped down to their essentials and observed before the work of understanding them begins. This process is at the core of the elemental nature present in Cannon's work, which Haberstroh has described (Yeats 105). The word is the beginning of language while, equally, the wood is the beginning of music. As the word sings, so does the wood.

Of equal importance to Cannon are the songs on whose backs tradition and memory are carried:

> For those who left my county,
> girls from Downings and the Rosses
> who followed herring boats north to Shetland
> gutting the sea's silver as they went
>
> or boys from Ranafast who took the Derry boat,
> who slept over a rope in a bothy,
> songs were their souls' currency
> the pure metal of their hearts. ("Carrying the Songs" 14)

The lyric poet's relationship to poetic tradition is similar to that of the singer and the instrumentalist to song and music. The poet has inherited an art and craft that is, in Cannon's case, oral, written, and bilingual; and she is both comfortable and adept in her role as one whose purpose is to carry the songs forward to another generation. Inherent here is the great instability caused by the constant revision of the song and tradition as it is passed from one singer to the next; however, with this process comes the freedom for the singer or poet to create something new in a distinctive, individual voice. This Eastern view of poetry that is part of Cannon's literary store has made it possible for her to thrive within the narrow, but rich, confines of her chosen form—the short lyric. Lessons learned from listening to traditional songs were reinforced, as she has pointed out, by her reading of Ezra Pound, a poet whose own work was profoundly influenced by Asian writing, Japanese in particular ("The Poetry of What Happens" 125). Writing of Pound's influence on succeeding generations of poets, Marjorie Perloff has noted:

> Whatever poets have made of the actual texture of the *Cantos*, it seems that Pound's poetic, as articulated in the famous essays, has become synonymous with modernism itself. Such axioms as "Use no superfluous word, no adjective which does not mean something" ("A Retrospect"); "The image is not an idea. It is a radiant node or cluster from which, and through which, and into which ideas are constantly rushing" (*Gaudier-Brzeska*); "Good writers are those who

keep the language efficient"; and "Poetry . . . is the most concentrated form of verbal expression" (*ABC of Reading*)—these aphorisms are now embedded in our critical vocabulary. (198)

Each of these aphorisms is applicable to Cannon's methodology. Her poems are precise, refined, and efficient, with no word wasted, and the composition of such work requires great patience. Also, Pound's "radiant node or cluster" is a notion that Cannon is fond of giving voice to, as is the case in "Hazelnuts":

> I thought that I knew what they meant
> when they said that wisdom is a hazelnut.
> You have to search the scrub
> for hazel thickets,
> gather the ripened nuts,
> crack the hard shells,
> and only then taste the sweetness at wisdom's kernel.
>
> But perhaps it is simpler.
> Perhaps it is we who wait in thickets
> for fate to find us
> and break us between its teeth
> before we can start to know anything. (*Carrying the Songs* 99)

Perloff suggests that there are three areas "in which Pound's legacy has been indisputable: (1) the drive toward precision, particularly immediacy—*le mot juste*; (2) the 'break[ing of] the pentameter' in favor of the 'musical' free verse line; and (3) the use of translation as the invention of a desired other" (198). Though all three of Pound's dicta have been incorporated into Cannon's aesthetics, it is the third that is of particular importance, given her belief that she is writing poetry in a borderland where at least two languages, and their variants, mingle. To live in the West of Ireland, given its history, is to belong to a linguistic world where translation is an integral part of everyday life and, hence, of poetry. From "'Taom'":

Surfacing from a fading language,
the word comes when needed.
A dark sound surges and ebbs,
its accuracy steadying the heart. (*Carrying the Songs* 60)

Frequently, in Cannon's world, words, experiences, sensations, and
objects are driven underground only to emerge later transformed. In
"Foundations" and "Shards," for example, mussel shells and broken
crockery, respectively, lie buried but surface to tell stories of the past.
By contrast, because it is deeply hidden and obscured from view, pollen
can wait interminably. And so she writes in "Pollen":

And this dust survives
through the deaths of ages.
It sleeps in deep layers of mud—
black, red and umber;
it sleeps under the wet pelt of a November hill
where long grass is the colour of fox;
it sleeps deep under lakes;
twelve metres down it survives,
dust of arctic meadows,
old and tough
as love. (*Carrying the Songs* 48)

Everything—hidden, concealed, buried, suspended—will retain its
energy. And even if the emotion is buried, figuratively speaking, so
deeply in rock that it is unable to come forth, it will still find a way to
send messages upward from the living, underground space that it has
created for itself. Cannon describes this notion in "*Viola d'Amore*":

Sometimes love does die,
but sometimes, a stream on porous rock,
it slips down into the inner dark of a hill,
joins with other hidden streams
to travel blind as the white fish that live in it.

It forsakes one underground streambed
for the cave that runs under it.
Unseen, it informs the hill,
and, like the hidden strings of the *viola d'amore,*
makes the hill reverberate,
so that people who wander there
wonder why the hill sings,
wonder why they find wells. (*Carrying the Songs* 95)

As Donna Potts has pointed out, Cannon has set many poems in the Burren in County Clare, a "huge expanse of about 300 kilometers of karstic limestone — the largest such area in Western Europe — which, despite massive glacial soil erosion, is home to a remarkable variety of plants" (46). Though one cannot easily see what gives life to these wonderful and distinctive plants, one is certainly made aware of the presence of a hidden force. It is as if a heart were beating in the center of the limestone, and the heart is the ultimate positive force in Cannon's work, one that contains the *omphalos* and the soul. Similar ways of seeing are evident in poetry from another Western tradition — the Native American — as will be evident in this short poem by Linda Hogan:

Sometimes the way to milk and honey is through the body.
Sometimes the way in is a song.
But there are three ways in the world: dangerous, wounding,
        and beauty.
To enter stone, be water.
To rise through hard earth, be plant
desiring sunlight, believing in water.
To enter fire, be dry.
To enter life, be food. ("The Way In" 1)

Throughout Cannon's poetry, bodies of water — from the sea to lakes to holy wells — recur and often work in tandem with other motifs, such as the hazelnuts mentioned earlier. Potts, in her essay on Cannon's first two collections, illustrates how this works:

In addition to the previously discussed associations of the well with the otherworld and hence with inspiration, the sacred tree, the *axis mundi*, was widely believed to unite earth to the underworld. Yeats regarded the hazel tree as the Celtic *axis mundi*. Such sacred water sources are also often linked to the fruit of certain trees, particularly the hazelnut, as in this poem ["Hazelnuts"]. Because the hazel was considered a fairy tree, its nuts a source of wisdom and its wood sacred to poets—used for wands and divining rods—it was taboo fuel on any hearth. (52)

Given the roles played by water, earth, divining rods, and trees, in the Christian tradition, one can explore Cannon's poems in this context. The Christian heritage does find a place in her work; however, it is not privileged, and its hierarchical view of the chain that links all living things to God is challenged.

An important source for Cannon when she was setting out as a poet was Kathleen Raine:

> One such book, in my own case, was Kathleen Raine's *Defending Ancient Springs* (1967), which I came across when I had been writing and publishing in journals for a few years. What I liked in it was Raine's rather unfashionable belief in the existence of an undeconstructible source for poetry, of the centrality of some sense of the spiritual at the heart of art and of the role of art in nurturing the human spirit. It accorded with intuitions which I had had about the violence of trying to deconstruct the core of beauty in, say, the early Irish nature lyrics, in terms of their historical, sociological, and psychological components. Call it by any other name, the synthesis of sound and rhythm which could alert or disarm the heart, which could acknowledge debts of passion, moments of candor, was in some sense miraculous. ("The Poetry of What Happens" 129–30)

Cannon's formal education in History and Politics at University College, Dublin, and Cambridge University had, she felt, impeded her progress as a poet, and in Raine she found a kindred spirit who had encountered similar problems when she first wrote poetry decades earlier. The two women were united by gender, by a shared interest in landscape and the outdoors, and by their studies at Cambridge. Raine, though we think of her as the quintessential English poet, was published by the Dolmen Press, visited Ireland frequently, and was an expert on Yeats. One will surely notice while reading *Defending Ancient Springs* how often Raine returns to the work of Yeats for confirmation, not only because he was Irish but also to be sure of her own literary and aesthetic footing.

Writing of her undergraduate days, Cannon recalls that "for an Irish student in the seventies to have spoken, or even thought, outside the terms of logical positivism was hardly possible" ("The Poetry of What Happens" 130). Equally, it was difficult "to admit to a spiritual dimension to human life" because to do so would be to cast in one's lot with the Catholic Church (130). For Cannon, the search began to locate a space outside of Catholic orthodoxy where the spiritual could thrive. On returning to Cambridge in the 1980s to study History, she found herself "thrown back upon language and what it offered," and she felt "that there was something extraordinarily brittle and short-lived about the truths yielded by historical research. It seemed to me that something was true only until fresh data became available or until its supporting ideology was supplanted by an alternative ideology. I found it exceedingly difficult to live with the implication that truth was relative and temporary" (131). In her heart, Cannon was certain that the "*felt* evidence of language . . . offered reassurance to the contrary," and she set out to explore this as a poet (131). To do so, she had to step outside of the logical positivist way of thinking. She could not have found a better primer than Raine's *Defending Ancient Springs*.

For Raine, positivist philosophy, together with the New Critical/ formalist prescription for the reading and writing of poetry that it influenced, is the enemy of creativity. She encountered the positivist influence firsthand at Cambridge in the 1920s and, looking back, concludes that "the Cambridge trend, then and since, has been anti-imaginative, for the very good reason that Cambridge humanism is a by-product of the Cambridge scientific schools and the positivist philosophy of Russell and Wittgenstein" (18). The scholars and poets who dominated the critical and literary debates while Raine was a student were giants in their fields—I. A. Richards, F. R. Leavis, William Empson, and others—and their theories would underline the critical and literary debate in the Anglophone world for decades afterward. At the time of her residence in Cambridge, Raine was too young to fully comprehend the revolution in reading and writing that was being urged on by these men. However, she clearly understood, as the result of "the scorched earth" policy employed to defeat those who disagreed with these new methodologies, that the poets whom she held in the highest esteem—Milton, Blake, Yeats, and Shelley, for example— had been relegated to a minor status (143–44). Writing of Vernon Watkins, one of the poets under consideration in *Defending Ancient Springs*, Raine notes that he "made a brief sortie into Cambridge as an undergraduate at William Empson's very college" before "he returned to Swansea after a term or two . . . perhaps he understood even then that tradition has more to give a poet than education has" (17–18).

Moya Cannon has written that "there is always a danger of becoming trapped permanently within the mode of thought fashionable in one's early twenties. It certainly took me a long time to accept the obvious—that there were some areas of life which reason could never comprehend or honor, which would turn to dust if approached analytically, but which could be honored in literature or in art generally— certain areas which could be better elucidated by rhyme than by reason" ("The Poetry of What Happens" 130). Fifty years earlier, Kathleen Raine had come to a similar realization. *Defending Ancient Springs* is both a look back in the direction of her teachers and a defiant work that pleads the case for another tradition: one, above all else, that privileges the imagination. To come across such a book when she did was a godsend for Cannon.

In addition to Watkins, *Defending Ancient Springs* includes essays on Edwin Muir, David Gascoyne, St. John Perse, Coleridge, and Shelley; on Yeats's debt to Blake; and on the roles played by symbols and myths in poetry. Raine's most sustained broadside against New Critical ideology is found in the "On the Symbol" chapter, where she declares that "the language of symbolic analogy is only possible upon the assumption that these multiple planes do in fact exist. Those for whom

the material world is the only plane of the real are unable to understand that the symbol—and poetry in the full sense is symbolic discourse, discourse by analogy—has as its primary purpose the evoca-
tion of one plane in terms of another; they must find other uses for
poetry or honestly admit that they have no use for it" (108). In other
words, she rejects the notion that the poem is a separate organic unit
best appreciated in isolation. For Raine, neither poems nor symbols
can have value if they are removed from their context—a context located in the world, in its resonant vocabulary and literature, and driven
by the imagination of the author. Underlying, informing, and supporting Raine's view of the poetic process is the work of Carl Jung:

> We do not know what the soul (or psyche) is, only that it is, and
> something of its inexhaustible riches; for it is here that we discover
> what Jung calls "the unending myth of death and rebirth, and of
> the multitudinous figures who weave in and out of the mystery.". . .
> Of this story no single life can realize more than a part; but be-
> neath our individual lives is the pooled experience of our inheri-
> tance, Jung's "collective unconscious" which declares itself, so he
> says, "only through the medium of creative fantasy." "It comes alive
> in the creative man, it reveals itself in the vision of the artist, in the
> inspiration of the thinker, in the inner experience of the mystic."
> The mythologies of all races are its embodiment; the psychologists
> are newcomers in a field long known to the poets, a fact they are apt
> to forget. (126–27)

As already has been pointed out, Cannon understood that "all" that
she was initially able to bring to the table of poetry was an offering of
"landscape, language, and place names, [and] that most tangible of
etymologies, the interface between language and landscape" ("The
Poetry of What Happens" 128). From Raine she learned that her instincts were sound, that her raw material was the considerable product of a rich literary heritage, and that there were universal and unchangeable truths in need of description for the generation for whom
Cannon's voice would speak. She would find her material both in the

extended world beyond the self, specifically in the West of Ireland, and in what Yeats referred to as "that age-long memoried self, that shapes the elaborate shell of the mollusk and the child in the womb, that teaches the birds to make their nests" (Raine 90). From Raine's arguments and from the example of her life as a poet, Cannon learned that she could trust her instincts and forsake some of the more decadent products of her university education. Like Watkins, she would trust tradition by looking to her own literature and her own landscape because, as Raine points out, "there can be no conflict between imagination and such traditional themes. On the contrary, the traditional symbols have at all times been at once the teachers of the imagination and the record of its insights. With every new insight there must be an accompanying discovery of the fitness and power of the old symbols; such a discovery is the natural, the inevitable consequence of our own insights into the world they embody" (137). Present throughout Cannon's work is a liberal use of archetypes contained within words—wells, wood, rock, bone—which opens up her poetry to Jungian interpretation. Finally, what Raine notes of Edwin Muir is applicable to Cannon: "he stands out . . . because of an unswerving inner certainty, an integrity, an indifference to fashion, that made him never seek to impress or please, but only to bear witness to the truth that was in him" (1).

Even the most cursory reading of Moya Cannon's poetry will uncover a strong ecological consciousness in her work. Examples abound almost in every poem, though perhaps no more so than in "Script," where a seal that has returned to the ocean from the beach has left a written report of its visit:

> We walked down the shore for a closer look.
> Dug hard into the sand,
> claw-marks
> recorded a breast-stroke,
> a perfect, cursive script
> which reached
> the ocean's lip. (*Carrying the Songs* 40)

The poem is homage to the seal's voice: its most important aspect is the script on the sand and not the poet's words on the page. Cannon is pushing for a striking revision of the theological great chain of being that for centuries has underlined Anglophone poetry and that was most memorably propounded by Pope:

> Vast chain of being! which from God began,
> Natures ethereal, human, angel, man,
> Beast, bird, fish, insect, what no eye can see,
> No glass can reach; from Infinite to thee,
> From thee to nothing.—On superior powers
> Were we to press, inferior might on ours. (*An Essay on Man* 131)

Simultaneously, she is pointing toward the ancient Gaelic Irish tradition where, as Potts and Cusick have made clear, different theological and literary ideologies prevailed that did not place "nature" in a secondary position to man. In this regard, she is again directed by Raine's injunction to look deeply into one's own tradition for guidance. Literally in "Script," the seal, a rich presence in the literature and mythology of the West of Ireland, is the teacher whose story must be attended to. Also, the seal reminds the poet that he/she does not need the poet's words because it is capable of producing its own art.

This kind of poem goes to the heart of contemporary ecological consciousness and is reminiscent of such American poets as Mary Oliver and Gary Snyder. Over the years, but particularly in her memoir, *Object Lessons,* Eavan Boland has written eloquently of the difficult journey that Irish women have had to make in order to become the authors of poems and rather than merely their subjects; here, Cannon takes this process a step further—the seal is not the subject, but the poet. In this respect, her attitude is simultaneously that of the feminist and the ecologist. In "Mountain," a poem centered on Ben Bulben, Cannon suggests that no writer can produce a work as great as what has come to us through nature. Also, she finds in the mountain the solid counter to "the brittle and short-lived . . . truths yielded by historical research" ("The Poetry of What Happens" 131):

> One singer was found by hunters on these green flanks
> and another chose them as a deep cradle for his bones
> but neither the Fianna's chroniclers nor Yeats
> did more than pay their respects
> to what was already there—
>
> a mountain
> which had already
> shaken off glaciers,
> carried a human cargo,
> known grace in stone. (*Carrying the Songs* 100)

Stone is not subject to the whims of historical revisionism or critical theory. These views of the natural world and of humans' relationship to it have much in common with Robinson Jeffers's outlook: "I believe the universe is one being, all its parts are different expressions of the same energy, and they are all in communication with each other, therefore parts of an organic whole. . . . It seems to me that this whole *alone* is worthy of the deeper love" (Kheel 136).

Writing of Cannon's ecological consciousness and how it relates to Irish writing, Cusick has noted:

> Cannon's poetic explorations courageously bring us to a new and important place of human engagement with the landscape that calls for humility in face of nature's intrinsic value—a value that exists quite independently of any attribution of cultural worth. . . . Despite such deeply rooted connections between language and material landscape in Ireland, too often the anthropocentric divide of culture dominates Irish place studies, thus positioning the Irish landscape as more a trope than a geographic reality. . . . Her poetry makes the landscape a subject before and above any political or personal debate and, in so doing, humbly recognizes the preeminence of the natural world. (59–65)

What Cannon asks of her reader is what Raine asked of herself—to look more deeply into one's tradition in order to know where one belongs. In the older Gaelic literary and beliefs systems, she has found another way of looking at nature to counter the views that had developed in English literature and that had become dogma in colonial and postcolonial Ireland: she has brought a Gaelic ecological consciousness into her own work and into present-day of Irish poetry. In her studies of poetry, languages, and nature—represented in her poetry—Cannon has proceeded in a highly objective and orderly manner, an indication that her painful studies at University College, Dublin, and at Cambridge did provide her with good value. In "Murdering the Language," she describes the intense excitement she felt as a child when she took sentences apart to learn the value of their individual components, and she concludes that since it is impossible to unlearn ingrained ways of thinking, the individual must accept imperfection:

> Laws learned by heart in school are the hardest to unlearn,
> but too much has been suffered since
> in the name of who governs whom.
> It is time to step outside the cold schools,
> to find a new, less brutal grammar
> which can allow what we know:
> that this northern shore was wrought
> not in one day, by one bright wave,
> but by tholing the rush and tug of many tides. (*Carrying the Songs* 88)

Potts and Cusick make undeniable claims for the primary role played by an ecological consciousness in Cannon's work. Does this indicate that she can be called an ecofeminist poet? Carolyn Merchant has noted that "the term *ecofeminisme* was coined by the French writer Françoise d'Eaubonne in 1974 to represent women's potential for bringing about an ecological revolution to ensure human survival on the planet" ("Ecofeminism and Feminist Theory" 100). Despite its political implications, the tenor of Cannon's work hardly lends itself to such an ideology. However, another mode of reading her poetry is to see it as an example of Deep Ecology. Marti Kheel has outlined what this theory proposes:

Both ecofeminism and deep ecology share in common an opposition to these value theories with their attendant notions of obligations and rights. The emphasis of both philosophies is not on an abstract or "rational" calculation of value but rather on the development of a new consciousness for all of life. Both ecofeminism and deep ecology may therefore be viewed as "deep" philosophies in the sense that they call for an inward transformation in order to attain an outward change. Deep ecologists employ the notion of self-realization to describe this inward transformation. As environmental philosophers Bill Devall and George Sessions explain, this process "begins when we cease to understand or see ourselves as isolated and narrow competing egos and begin to identify with other humans from our family and friends to, eventually, our species. But the deep ecology sense of Self requires a further maturity and growth, an identification which goes beyond humanity to include the nonhuman world." (128)

This ideology accommodates Cannon's vision, though for her, as well as for Raine, an inward transformation has less to do with change and more with coming to recognize the diverse traditions to which it belongs. Kheel goes on to list some of the differences between ecofeminism and Deep Ecology:

There is a significant distinction between ecofeminism and deep ecology, however, in their understanding of the root cause of our environmental malaise. For deep ecologists, it is the anthropocentric worldview that is foremost to blame. The two norms of deep ecology—self-realization and biospherical egalitarianism—are thus designed to redress this self-centered worldview. Ecofeminists, on the other hand, argue that it is the androcentric worldview that deserves primary blame. For ecofeminists, it is not just "humans" but men and the masculinist worldview that must be dismantled from their privileged place. (129)

In the Irish context, the ecofeminist view is complicated by colonization; in many respects, Irishmen had no power to implement political or environmental policy. At the same time, it is clear that the Catholic Church promoted a great-chain-of-being ideology that served to distance humans from nature. Because of the enormous wealth that has been generated as a result of the Celtic Tiger, the environment has been seriously degraded by "development." A cursory look through the newspapers will reveal that almost all of these developers are men! In this respect, Cannon's interest in place and her sense of the landscape as a sacred space is cautionary and prophetic: she is providing an inventory of an endangered world.

A further ecological category is bioregionalism, which Michael E. Zimmerman has described as follows:

> Deep ecologists like Gary Snyder put such compassion into practice by attempting to "reinhabit" the land and to reestablish appropriate humanity-nature relationships in light of the particular character and possibilities of the area in which they find themselves. The bioregional movement, favored by deep ecologists, is an example of the growing conviction that only by living in a *particular* place, with *particular* relationships with people and the landscape, can humanity learn to produce goods and dispose of waste in ways that respect all who are affected. (150)

In Snyder's case, he has settled onto his land in the foothills of the Sierra Nevada, California, becoming involved in his local community, and this life in all of its micro and macro aspects has played a central part in his work, most famously, *Turtle Island* (1974). Cannon, who now lives in Galway's city center, is herself a committed bioregionalist who pays close attention to her immediate surroundings and records what she observes. For example, in "Nest":

> A brown wheel of reeds and broken willow
> turns somnolently in a corner above the weir.
> How long will that current hold it
> before the flow sweeps it over?

> Two Coke cans and a fast-food carton
> are wound into the heart of it.

Out of habit,
god goes on making nests. (*Carrying the Songs* 77)

Even though we can discern from her poetry and prose her priorities and beliefs, it would be a mistake to pigeonhole her into one or more constructs. As a poet, Cannon is looking out at the West of Ireland from various vantage points—from the top of a mountain, from a schoolroom where her father teaches, from the harbor or Long Walk in Galway, from a car parked by the side of the road, from her kitchen window. She is also looking inward into the self, into the center of the mountain where its heart beats, and into the collective unconscious that is our common inheritance. Just as the light is constantly changing in the West of Ireland, so, too, is the mind and perspective of the poet; therefore, because the landscape is large and the mind is in flux, no one theory can adequately contain all that it comprises. For her part, Moya Cannon seeks to record found parts of what endures.

BIBLIOGRAPHY

Aalen, F. H. A., Kevin Whelan, and Matthew Stout, eds. *Atlas of the Irish Rural Landscape*. Cork: Cork University Press, 1997.

Adams, Lee, and Buck Rainey. *Shoot-Em-Ups: The Complete Guide to Westerns of the Sound Era*. New Rochelle, N.Y.: Arlington House, 1995.

Akerman, James R., and Robert W. Karrow, eds. *Maps: Finding Our Place in the World*. Chicago: University of Chicago Press, 2007.

Alexander, Meena. "Dorothy Wordsworth: The Grounds of Writing." *Women's Studies* 14 (1988): 195–210.

———. *Women in Romanticism*. Basingstoke: Macmillan, 1989.

Alexandre, Veronique. "Tim Robinson and the Aran Landscape." *Imaginaires: Revue de Centre de recherche sur l'imaginaire dans les littératures de langue anglaise* 5.5 (2000): 121–33.

Allen, Gilbert. "Passionate Detachment in the Lyrics of Jeffers and Yeats." *Robinson Jeffers and a Gallery of Writers: Essays in Honor of William H. Nolte*. Ed. William B. Thesing. Columbia: University of South Carolina Press, 1995. 60–68.

Allen, Paula Gunn. *The Sacred Hoop: Recovering the Feminine in American Indian Traditions*. Boston: Beacon, 1986.

Andrews, J. H. *A Paper Landscape: The Ordnance Survey in Nineteenth Century Ireland*. Oxford: Clarendon Press, 1975.

Anzaldúa, Gloria. *The Gloria Anzaldúa Reader*. Ed. AnaLouise Keating. Durham and London: Duke University Press, 2009.

Appleyard, Donald, Kevin Lynch, and John R. Myer. *The View from the Road*. Cambridge: M.I.T. Press, 1964.

Armbruster, Karla, and Kathleen R. Wallace, eds. *Beyond Nature Writing: Expanding the Boundaries of Ecocriticism.* Charlottesville: University Press of Virginia, 2001.

Artaud, Antonin. *Selected Writings.* Trans. Helen Weaver. New York: Farrar, Straus and Giroux, 1976.

———. *The Theatre and Its Double.* Trans. Mary Caroline Richards. New York: Grove, 1958.

Attis, David. "Science and Irish Identity: The Relevance of Science Studies for Irish Studies." *New Voices in Irish Criticism.* Ed. P. J. Mathews. Dublin: Four Courts Press, 2000. 133–41.

Banville, John. *The Book of Evidence.* New York: Warner, 1991.

Barrell, John. *The Idea of Landscape and the Sense of Place, 1730–1840: An Approach to the Poetry of John Clare.* Cambridge: Cambridge University Press, 1972.

Barry, Terry, ed. *A History of Settlement in Ireland.* London: Routledge, 1988.

Barsam, Richard. *The Vision of Robert Flaherty: The Artist as Myth and Filmmaker.* Bloomington and Indianapolis: Indiana University Press, 1998.

Bate, Jonathan. *Romantic Ecology: Wordsworth and the Environmental Tradition.* London: Routledge, 1991.

———. *The Song of the Earth.* Cambridge, Mass.: Harvard University Press, 2000.

Benjamin, Walter. *Charles Baudelaire: A Lyric Poet in the Era of High Capitalism.* Trans. Henry Zohn. London: New Left Books, 1973.

———. *Illuminations.* Ed. Hannah Arendt. Trans. Henry Zohn. London: Jonathan Cape, 1970.

Benson, Jackson J. *Wallace Stegner: A Study of the Short Fiction.* New York: Twayne, 1998.

Bernard, Jami. *Quentin Tarantino: The Man and His Movies.* New York: Harper Perennial, 1995.

Berry, Wendell. *The Gift of Good Land.* San Francisco: North Point Press, 1981.

———. *Standing by Words.* San Francisco: North Point Press, 1983.

Black, Jeremy. *Britain since the Seventies: Politics and Society in the Consumer Age.* London: Reaktion Books, 2004.

———. *Maps and Politics.* Chicago: University of Chicago Press, 1997.

Boland, Eavan. "The Achill Woman." *Outside History.* Manchester: Carcanet Press, 1990. 27–28.

———. "New Wave 2: Born in the 1950s; Irish Poets of the Global Village." *Irish Poetry since Kavanagh: The Thomas Davis Lectures.* Ed. Theo Dorgan. Dublin: Four Courts Press, 1996. 136–46.

———. *Object Lessons: The Life of the Woman and the Poet in Our Time.* New York: Norton, 1995.

———. "That the Science of Cartography Is Limited." *In a Time of Violence.* New York: Norton, 1994. 7–8.

Bolger, Dermot, ed. *Druids, Dudes and Beauty Queens: The Changing Face of Irish Theatre.* Dublin: New Island Books, 2001.

Bond, Edward. *Saved.* London: Methuen, 2000.

Bornstein, George, ed. *Ezra Pound among the Poets.* Chicago: University of Chicago Press, 1985.

Bouzereau, Laurent. *Ultra Violent Movies from Sam Peckinpah to Quentin Tarantino.* Secaucus, N.J.: Citadel Press, 1996.

Brady, Mary Pat. *Extinct Lands, Temporal Geographies: Chicana Literature and the Urgency of Space.* Durham and London: Duke University Press, 2002.

Brecht, Bertolt. *Brecht on Theatre.* Trans. John Willett. New York: Hill and Wang, 1964.

Brewer, Gay. *David Mamet and Film: Illusion/Disillusion in a Wounded Land.* Jefferson, N.C.: McFarland and Company, 1993.

Bryson, J. Scott, ed. *Ecopoetry: A Critical Introduction.* Salt Lake City: University of Utah Press, 2002.

Buell, Lawrence. *The Environmental Imagination: Thoreau, Nature Writing, and the Formation of American Culture.* Cambridge: Harvard University Press, 1995.

Burke, Patrick. "'Like the Cat-astrophe of the Old Comedy': The Animal in *The Lieutenant of Inishmore.*" *The Theatre of Martin McDonagh: A World of Savage Stories.* Ed. Lilian Chambers and Eamonn Jordan. Dublin: Carysfort Press, 2006. 155–61.

Calder, Jenni. *There Must Be a Lone Ranger.* London: Hamish Hamilton, 1974.

Campbell, Andrea, ed. *New Directions in Ecofeminist Literary Criticism.* Newcastle: Cambridge Scholars Publishing, 2008.

Campbell, Neil. *The Rhizomatic West: Representing the American West in a Transnational, Global, Media Age.* Lincoln: University of Nebraska Press, 2008.

Campbell, Sueellen. "The Land and Language of Desire: Where Deep Ecology and Post-Structuralism Meet." *The Ecocriticism Reader: Landmarks in Literary Ecology.* Ed. Cheryll Glotfelty and Harold Fromm. Athens: University of Georgia Press, 1996. 124–36.

Cannon, Moya. *Carrying the Songs.* Manchester: Carcarnet Press, 2007.

———. *Oar.* Rev. ed. Loughcrew, Co. Meath: Gallery Press, 2000. Galway: Salmon Publishing, 1990.

————. *The Parchment Boat.* Loughcrew, Co. Meath: Gallery Press, 1997.

————. "The Poetry of What Happens." *My Self, My Muse.* Ed. Patricia Boyle Haberstroh. Syracuse, N.Y.: Syracuse University Press, 2001. 124–32.

Carpenter, Andrew, ed. *Place, Personality and the Irish Writer.* Gerrards Cross: Colin Smythe, 1977.

Chambers, Lilian, and Eamonn Jordan, eds. *The Theatre of Martin McDonagh: A World of Savage Stories.* Dublin: Carysfort Press, 2006.

Charyn, Jerome. *Raised by Wolves: The Turbulent Art and Times of Quentin Tarantino.* New York: Thunder's Mouth Press, 2006.

Chatwin, Bruce. *In Patagonia.* New York: Penguin, 1988.

————. *On the Black Hill.* New York: Viking, 1982.

————. *The Songlines.* New York: Penguin, 1988.

Christ, Carol P. "Rethinking Theology and Nature." *Reweaving the World: The Emergence of Ecofeminism.* Ed. Irene Diamond and Gloria Feman Orenstein. San Francisco: Sierra Club Books, 1990. 58–69.

Christensen, Laird, Mark C. Long, and Fred Waage, eds. *Teaching North American Environmental Literature.* New York: Modern Language Association of America, 2008.

Christmas, Linda. *Chopping Down the Cherry Trees: A Portrait of Britain in the Eighties.* London: Viking, 1989.

Cleary, Joe, and Claire Connolly, eds. *The Cambridge Companion to Irish Culture.* Cambridge: Cambridge University Press, 2005.

Collins, Timothy. "The Clare Island Survey of 1909–11: Participants, Papers and Progress." *New Survey of Clare Island.* Ed. Críostóir Mc Cárthaigh and Kevin Whelan. Vol. 1. Dublin: Royal Irish Academy, 1999. 1–33.

Comer, Krista. *Landscapes of the New West: Gender and Geography in Contemporary Women's Writing.* Chapel Hill and London: University of North Carolina Press, 1999.

Conrad, Joseph. *Heart of Darkness.* New York: Signet, 1997.

Cook, Barbara, ed. *Women Writing Nature.* Lanham, Md.: Lexington Press, 2008.

Cook-Lynn, Elizabeth. *Why I Can't Read Wallace Stegner and Other Essays.* Madison: University of Wisconsin Press, 1996.

Curtis, Jim. *Rock Eras: Interpretations of Music and Society, 1954–1984.* Bowling Green, Ohio: Bowling Green State University Popular Press, 1987.

Cusick, Christine. "'Our Language Was Tidal': Moya Cannon's Poetics of Place." *New Hibernia Review* 9.1 (Earrach/Spring 2005): 59–76.

Darby, Wendy Joy. *Landscape and Identity: Geographies of Nation and Class in England.* Oxford: Berg, 2000.

Dean, Joan FitzPatrick. "Martin McDonagh's Stagecraft." *Martin McDonagh: A Casebook.* Ed. Richard Rankin Russell. London and New York: Routledge, 2007. 25–40.

Deane, Seamus. *Celtic Revivals.* Winston-Salem, N.C.: Wake Forest University Press, 1985.

Delanty, Greg. *Southward.* Baton Rouge: Louisiana University Press, 1992.

Devall, Bill, and George Sessions. *Deep Ecology: Living as if Nature Mattered.* Salt Lake City: Peregrine Smith, 1985.

Diamond, Irene, and Gloria Feman Orenstein. *Reweaving the World: The Emergence of Ecofeminism.* San Francisco: Sierra Club Books, 1990.

Dorling, Daniel, and David Fairbairn. *Mapping: Ways of Representing the World.* Harlow: Longman, 1997.

Doyle, Maria. "Breaking Bodies: The Presence of Violence in Martin McDonagh's Stage." *Martin McDonagh: A Casebook.* Ed. Richard Rankin Russell. London and New York: Routledge, 2007. 92–110.

Elder, John. *Imagining the Earth: Poetry and the Vision of Nature.* Urbana and Chicago: University of Illinois Press, 1985.

———. "The Poetry of Experience." *Beyond Nature Writing: Expanding the Boundaries of Ecocriticism.* Ed. Karla Armbruster and Kathleen R. Wallace. Charlottesville: University Press of Virginia, 2001. 312–24.

English, Richard. *Armed Struggle: The History of the IRA.* Oxford: Oxford University Press, 2003.

Enzensberger, Hans Magnus. *Eine literarische Landkarte.* Munich: Wilhelm Goldmann Verlag, 1999.

Evans, E. Estyn. *Irish Folk Ways.* London: Routledge and Kegan Paul, 1957.

———. *The Personality of Ireland: Habitat, Heritage and History.* Cambridge: Cambridge University Press, 1973.

Evernden, Neil. "Beyond Ecology: Self, Place, and the Pathetic Fallacy." *The Ecocriticism Reader: Landmarks in Literary Ecology.* Ed. Cheryll Glotfelty and Harold Fromm. Athens: University of Georgia Press, 1996. 92–104.

Eyman, Scott. *Print the Legend: The Life and Times of John Ford.* New York: Simon and Schuster, 1999.

Fenin, George N., and William K. Everson. *The Western: From Silents to the Seventies.* New York: Grossman, 1973.

Fish, Stanley. *Doing What Comes Naturally: Change, Rhetoric, and the Practice of Theory in Literary and Legal Studies.* Oxford: Clarendon Press, 1989.

Fleming, Deborah. "Landscape and the Self in W. B. Yeats and Robinson Jeffers." *Ecopoetry: A Critical Introduction.* Ed. J. Scott Bryson. Salt Lake City: University of Utah Press, 2002. 39–47.

Foakes, R. A. *Shakespeare and Violence.* Cambridge: Cambridge University Press, 2003.

Foster, John Wilson. "Natural History, Science and Culture." *Irish Review* 9 (1990): 61–69.

———. "Natural Science and Irish Culture." *Eire-Ireland* 26.2 (1991): 92–103.

———, ed. *Nature in Ireland.* Dublin: Lilliput Press, 1997.

Foster, Verna A. "(Up)staging the Staging of Ireland: Martin McDonagh's *The Cripple of Inishmaan.*" *Nua: Studies in Contemporary Irish Writing* 5.1 (Fall 2006): 25–33.

Fradkin, Philip L. *Wallace Stegner and the American West.* New York: Knopf, 2008.

Friel, Brian. *Translations.* London: Faber and Faber, 1981.

Frye, Northrop. *The Educated Imagination.* Toronto: CBC, 1961.

Gallagher, Tag. *John Ford: The Man and His Films.* Berkeley: University of California Press, 1986.

Gilbert, Roger. *Walks in the World: Representation and Experience in Modern American Poetry.* Princeton: Princeton University Press, 1991.

Glotfelty, Cheryll, and Harold Fromm, eds. *The Ecocriticism Reader: Landmarks in Literary Ecology.* Athens: University of Georgia Press, 1996.

Golding, William. *Lord of the Flies.* London: Faber and Faber, 1954.

Goodby, John. *Irish Poetry since 1950: From Stillness into History.* Manchester: Manchester University Press, 2000.

Grassian, Daniel. *Understanding Sherman Alexie.* Columbia: University of South Carolina Press, 2005.

Graulich, Melody, and Stephen Tatum, eds. *Reading* The Virginian *in the New West.* Lincoln: University of Nebraska Press, 2003.

Grazia, Margreta, and Stanley Wells. *The Cambridge Companion to Shakespeare.* Cambridge: Cambridge University Press, 2001.

Grene, Nicholas. "Ireland in Two Minds: Martin McDonagh and Conor McPherson." *The Theatre of Martin McDonagh: A World of Savage Stories.* Ed. Lilian Chambers and Eamonn Jordan. Dublin: Carysfort Press, 2006. 43–59.

Griffin, Susan. *Made from This Earth.* New York: Harper and Row, 1982.

———. *Woman and Nature: The Roaring Inside Her.* New York: Harper and Row, 1978.

Griffith, Richard. *The World of Robert Flaherty.* Boston: Little, Brown, 1953.

Haberstroh, Patricia Boyle. *Women Creating Women: Contemporary Irish Women Poets.* Syracuse, N.Y.: Syracuse University Press, 1996.

———. "Women Poets of the West: Moya Cannon and Mary O'Malley." *Nua: Studies in Contemporary Irish Writing* 2.1–2 (1998–1999): 180–91.

Harley, J. B., and David Woodward. *Cartography in the Traditional East and Southeast Asian Societies. The History of Cartography.* Vol. 2, bk. 2. Chicago: University of Chicago Press, 1994.

Hazlitt, William. *Selected Writings.* Ed. Ronald Blythe. Harmondsworth: Penguin, 1970.

Heaney, Seamus. "Digging." *Death of a Naturalist.* London: Faber and Faber, 1966. 1–2.

———. "Faith, Hope and Poetry." *Preoccupations: Selected Prose, 1968–1978.* New York: Noonday Press, 1980. 217–20.

———. "The God in the Tree: Early Irish Nature Poetry." *Preoccupations: Selected Prose, 1968–1978.* New York: Noonday Press, 1980. 181–89.

———. "Mossbawn." *Preoccupations: Selected Prose, 1968–1978.* New York: Noonday Press, 1980. 17–27.

Henry, Tricia. *Break All Rules! Punk Rock and the Making of a Style.* Ann Arbor, Mich.: UMI Research Press, 1989.

Hine, Robert V., and John Mack Faragher. *The American West: A New Interpretive History.* New Haven: Yale University Press, 2000.

Hogan, Linda. *Rounding the Human Corners.* Minneapolis: Coffee House Press, 2008.

Howarth, William. "Some Principles of Ecocriticism." *The Ecocriticism Reader: Landmarks in Literary Ecology.* Ed. Cheryll Glotfelty and Harold Fromm. Athens: University of Georgia Press, 1996. 69–91.

Huber, Werner. "The Early Plays: Martin McDonagh, Shooting Star and Hard Man from South London." *The Theatre of Martin McDonagh: A World of Savage Stories.* Ed. Lilian Chambers and Eamonn Jordan. Dublin: Carysfort Press, 2006. 13–26.

Hunt, Leon. *British Low Culture: From Safari Suits to Sexploitation.* London and New York: Routledge, 1998.

Hutchinson, Clive D. *Birds of Ireland.* Calton, Staffordshire: T. and A. D. Poyser, 1989.

James, Clive. *Glued to the Box: Television Criticism from the Observer, 1979–82.* London: Cape, 1983.

Jarvis, Robin. *Romantic Writing and Pedestrian Travel.* Basingstoke and London: Macmillan, 1997.

Jeffares, A. Norman. "Place, Space and Personality and the Irish Writer." *Place, Personality and the Irish Writer*. Ed. Andrew Carpenter. Gerrards Cross: Colin Smythe, 1977. 11–40.

Jeffers, Robinson. *Selected Poetry*. Ed. Tim Hunt. Stanford, Calif.: Stanford University Press, 2001.

Johnson, James H. *The Human Geography of Ireland*. Chichester: John Wiley, 1994.

Jordan, Eamonn. "War on Narrative: *The Pillowman*." *The Theatre of Martin McDonagh: A World of Savage Stories*. Ed. Lilian Chambers and Eamonn Jordan. Dublin: Carysfort Press, 2006. 174–97.

Joyce, James. *Ulysses*. The Corrected Text. New York: Vintage, 1986.

Kaplan, E. Ann. *Trauma Culture: The Politics of Terror and Loss in Media and Literature*. New Brunswick, N.J.: Rutgers University Press, 1995.

Kelman, James. *How Late It Was, How Late*. London: Secker and Warburg, 1994.

Kennedy, P. G., R. F. Ruttledge, and C. F. Scroope. *Birds of Ireland*. Edinburgh: Oliver and Boyd, 1954.

Kheel, Marti. "Ecofeminism and Deep Ecology: Reflections on Identity and Difference." *Reweaving the World: The Emergence of Ecofeminism*. Ed. Irene Diamond and Gloria Feman Orenstein. San Francisco: Sierra Club Books, 1990. 128–37.

Kiberd, Declan. *Inventing Ireland: The Literature of the Modern Nation*. Cambridge, Mass.: Harvard University Press, 1995.

———. *Irish Classics*. Cambridge, Mass.: Harvard University Press, 2001.

———. "John McGahern's *Amongst Women*." *Language and Tradition in Ireland: Continuities and Displacements*. Ed. Maria Tymoczko and Colin Ireland. Amherst and Boston: University of Massachusetts Press, 2003. 195–213.

Kirkpatrick, Bethany. "My Body, My People, My Land: Healing the Bonds That Are Broken in Linda Hogan's *Solar Storms*." *New Directions in Ecofeminist Literary Criticism*. Ed. Andrea Campbell. Newcastle: Cambridge Scholars Publishing, 2008. 1–14.

Kirkpatrick, Kathryn. "'A Maturation of Starlings in a Rowan Tree': Finding Gary Snyder in Paula Meehan's Eco-Political Poetics." *An Sionnach: A Journal of Literature, Culture, and the Arts* 5.1–2 (Fall 2009): 195–207.

———, ed. *Border Crossings: Irish Women Writers and National Identities*. Tuscaloosa and London: University of Alabama Press, 2000.

Kitses, Jim. *Horizons West: Anthony Mann, Budd Boetticher, Sam Peckinpah: Studies in Authorship within the Western.* London: BFI Publishing, 1969.

Kollin, Susan, ed. *Postwestern Cultures: Literature, Theory, Space.* Lincoln: University of Nebraska Press, 2007.

Ladino, Jennifer. "New Frontiers for Ecofeminism: Women, Nature and Globalization in Ruth L. Ozeki's *My Year of Meats.*" *New Directions in Ecofeminist Literary Criticism.* Ed. Andrea Campbell. Newcastle: Cambridge Scholars Publishing, 2008. 124–47.

Lahr, John. "Write, Stop, Pivot, Punch." *The Guardian.* Section G2, p. 23. August 7, 2008.

Lanters, José. "The Identity Politics of Martin McDonagh." *Martin McDonagh: A Casebook.* Ed. Richard Rankin Russell. London and New York: Routledge, 2007. 9–24.

Lawrence, D. H. *Studies in Classic American Literature.* New York: Penguin, 1977.

Lawrence, Karen. *The Odyssey of Style in* Ulysses. Princeton: Princeton University Press. 1981.

Least Heat-Moon, William. *PrairyErth.* Boston: Houghton Mifflin, 1991.

Lee, Cordell D. K. "Chinese Maps in Political Culture." *Cartography in the Traditional East and Southeast Asian Societies. The History of Cartography.* Vol. 2, bk. 2. Ed. J. B. Harley and David Woodward. Chicago: University of Chicago Press, 1994. 70–85.

Leerssen, Joep. *Remembrance and Imagination: Patterns in the Historical and Literary Representation of Ireland in the Nineteenth Century.* Cork: Field Day/Cork University Press, 1996.

Lenihan, John H. *Showdown: Confronting Modern America in the Western Film.* Urbana: University of Illinois Press, 1980.

Lewis, Nathaniel. *Unsettling the Literary West: Authenticity and Authorship.* Lincoln: University of Nebraska Press, 2003.

Lonergan, Patrick. "'Never Mind the Shamrocks': Globalizing Martin McDonagh." *Martin McDonagh: A Casebook.* Ed. Richard Rankin Russell. London and New York: Routledge, 2007. 149–77.

Longley, Edna. "'The Business of the Earth': Edward Thomas and Ecocentrism." *Poetry and Posterity.* Tarset, Northumberland: Bloodaxe Books, 2000. 23–51.

Love, Glen A. "Revaluing Nature: Toward an Ecological Criticism." *Western American Literature* 25.3 (1990): 201–15.

Luckhurst, Mary. "Martin McDonagh's *Lieutenant of Inishmore:* Selling (-Out) to the English." *The Theatre of Martin McDonagh: A World of Savage Stories.* Ed. Lilian Chambers and Eamonn Jordan. Dublin: Carysfort Press, 2006. 116–29.

Lysaght, Seán. *The Clare Island Survey.* Loughcrew, Co. Meath: Gallery Press, 1991.

———. *Erris.* Loughcrew, Co. Meath: Gallery Press, 2002.

———. *The Mouth of a River.* Loughcrew, Co. Meath: Gallery Press, 2007.

———. *Noah's Irish Ark.* Dublin: Dedalus Press, 1989.

———. *Robert Lloyd Praeger: The Life of a Naturalist.* Dublin: Four Courts Press, 1998.

———. *Scarecrow.* Loughcrew, Co. Meath: Gallery Press, 1998.

Mac Giollarnáth, Seán. "List of Irish Names of Birds." *Birds of Ireland.* By P. G. Kennedy et al. Edinburgh: Oliver and Boyd, 1954. 422–25.

Maher, Eamon. *John McGahern: From the Local to the Universal.* Dublin: The Liffey Press, 2003.

Mannion, John. *Irish Settlements in Eastern Canada: A Study of Cultural Transfer and Adaption.* Toronto and Buffalo: University of Toronto Press, 1974.

Marples, Morris. *Shanks's Pony: A Study of Walking.* London: J. M. Dent, 1959.

McBride, Joseph. *Searching for John Ford: A Life.* New York: St. Martin's Press, 2001.

McCabe, Patrick. *The Butcher Boy.* New York: Fromm, 1992.

McDonagh, John, and Joan Fitzpatrick Dean. *Studies in the Drama of Martin McDonagh.* Working Papers in Irish Studies, 02/3-2. Ft. Lauderdale, Fla.: Nova Southeastern University, 2002.

McDonagh. Martin. *The Beauty Queen of Leenane and Other Plays.* New York: Vintage, 1998.

———. *The Cripple of Inishmann.* New York: Vintage, 1998.

———. *In Bruges.* Los Angeles: Universal/Focus Features, 2007.

———. *The Lieutenant of Inishmore.* London: Methuen, 2001.

———. *The Pillowman.* London: Faber and Faber, 2003.

———. *Six Shooter.* Irish Film Board/Film Four/A Missing in Action Films and Funny Farm Films, 2005.

McGahern, John. *Amongst Women.* New York: Penguin, 1990.

———. *The Barracks.* London: Faber and Faber, 1963.

———. "The Church and Its Spire." *Love of the World: Essays.* Ed. Stanley Van Der Ziel. London: Faber and Faber, 2009. 133–48.

———. *Collected Stories.* London: Faber and Faber, 1992.

———. *Creatures of the Earth: New and Selected Stories.* London: Faber and Faber, 2006.

———. *The Dark.* London: Faber and Faber, 1965.

———. "Dubliners." *James Joyce: The Artist and the Labyrinth.* Ed. Augustine Martin. London: Ryan Publishing, 1990. 63–72.

———. *High Ground.* New York: Penguin, 1993 [1985].

———. *The Leavetaking.* Revised edition. London: Faber and Faber, 1984 [1st. ed. 1974].

———. *Love of the World: Essays.* Ed. Stanley Van Der Ziel. London: Faber and Faber, 2009.

———. *Memoir.* London: Faber and Faber, 2005.

———. *Nightlines.* London: Faber and Faber, 1970.

———. *The Pornographer.* London: Faber and Faber, 1979.

———. "The Solitary Reaper." *Love of the World: Essays.* Ed. Stanley Van Der Ziel. London: Faber and Faber, 2009. 87–95.

———. "The Stories of Alistair MacLeod." *Love of the World: Essays.* Ed. Stanley Van Der Ziel. London: Faber and Faber, 2009. 208–12.

———. *That They May Face the Rising Sun.* London: Faber and Faber, 2002. Published as *By the Lake* in the United States. New York: Knopf, 2002.

McGregor, Robert Kuhn. *A Wider View of the Universe: Henry Thoreau's Study of Nature.* Urbana and Chicago: University of Illinois Press, 1997.

McKenna, Bernard. "Such Delvings and Exhumations: The Quest for Self-Actualization in Mary O'Malley's Poetry." *Contemporary Irish Women Poets: Some Male Perspectives.* Ed. Alexander G. Gonzalez. Westport, Conn.: Greenwood Press, 1999. 151–72.

Medved, Michael. *Hollywood vs. America: Popular Culture and the War on Traditional Values.* New York: HarperCollins, 1992.

Meehan, Paula. *Painting Rain.* Winston-Salem, N.C.: Wake Forest University Press, 2009.

Merchant, Carolyn. *The Death of Nature: Women, Ecology, and the Scientific Revolution.* San Francisco: Harper and Row, 1981.

———. "Ecofeminism and Feminist Theory." *Reweaving the World: The Emergence of Ecofeminism.* Ed. Irene Diamond and Gloria Feman Orenstein. San Francisco: Sierra Club Books, 1990. 100–105.

Messenger, John C. *Inis Beag: Isle of Ireland.* New York: Holt, Rinehart and Winston, 1969.

Meyer, Kuno. *Ancient Irish Poetry.* London: Constable, 1911.

Miola, Robert S. *Shakespeare's Reading.* Oxford: Oxford University Press, 2000.

Momaday, N. Scott. *The Man Made of Words: Essays, Stories, Passages.* New York: St. Martin's Griffin, 1997.

———. *The Way to Rainy Mountain.* Albuquerque: University of New Mexico Press, 1969.

Morash, Christopher. *A History of Irish Theatre, 1601–2000.* Cambridge: Cambridge University Press, 2002.

Munro, Alice. "Boys and Girls." *Dance of the Happy Shades.* New York: Vintage, 1998. 111–27.

Murphy, Patrick D. *Literature, Nature and Other: Ecofeminist Critiques.* Albany: State University of New York Press, 1995.

Murphy, Richard. *Collected Poems.* Winston-Salem, N.C.: Wake Forest University Press, 2001.

———. *The Kick.* London: Granta Books, 2002.

Naipaul, V. S. *A Bend in the River.* New York: Vintage, 1989.

———. *Half a Life.* London: Picador, 2001.

Nash, Roderick. *Wilderness and the American Mind.* 3rd ed. New Haven and London: Yale University Press, 1982.

Nehring, Neil. *Flowers in the Dustbin: Culture, Anarchy, and Postwar England.* Ann Arbor: University of Michigan Press, 1993.

Ní Dhomhnaill, Nuala, and Paul Muldoon, trans. *Pharoah's Daughter.* Winston-Salem, N.C.: Wake Forest, 1990.

Norris, Kathleen. *Dakota: A Spiritual Geography.* New York: Ticknor and Fields, 1993.

O'Connor, Frank. *The Lonely Voice.* Cleveland: World Publishing, 1963.

Ó hEithir, Breandán. "Introduction." *An Aran Reader.* Ed. Breandán Ó hEithir and Ruart Ó hEithir. Dublin: Lilliput Press, 1991. 1–9.

Ó Laoire, Lillis. *On a Rock in the Middle of the Ocean: Songs and Singers in Tory Island, Ireland.* Lanham, Md.: The Scarecrow Press, 2005.

Olson, Charles. "Projective Verse." *Postmodern American Poetry.* Ed. Paul Hoover. New York: Norton, 1994. 613–21.

Olsson, Gunnar. *Abysmal: A Critique of Cartographic Reason.* Chicago: University of Chicago Press, 2007.

O'Malley, Mary. *Asylum Road.* Cliffs of Moher, Co. Clare: Salmon Publishing, 2001.

———. "'Between the Snow and the Huge Roses.'" *My Self, My Muse.* Ed. Patricia Boyle Haberstroh. Syracuse, N.Y.: Syracuse University Press, 2001. 34–45.

———. *The Boning Hall: New and Selected Poems.* Manchester: Carcarnet Press, 2002.

———. *A Consideration of Silk.* Galway: Salmon Publishing, 1990.

———. *The Knife in the Wave.* Cliffs of Moher, Co. Clare: Salmon Publishing, 1997.

———. *A Perfect V.* Manchester: Carcarnet Press, 2006.

———. *Where the Rocks Float.* Dublin: Salmon Publishing, 1993.

Ó Muraíle, Nollaig. "The Place-Names of Clare Island." *New Survey of Clare Island.* Ed. Críostóir Mac Cárthaigh and Kevin Whelan. Vol. 1. Dublin: Royal Irish Academy, 1999. 99–139.

O'Toole, Fintan. "A Mind in Connemara: The Plays of Martin McDonagh." *The New Yorker.* March 6, 2006, 40–47.

Papanikolas, Zeese. "The Cowboy and the Gaucho." *Reading* The Virginian *in the New West.* Ed. Melody Graulich and Stephen Tatum. Lincoln: University of Nebraska Press, 2003. 176–97.

Parks, Rita. *The Western Hero in Film and Television: Mass Media Mythology.* Ann Arbor, Mich.: UMI Research Press, 1982.

Pelan, Rebecca. *Two Irelands: Literary Feminisms North and South.* Syracuse, N.Y.: Syracuse University Press, 2005.

Perloff, Marjorie. "The Contemporary of Our Grandchildren: Pound's Influence." *Ezra Pound among the Poets.* Ed. George Bornstein. Chicago: University of Chicago Press, 1985. 195–229.

Peterson, Roger Tory, Guy Mountfort, and P. A. D. Hollom. *A Field Guide to the Birds of Britain and Europe.* 4th ed. Boston: Houghton Mifflin, 1983.

Phillipps, John. *Transgender on Screen.* Basingstoke: Palgrave MacMillan, 2006.

Plant, Judith. "Searching for Common Ground: Ecofeminism and Bioregionalism." *Reweaving the World: The Emergence of Ecofeminism.* Ed. Irene Diamond and Gloria Feman Orenstein. San Francisco: Sierra Club Books, 1990. 155–61.

Pope, Alexander. *An Essay on Man.* Ed. Martin Price. *The Selected Poetry of Pope.* New York: Meridian, 1980. 123–63.

Potts, Donna. "Water from Stone: The Spirit of Place in Moya Cannon's Poetry." *An Sionnach* 3.2 (Fall 2007): 46–54.

Praeger, Robert Lloyd. "General Introduction and Narrative." *Proceedings of the Royal Irish Academy.* Vol. 31.1. Dublin: Hodges, Figgis, 1915. 1–12.

———. *Irish Landscape/Gnéithe na hÉireann. Irish Life and Culture 4.* Dublin: Cultural Relations Committee, 1953.

———. *The Way that I Went: An Irishman in Ireland.* Dublin: Hodges, Figgis; London: Methuen, 1937.

Quetchenbach, Bernard W. *Back from the Far Field: American Nature Poetry in the Late Twentieth Century.* Charlottesville: University Press of Virginia, 2000.

Raine, Kathleen. *Collected Poems, 1935–1980.* London: George Allen and Unwin, 1981.

———. *Defending Ancient Springs.* London: Oxford University Press, 1967.

———. *The Inner Journey of the Poet.* New York: George Braziller, 1982.

Ramsey, Patrick. "Fragrant Necrophilia." *The Irish Review* 15 (Spring 1994): 148–54.

Rees, Catherine. "The Politics of Morality: Martin McDonagh's *The Lieutenant of Inishmore.*" *The Theatre of Martin McDonagh: A World of Savage Stories.* Ed. Lilian Chambers and Eamonn Jordan. Dublin: Carysfort Press, 2006. 130–40.

Rich, Adrienne. "Diving into the Wreck." *Adrienne Rich's Poetry and Prose.* Ed. Barbara Charlesworth Gelpi and Albert Gelpi. New York: Norton, 1993. 53–55.

———. "North American Time." *Adrienne Rich's Poetry and Prose.* Ed. Barbara Charlesworth Gelpi and Albert Gelpi. New York: Norton, 1993. 114–18.

Ricou, Laurie. *The Arbutus/Madrone Files: Reading the Pacific Northwest.* Corvallis: Oregon State University Press, 2002.

Robertson, David. *Real Matter.* Salt Lake City: University of Utah Press, 1997.

Robinson, Tim. *Conamara Theas: Áit agus Anam.* Aistriú a Rinne Liam Mac Con Iomaire. Baile Átha Cliath: Coiscéim, 1992.

———. *Connemara: The Last Pool of Darkness.* Dublin: Penguin Ireland, 2008.

———. *Connemara: Part 1, Introduction and Gazetteer.* Roundstone, Co. Galway: Folding Landscapes, 1980.

———. *Mapping South Connemara Parts 1–29.* Roundstone, Co. Galway: Folding Landscapes, 1985.

———. *Mementos of Mortality: The Cenotaphs and Funerary Cairns of Árainn.* With Photographs by Gilbert Stucky. Roundstone, Co. Galway: Folding Landscapes, 1991.

———. *My Time in Space.* Dublin: Lilliput Press, 2001.

———. *Olwen Fouéré in the Bull's Wall.* Clonmel, Co. Tipperary: Coracle, 2001.

———. *Setting Foot on the Shores of Connemara and Other Writings.* Dublin: Lilliput Press, 1996.

———. *Spás, Am, Conamara.* Aistriú a Rinne Liam Mac Con Iomaire. Baile Átha Cliath: Coiscéim, 1993.

———. *Stones of Aran: Labyrinth.* Dublin: Lilliput Press, 1995.

———. *Stones of Aran: Pilgrimage.* Dublin: Lilliput Press, 1986.

———. *Tales and Imaginings.* Dublin: Lilliput Press, 2002.

———. *The View from the Horizon.* Clonmel, Co. Tipperary: Coracle, 1997.

———, ed. and introd. *The Aran Islands.* By J. M. Synge. London: Penguin, 1992.

———, ed. and introd. *Connemara after the Famine: Journal of a Survey of the Martin Estate by Thomas Colville Scoot, 1853.* Dublin: Lilliput Press, 1995.

Rosendale, Steven, ed. *The Greening of Literary Scholarship: Literature, Theory, and the Environment.* Iowa City: University of Iowa Press, 2002.

Rosowski, Susan J. *Birthing a Nation: Gender, Creativity, and the West in American Literature.* Lincoln and London: University of Nebraska Press, 1999.

Rotella, Guy. *Reading and Writing Nature.* Boston: Northeastern University Press, 1991.

Rusinko, Susan. *British Drama, 1950 to the Present: A Critical History.* Boston: Twayne, 1989.

Russell, Richard Rankin, ed. *Martin McDonagh: A Casebook.* London and New York: Routledge, 2007.

Ryden, Kent C. *Mapping the Invisible Landscape: Folklore, Writing, and the Sense of Place.* Iowa City: University of Iowa Press, 1993.

Sampson, Denis. *Outstaring Nature's Eye: The Fiction of John McGahern.* Washington, D.C.: Catholic University of America Press, 1993.

Sandbrook, Dominic. *Never Had It So Good: A History of Britain from Suez to the Beatles.* London: Abacus, 2006.

Sanders, Scott Russell. "Speaking a Word for Nature." *The Ecocriticism Reader: Landmarks in Literary Ecology.* Ed. Cheryll Glotfelty and Harold Fromm. Athens: University of Georgia Press, 1996. 182–95.

Schaffer, Peter. *Equus.* London: Deutsch, 1973.

Scharnhorst, Gary. "Wister and the Great Railway Strike of 1894." *Reading The Virginian in the New West.* Ed. Melody Graulich and Stephen Tatum. Lincoln: University of Nebraska Press, 2003. 113–25.

Schneider, Richard J. *Thoreau's Sense of Place: Essays in American Environmental Writing.* Iowa City: University of Iowa Press, 2000.

Scigaj, Leonard M. *Sustainable Poetry: Four American Ecopoets.* Lexington: University of Kentucky Press, 1999.

Shakespeare, Nicholas. *Bruce Chatwin.* New York: Doubleday, 2000.

Sides, Hampton. *Blood and Thunder: An Epic of the American West.* New York: Doubleday, 2006.

Sierz, Alex. *In-Yer-Face Theatre: British Drama Today.* London: Faber and Faber, 2001.

Sinclair, Andrew. *John Ford.* New York: Dial, 1974.

Slotkin, Richard. *The Fatal Environment: The Myth of the Frontier in the Age of Industrialization, 1800–1890.* New York: Atheneum, 1985.

———. *Gunfighter Nation: The Myth of the Frontier in Twentieth-Century America.* New York: HarperPerennial, 1993.

———. *Regeneration through Violence: The Mythology of the American Frontier, 1600–1860.* Middletown, Conn.: Wesleyan University Press, 1973.

Smyth, Gerry. *Decolonization and Irish Criticism: The Construction of Irish Literature.* London: Pluto Press, 1998.

Smyth, William J. *Map-making, Landscapes and Memory: A Geography of Colonial and Early Modern Ireland, c. 1530–1750.* Notre Dame, Ind.: University of Notre Dame Press, 2006.

Smyth, William J., and Kevin Whelan. *Essays on the Historical Geography of Ireland.* Cork: Cork University Press, 1988.

Snyder, Gary. "Blue Mountains Constantly Walking." *The Gary Snyder Reader: Prose, Poetry, and Translations.* Washington, D.C.: Counterpoint, 1999. 200–213.

———. *The Gary Snyder Reader: Prose, Poetry, and Translations.* Washington, D.C.: Counterpoint, 1999.

———. *Turtle Island.* New York: New Directions, 1974.

Solnit, Rebecca. *Wanderlust: A History of Walking.* New York: Viking Penguin, 2000.

Stephens, Michael. *The Brooklyn Book of the Dead.* Normal, Ill.: Dalkey Archive Press, 1994.

———. *Green Dreams: Essays under the Influence of the Irish.* Athens: University of Georgia Press, 1994.

———. *Season at Coole.* Elmwood Park, Ill.: Dalkey Archive Press, 1984.

Stevens, George (dir). *Shane.* Los Angeles: Paramount, 1953.

Stevens, Wallace. *Collected Poems.* New York: Knopf, 1954.

———. *The Necessary Angel: Essays on Reality and the Imagination.* New York: Vintage, 1951.

Synge, J. M. *The Aran Islands.* Ed. Robin Skelton. Oxford: Oxford University Press, 1979.

Thoreau, Henry David. "Walking." *Great Short Works of Henry David Thoreau.* Ed. Wendell Glick. New York: Harper and Row, 1982. 294–309.

Thubron, Colin. "A Prince of the Road." *New York Review of Books.* Vol. 55, 1, January 17, 2008, 29–31.

———. *Mirror to Damascus.* Boston: Little, Brown, 1967.

Tompkins, Jane. *West of Everything: The Inner Life of Westerns.* New York: Oxford University Press, 1992.

Truska, Jon. *Billy the Kid: A Bio-Bibliography.* Westport, Conn.: Greenwood Press, 1983.

Turchi, Peter. *Maps of the Imagination: The Writer as Cartographer.* San Antonio, Tex.: Trinity University Press, 2004.

Tuttle, Jennifer S. "Indigenous Whiteness and Wister's Invisible Indians." *Reading* The Virginian *in the New West.* Ed. Melody Graulich and Stephen Tatum. Lincoln: University of Nebraska Press, 2003. 89–112.

Utley, Robert M. *Billy the Kid: A Short and Violent Life.* Lincoln: University of Nebraska Press, 1989.

Voous, K. H. *List of Recent Holarctic Bird Species.* London: Academic Press, 1977.

Voros, Gyorgyi. *Notations of the Wild: Ecology in the Poetry of Wallace Stevens.* Iowa City: University of Iowa Press, 1997.

Wallace, Anne D. *Walking, Literature, and English Culture: The Origins and Uses of Peripatetic in the Nineteenth Century.* Oxford: Clarendon Press, 1993.

Weekes, Ann Owens. *Irish Women Writers: An Uncharted Tradition.* Lexington: University Press of Kentucky, 1990.

Westbrook, Max. "Afterword." *The Virginian.* By Owen Wister. New York: Signet, 1979. 318–31.

Wheatley, David. "Irish Poetry in the Twenty-First Century." *The Cambridge Companion to Contemporary Irish Poetry.* Ed. Matthew Campbell. Cambridge: Cambridge University Press, 2003. 250–67.

Whelan, Kevin. "Landscape and Society on Clare Island, 1700–1900." *New Survey of Clare Island.* Ed. Críostóir Mac Cárthaigh and Kevin Whelan. Vol. 1. Dublin: Royal Irish Academy, 1999. 73–98.

White, Richard. *"It's Your Misfortune and None of My Own": A History of the American West.* Norman: University of Oklahoma Press, 1991.

Whyte, James. *Strategies of Transcendence: History, Myth and Ritual in the Fiction of John McGahern.* New York: Edwin Mellen, 2002.

Williams, Raymond. *The Country and the City*. London: Chatto and Windus, 1973.

Wister, Owen. *The Virginian*. New York: Signet, 1979.

Woods, Paul A. *King Pulp: The World of Quentin Tarantino*. London: Plexus, 1998.

Woodward, David, ed. *Art and Cartography: Six Historical Essays*. Chicago: University of Chicago Press, 1987.

Wordsworth, William. "Tintern Abbey." *The Norton Anthology of English Literature*. 7th ed. Ed. M. H. Abrams et al. Vol. 2. New York: Norton, 2000. 235–38.

Wrobel, David M. *Promised Lands: Promotion, Memory, and the Creation of the American West*. Lawrence: University Press of Kansas, 2002.

Yeats, W. B. *The Yeats Reader*. Rev. ed. Ed. Richard J. Finneran. New York: Scribner, 2002.

Zimmerman, Michael E. "Deep Ecology and Ecofeminism: The Emerging Dialogue." *Reweaving the World: The Emergence of Ecofeminism*. Ed. Irene Diamond and Gloria Feman Orenstein. San Francisco: Sierra Club Books, 1990. 138–54.

INDEX

Aalen, F. H. A., 28
Aberley, Doug, 21–22
Achebe, Chinua, 39
"Achill Woman, The" (Boland), 79
Akhmatova, Anna, 78
Alexie, Sherman, 127
Allen, Gilbert, 55
American West
    Kitses on, 108
    mythologizing, 136–37
    reimagining by women writers,
        81–82, 83
    violence in, 118
    wilderness of, 67
Ammons, A. R., 54
"Among School Children" (Yeats),
    161
Amongst Women (McGahern), 87
    elegizing the West, 80
    female characters in, 97, 99
    "Gold Watch" and, 102
    male characters in, 103, 131
    names of characters, 89
    themes initially in *High Ground*,
        88
    violence in, 114

Anglo-Irish
    McGahern on, 97, 106
    Murphy on, 55, 66–67
animals
    abuse in Irish drama, 125, 126
    cruelty to in McGafern, 110
Aosdána
    O'Malley member of, 71
    Robinson member of, 39
Aran Islands, The (Synge), 34
Arbutus, The/Madrone Files:
        Reading the Pacific Northwest
    (Ricou), 59
archetypes in Cannon, 170
"Ardilaun" (Murphy), 57–58
Artaud, Antonin, 31, 124
ASLE (Association for the Study
    of Literature and the
    Environment), 53
Asylum Road (O'Malley), 71
Atlas of the Irish Rural Landscape
    (Aalen, Lohelan, and Stout,
    eds.), 28–29
Attis, David
    on early scientists in Ireland, 145
    on science and culture, 149

Attis, David (*cont.*)
   on science and literature,
      140–41

*Back from the Far Field: American
   Nature Poetry in the Late
   Twentieth Century*
   (Quetchenbach), 54
"Ballad, A" (McGahern), 95, 102
"Ballinspittle Banshee, The"
   (Lysaght), 154
"Bank Holiday" (McGahern), 91
   as Dublin story, 90, 93, 96
   male characters and, 93, 94, 102
   in organization of *High Ground,*
      88
Banshees of Inisheer, The
   (McDonagh), 114
Banville, John, 114
Barracks, The (McGahern), 89, 102,
   103
Barrett, Gillian, 29–30
Bate, John, 54
Battle of Aughrim, The (Murphy),
   55
Beauty Queen of Lennane, The
   (McDonagh), 113, 125
Beckett, J. C., 26
"Before Anthropology" (Lysaght),
   154
Behan, Brendan, 121
Behanding in Spokane, A
   (McDonagh), 114
Belfast Naturalists' Field Club,
   142
Bend in the River, A (Naipaul),
   127
Benjamin, Walter, 5–6

Berry, Wendell
   ecocriticism and, 53, 54
   influence of environment on
      work of, 61
   on relationship of action,
      creativity, and language, 62
bilingualism in O'Malley, 78–79
Billy the Kid, 130
bioregionalism, 175
Birds of Ireland (Kennedy, Rutledge,
   and Scrope), 140, 141,
   148–49, 151
*Birthing a Nation: Gender,
   Creativity, and the West in
   American Literature*
   (Rosowski), 82
Black, Jeremy, 124, 125
Black Elk Speaks, 13
Blake, William, 90
"Blue Mountains Constantly
   Walking" (Snyder), 6
Bly, Robert, 54
boats
   in poems by Murphy, 76, 77
   in poems by O'Malley, 73–74
bodies of water in Cannon, 165
Boland, Eavan
   attitude to the West, 79, 80
   on being a woman poet in
      Dublin, 83–84
   Cannon and, 158, 171
   influence on O'Malley, 78, 79
   methodology used in *Object
      Lessons,* 38–39
   O'Malley compared to, 77,
      79–80, 84
   in Smyth's epigraphs, 26
   on women's poetry, 79

Böll, Heinrich, 137
Bond, Edward, 126
Boning Hall, The: New and Selected Poems (O'Malley), 71
Book of Evidence, The (Banville), 114
"Boys and Girls" (Munro), 73, 101
Bryson, J. Scott, 54, 65–66
Buddhism
    influence on Murphy, 57
    Zen consciousness in Robinson, 10
Burke, Patrick, 126
Butcher Boy, The (McCabe), 114

Calder, Jenni, 128
Cannon, Moya, 157–76
    biography, 157
    ecofeminist reading, 54
    ecology in work of, 158, 170, 172, 173–74
    and Gaelic Irish tradition, 171, 173
    Heaney and, 158, 160
    Hogan compared to, 165
    influenced by Murphy, 52
    landscape in work of, 158–59, 160, 165
    and music, 161–62
    O'Malley compared to, 78
    Raine and, 169, 171
Carbery, Ethna, 31
cartography, 1
    compared to literary studies, 18
    Robinson and, 2
    written *versus* oral, 24–25
    See also map-making; mapping; maps

Catholic Church, Cannon and, 167
"Ceist na Teangan" (Ní Dhomhnaill), 151
Celan, Paul, 78
Chambers, Lilian, 117, 118
characters in McGahern
    female, 98, 99–100
    male, 102–8, 131
    names of, 89
Charles Baudelaire: A Lyric Poet in the Era of High Capitalism (Benjamin), 5–6
Charyn, Jerome, 121
Chatwin, Bruce, 42–43
    Robinson compared to, 40, 44–46
    Shakespeare, Nicholas, on, 44, 45
children, violence toward, 126
"Chough" (Lysaght), 152–53
Christian tradition in Cannon, 166
"Church and Its Spire, The" (McGahern), 96
circular motion
    Aran Islanders and, 13–14
    Robinson and, 12–13
Clare Island Survey (Lysaght), 139–56
"Clare Island Survey" (Lysaght), 140
    on Praeger, 144–45
Clare Island Survey (Royal Irish Academy, 1911–1915), 139, 142–44, 151
Clarke, Austin
    on birthplace of scientist, 141
    Ó Direáin compared to, 35
"Cleggan Disaster, The" (Murphy), 76

"Coda" (Lysaght), 140, 155
Coleridge, Samuel Taylor
    Jarvis on, 14–15
    Robinson compared to, 15
Colgan, N., 145
Collected Poems (Murphy), 51
Collected Stories (McGahern), 87, 88
Collins, Pat, 89
Collins, Timothy, 142–43
colonized spaces, Eurocentric
    versions of, 39
Comer, Krista, 83
Common Ground, 22
community and ecocriticism, 67
*Connemara: The Last Pool of
    Darkness* (Robinson), 16
Conrad, Joseph
    McDonagh compared to, 115
    McGahern compared to, 103
consciousness, ecological
    of Cannon, 172, 173
    of Heaney, 52
    of Murphy, 51
Consideration of Silk, A (O'Malley),
    71
"Conversion of William Kirkwood,
    The" (McGahern), 97, 99
    on Catholic clergy, 94
    female characters in, 98–99
    Munro's "Boys and Girls"
        compared to, 101
    on Protestants, 95
    in timeline of *High Ground*, 88
Cook-Lynn, Elizabeth, 32, 81
Country and the City, The
    (Williams), 6
"Country Funeral, The"
    (McGahern), 87, 109
    compared to "Wheels," 88

"Countrywoman Remembers, The"
    (O'Malley), 72–73
"Creamery Manager, The"
    (McGahern), 87, 109
"Creatures of the Earth"
    (McGahern), 87, 109
    cruelty to animals, 110
*Creatures of the Earth: New and
    Selected Stories* (McGahern),
    87
Cripple of Inishmaan, The
    (McDonagh), 113
"Crossing the Line" (McGahern),
    94, 95, 106
culture
    inheritance of McDonagh, 117
    McDonagh's plays and
        American, 118
    oral, 38
Cusick, Christine, 171
    on Cannon, 159
    on Cannon's ecological
        consciousness, 172, 173

Dakota: A Spiritual Geography
    (Norris), 82
Dark, The (McGahern), 103
Dean, Joan FitzPatrick, 120, 136
Deane, Seamus
    on Synge, 33
    on *Translations*, 152
Death of a Naturalist (Heaney), 75
"Declensions" (Lysaght), 150
Deep Ecology, 173–74
deepmap of Inishmore, 3–4, 11, 21,
    22
Defending Ancient Springs (Raine),
    166, 167–68
Delanty, Greg, 150

Desert Notes (Lopez), 3
Dharma Bums, The (Kerouac), 10–11
"Digging" (Heaney), 75
"Diving into the Wreck" (Rich), 77
Dolmen Press, 51, 76, 167
Donoghue, Denis, 54–55
Dorling, Daniel, 17, 18, 19
Doyle, Maria, 120
Drever, Timothy. *See* Robinson, Tim
Dromgoole, Dominic, 119
Dublin
    in McGahern's work, 88, 90, 91,
      92, 96
    shaping Joyce's *Ulysses,* 8
    woman poets in, 83–84
Dubliners (Joyce)
    Joyce on, 95
    McGahern's engagement with,
      92
"Dublinia" (O'Malley), 81

ecocriticism
    as ideal mode for reading Irish
      literature, 68
    in the United States, 53, 54–55
Ecocriticism Reader (Glotfelty and
    Fromm, eds.), 53
ecofeminism, 54
    defining, 173–74
    as mode of reading women poets
      from the West of Ireland, 54
ecology, 51
    Anglo-Irish and, 67
    in Cannon, 158, 170, 173–74
    —Cusick on, 172
    in Heaney, 52
    link to literature, 52
    in Murphy, 65, 67
    and reimagining of space, 59

ecopoetics, urban Irish, 63–64
ecopoetry, 51–69
Ecopoetry: A Critical Introduction
    (Bryson, ed.), 54, 65–66
"Eddie Mac" (McGahern)
    male characters and, 102
    on Protestants, 95
    Sampson on, 97–98
    in timeline of *High Ground,* 88
Einstein, Albert, 47
Elder, John, 53
Enzenberger, Hans Magnus, 45
Erris (Lysaght), 139, 156
"Erris" (Lysaght), 155–56
Evans, E. Estyn, 27, 28

Fairbairn, David, 17, 18, 19
Fanon, Franz, 33
Farrell, Colin, 114
Feamainn Bhealtaine (Mayweed)
    (Ó Direáin), 35, 37
films, reading McDonagh's plays
    in relation to contemporary,
      120, 122
Flaherty, Robert, 2, 34
Flaubert, Gustave, 92
Foakes, R. A., 134–35
Folding Landscapes (publishing
    house), 15–16
Ford, John, 132–33, 137
Foster, John Wilson, 54
"Foundations" (Cannon), 164
Friel, Brian
    Kiberd on, 151
    Lysaght compared to, 151
    McGahern compared to, 94
    on Ordnance Surveys, 20, 145
Fromm, Harold, 53
"Fuchsia Blaze, The" (Delanty), 150

Gaelic Irish tradition, Cannon and, 171, 173
García Lorca, Federico, 78
geographers, 17, 18
    interdisciplinarity of, 23
    Swedish, 22–23
geography's alignment with literature, 26
Glotfelty, Cheryll, 53
Glück, Louis, 54
Glued to the Box (James), 123
"God Who Eats Corn, The" (Murphy), 56
Golding, William, 56–57
"Gold Watch" (McGahern)
    characters names in, 89
    male characters and, 102, 103
    setting of, 90, 91
Goodby, John, 85–86
Greening of Literary Scholarship, The: Literature, Theory, and the Environment (Rosendale), 52–53
Gregory, Lady Augusta, 31, 83, 137
Grene, Nicholas, 119
Grennan, Eamon
    Lysaght compared to, 155
    and West of Ireland, 69
Gunfighter Nation: The Myth of the Frontier in Twentieth-Century America (Slotkin), 118

Haberstroh, Patricia Boyle
    on Cannon, 157–58, 161
    on Irish women's poetry, 77–78
Hägerstrand, Torsten, 22
Harley, Brian, 17–18

Harris, Richard, 121
"Hazelnuts" (Cannon), 163
Hazlitt, William, 10
Heaney, Seamus
    Cannon and, 158, 160
    ecological consciousness in, 52
    and Inishmore, 31
    link of Gaelic and Japanese poetry, 59
    on Mandelstam, 66
    on monasticism and nature poetry, 58
    O'Malley compared to, 75
    in Smyth's epigraphs, 26
Heart of Darkness (Conrad), 127
Henry, Paul, 137
Henry, Tricia, 118, 124
Higgins, Rita Ann, 78
High Ground (McGahern), 87–111
"High Ground" (McGahern), 93–94, 102
High Island (Murphy), 52, 56–60
    clarity and depth of description in, 64
    ecological discovery in, 65
    poetic structure, 57–58
history
    alignment with geography, 26
    exploration by Murphy, 55
Hogan, Linda
    Cannon compared to, 165
    ecocriticism and, 54
house building, Snyder and Murphy and, 68
houses in Murphy's work, 55
How Late It Was, How Late (Kelman), 126
Huber, Werner, 119

Hughes, Ted, 78
Husserl, Edmund, 7

images in Cannon, 158
*Imagining the Earth: Poetry and the
Vision of Nature* (Elder), 53
In Bruges (film, McDonagh), 114
indigenous worlds, connections to,
60
Inishmore, 1
deepmap of, 3–4, 11, 21, 22
Robinson's first maps of the
island, 2
"In the Burren" (Lysaght), 153
"in-yer-face" movement, 115
Irish Museum of Modern Art
(Dublin), 46–47
Irish Review, The, 84
*Irish Settlements in Eastern Canada:
A Study of Cultural Transfer
and Adaptation* (Mannion),
28, 30
island, concept of, 59
isolation, Murphy and, 57, 59
*"It's Your Misfortune and None of my
Own": A New History of the
American West* (White), 118

James, Clive, 123
Jarvis, Robin, 6
on alignment of walking and
writing, 10, 14, 16
"Jealousy" (O'Malley), 73
Jeffers, Robinson
Cannon compared to, 172
ecocriticism and, 55
Lysaght compared to, 153
Western-ness of, 55

Jeffers, Una, 55
Jordan, Eamonn, 117, 118
Joyce, James, 31
Cannon and, 160
McDonagh compared to, 117
See also Dubliners (Joyce); *Ulysses*
(Joyce)
Jung, Carl, 169

Kavanagh, Patrick
hard realism of, 105
Lysaght and Praeger compared
to, 141
McGahern on, 93
O'Malley compared to, 84
Kelman, James, 126
Kheel, Marti, 173–74
Kiberd, Declan
on Friel's *Translations,* 151
on McGahern's attitude to the
West, 80
on Revival women writers, 83
on Synge and Aran Islands, 33
Kick, The (Murphy), 52, 76
ecological discovery in, 65
Kinsella, Thomas, 35
Kirkpatrick, Kathryn, 64
Kitses, Jim, 108
Knife in the Wave, The (O'Malley), 71

landscape
in Cannon's work, 158–59, 160
—bodies of water, 165
O'Malley on, 72
*Landscapes of the New West:
Gender and Geography in
Contemporary Women's
Writing* (Comer), 83

language
  bilingualism in O'Malley,
    78–79
  in Cannon, 159
  importance of Irish names for
    Lysaght, 148
  McDonagh
  —bad language, 126
  —manipulation of Irish speech,
    122
Lanters, José, 120
"Last Galway Hooker, The"
    (Murphy), 76
Lawless, Emily, 31
Lawrence, D. H., 103
Lawrence, Karen, 8
Least Heat-Moon, William,
    3, 4, 11–12
Leavetaking, The (McGahern),
    89
Lee, Spike, 120
Leigh Fermor, Patrick, 40, 46
Lenihan, John H., 130–31
Lévi-Strauss, Claude, 28
Lewis, C. S., 56
Lieutenant of Inishmore, The
    (McDonagh)
  characters in, 128–29, 131
  Rees on, 126–27
  as revenge play, 135
  violence in, 118, 120, 125
  West of Ireland setting of, 113
  The Wild Bunch compared to,
    128, 134
"Like All Other Men"
    (McGahern), 90
"Lines for a New House"
    (Lysaght), 156

"List of Irish Names for Birds"
    (Mac Giollarnáth), 141, 148
Literary Revival, 82, 83
  imagined West, 137
Lonergan, Patrick, 119, 120, 122
Lonesome West, The (McDonagh),
    113
Longley, Edna, 54
Longley, Michael, 31, 69
  Lysaght compared to, 155
Lopez, Barry, 3
Lord of the Flies (Golding), 56–57
Love, Glen A., 52–53
"Love of the World" (McGahern),
    87
  on splendor of West of Ireland,
    110
  violence in, 103, 109–10
Lucas, George, 128
Luckhurst, Mary, 119–20
"Lullaby" (O'Malley), 76
Lydon, John (Johnny Rotten),
    125
Lysaght, Seán, 139–56
  biography, 139
  Friel compared to, 151
  Grennan compared to, 155
  influenced by Murphy, 52, 64
  Jeffers compared to, 153
  Kavanagh compared to, 141
  Longley, Michael, compared to,
    155
  Praeger as father figure, 146
  Praeger compared to, 140–41

Mac Giollarnáth, Seán, 141, 148
MacLeod, Alistair, 110
MacNeill, John (Eoin), 145

Maher, Eamon
  on "Gold Watch," 102
  on McGahern's *Collected Stories,*
    88, 106
Mahon, Derek, 31
"Maighdean Mhara, The"
    (O'Malley), 74
Mandelstam, Osip, 66
Mannion, John, 17, 28, 30
Man of Aran (Flaherty), 2
"Manx Shearwater" (Lysaght), 140
map-making
  as distinguished from mapping,
    19
  early tools of, 25
  political-postcolonial context
    of, 20
*Map-making, Landscapes and
    Memory: A Geography of
    Colonial and Early Modern
    Ireland c. 1530–1750*
    (Smyth), 23
mapping
  as distinguished from map-
    making, 19
  Gaelic sense of, and memory, 24
  and walking as decolonizing
    act, 25–26
Mapping the Invisible Landscape
    (Ryden), 31
*Mapping: Ways of Representing
    the World* (Dorling and
    Fairbairn), 17, 18, 19
maps
  limits of, 3
  and memory, 24, 43
  See also deepmap of Inishmore;
    map-making; mapping

Marples, Morris, 5
Marsh, G. P., 28
Martin McDonagh: A Casebook
    (Russell, ed.), 119
masculinity in McDonagh's plays,
    124
Matthiessen, Peter, 13
McBreen, Joan, 78
McCabe, Patrick, 114
McCann, Colum, 69
McDonagh, Martin, 113–38
  family of, 115–16
  ill-mannered behavior, 121
  Joyce compared to, 117
  and language, 122, 126
  Naipaul compared to, 127
  Peckinpah and, 118, 128, 132
  on republicanism, 133
  Stephens compared to, 116
  Tarantino and, 118, 121, 122,
    128
  tuned in to worldwide
    developments, 84
  violence in works of, 114–15,
    118, 119, 120, 125
  on West of Ireland, 114, 127
McGahern, John, 87–111
  Dublin in work of, 88, 90, 91,
    92, 96
  influenced by MacLeod, 110
  literary influences on, 92
  on Protestants, 95
  violence in works of, 109–10,
    114, 131
  on West of Ireland, 80, 96,
    110–11
  Wister compared to, 104–5,
    109, 131

McKenna, Bernard, 83
McMurtry, Larry, 105
"Meadow Pipit" (Lysaght), 148
Meaney, Colm, 114
Meehan, Paula, 63–64, 67
    influenced by Snyder, 64
    O'Malley compared to, 77
Memoir (McGahern), 87, 89, 102
memory and maps, 24, 43
men, O'Malley's celebration of lives
    of, 72
Merchant, Carolyn, 173
Merwin, W. S.
    ecocriticism and, 54
    on relationship of action,
        creativity and language, 62
Meyer, Kuno, 60
Miola, Robert S.
    on Renaissance readers, 121
    on revenge plays, 136
Mirror to Damascus (Thubron),
    40–41
Momaday, N. Scott, 3–4
Montague, John, 78
Moore, George, 92, 93
Morash, Christopher, 119
"Mountain" (Cannon), 171–72
Mouth of a River, The (Lysaght),
    139
Muir, Edwin, 170
Munro, Alice
    McGahern compared to, 101
    O'Malley compared to, 73
"Murdering the Language"
    (Cannon), 173
Murphy, Richard, 51–69
    on Anglo-Irish, 55, 66–67
    biography, 56

house building, 68
influence
    —on Cannon, 52
    —on Lysaght, 52, 64
    —on O'Malley, 52, 76, 77
influenced by Praeger, 64
and isolation, 57, 59
Lysaght compared to, 155
O'Malley's "Tracing" dedicated
    to, 75
Snyder compared to, 52, 59, 60,
    68
"tang and clarity" in poetry of,
    60–61
Yeats compared to, 55–56
music
    Cannon and, 161–62
    in O'Malley's poetry, 84–85
mythology
    of American West, 136–37
    in O'Malley, 84
My Time in Space (Robinson), 22

"Na Beanna Beola/The Twelve
    Pins, Connemara"
    (O'Malley), 72
Naipaul, V. S., 127
Nash, Roderick, 53
"Naturalist" (Lysaght), 153–54
Neruda, Pablo, 78
"Nest" (Cannon), 175–76
New Criticism, 18
    Murphy and, 66
    Raine and, 167–68
New Survey of Clare Island (Royal
    Irish Academy, 1999–2005),
    139, 145–46
New York Dolls, 124

New Yorker, The, 113
Ní Dhomhnaill, Nuala, 151
   O'Malley compared to, 84
Nightlines (McGahern), 88
Noah's Irish Ark (Lysaght), 139, 153
Norris, Kathleen, 82
"North American Time" (Rich), 77
*Notations of the Wild: Ecology in the
   Poetry of Wallace Stevens*
   (Voros), 54–55

Oar (Cannon), 157
*Object Lessons: The Life of the
   Woman and the Poet in Our
   Time* (Boland), 38–39,
   83–84, 171
O'Connor, Frank, 94
Ó Direáin, Máire, 30, 34
Ó Direáin, Máirtín
   and Inishmore, 31
   Robinson and, 34, 35, 37
O'Flaherty, Liam
   and Inishmore, 31
   Robinson on, 34
Ó hEithir, Breandán, 31–32, 33
Ó Laoire, Lillis, 25
"Oldfashioned" (McGahern), 91,
   95, 101
   Anglo-Irish in, 106
   male characters and, 102, 103
Oliver, Mary
   Cannon compared to, 171
   ecocriticism and, 54
Olson, Charles, 8
Olsson, Gunner, 22–23
O'Malley, Mary, 71–86
   bilingualism, 78–79
   boats in works of, 73–74

Boland compared to, 77, 79–80,
   84
ecofeminist reading, 54
Heaney compared to, 75
literary influences, 78
—Boland, 79
—Murphy, 52, 76, 77
and music, 84–85
Norris compared to, 82
*On a Rock in the Middle of the Ocean:
   Songs and Singers in Tory
   Island, Ireland* (Ó Laoire), 25
"On the Symbol" (Raine), 168
Ordnance Surveys, 17
   Friel on, 20, 145
   Robinson on, 20–21
Ó Searcaigh, Cathal, 28
O'Toole, Fintan, 113, 115
"Our Worlds" (Cannon), 159–60

Painting Rain (Meehan), 63–64
Papanikolas, Zeese, 109
"Parachutes" (McGahern)
   as Dublin story, 90, 96
   male characters and, 102
   in organization of *High Ground,*
   88
Parchment Boat, The (Cannon), 157
Pearse, Patrick, 31
Peckinpah, Sam
   influence on McDonagh, 118
   McDonagh compared to, 128,
   132
   work as commentary on Ford,
   132–33
Perfect V, A (O'Malley), 71
Perloff, Marjorie, 162–63
Pessoa, Fernando, 78

Pfister, Manfred, 45
"Pine Tree Tops" (Snyder), 61–62
Playboy of the Western World, The
(Synge), 105, 131
poetry
Eastern influence on, 59, 162
ecopoetry, 51–69
form in Cannon, 157–58
integral part of natural world,
75
of Irish women, 77–79
Native American, 165
scarecrow as device, 155
structure in Murphy, 57–58,
60–61
"Poetry Harlots, The" (O'Malley),
85
"Poetry of What Happens, The"
(Cannon), 158
"Pollen" (Cannon), 164
"Poor People" (O'Flaherty), 37
Pope, Alexander, 171
positivism, Raine and, 167
Potts, Donna, 165–66, 171, 173
Pound, Ezra
Cannon and, 158
Perloff on, 162–63
Praeger, Robert Lloyd
biography by Lysaght, 139, 147,
156
on early rising, 151–52
interest in Irish names, 146
Lysaght compared to, 140–41
Murphy influenced by, 64
and Survey of Clare Island,
142–44
PrairyErth (Least Heat-Moon), 3,
11–12
"Projective Verse" (Olson), 8

Protestants
McGahern on, 95
See also Anglo-Irish
Proust, Marcel, 92
Pulp Fiction (film, Tarantino), 120
punk rock, McDonagh and, 117,
118, 124

Quetchenbach, Bernard W., 54

Raine, Kathleen, 158, 166–69
Cannon and, 169, 171
Ramelli, Agostino, 121
Ramsey, Patrick, 84
Rees, Catherine, 117, 126
regional studies, 27–28
"Revaluing Nature: Toward an
Ecological Criticism" (Love),
52–53
revenge
in Peckinpah's work, 128
plays of, 118, 128, 135, 136
Rich, Adrienne
ecocriticism and, 54
feminist poetics and, 77
Ricou, Laurie, 59
Robinson, Tim, 1–49
Chatwin compared to, 40,
44–46
on circular motion, 12–13
Coleridge compared to, 15
Least Heat-Moon compared to,
3–4, 11–12
Ó Direáin, Máirtín, and, 34, 35,
37
Romantic ideology of, 36
Smyth compared to, 23–24
style, 9–10
and walking, 1, 10, 46

Romantic Writing and Pedestrian Travel (Jarvis), 6
Rosendale, Steven, 52–53
Rosowski, Susan J., 82
Ross, Martin, 31
Rotella, Guy, 54
Rough Field, The (Montague), 78
Rousseau, Jean-Jacques, 7
Russell, Richard Rankin, 119
Ryden, C., 31

Said, Edward, 39
"Sailing to Byzantium" (Yeats), 152, 153
Sampson, Denis, on McGahern
    on "Eddie Mac," 97–98
    on female characters, 99
    on *High Ground*, 88, 93
    on "Like All Other Men," 90
Sandbrook, Dominic, 40
Saved (Bond), 126
Scarecrow (Lysaght), 139
scarecrow as poetic device, 155
Scigaj, Leonard M., 54, 69
"Scríob" (Cannon), 160
"Script" (Cannon), 170, 171
"Second Plantation of Connaught, The" (O'Malley), 78–79, 80–81
Seneca, 136
Sesso, Oda, 58
Setting Foot on the Shores of Connemara (Robinson), 2, 20
"Severed Head, The" (Montague), 78
sexuality in McDonagh's plays, 124
Shakespeare, Nicholas, 44, 45

Shakespeare, William
    McDonagh compared to, 118
    violence in, 134–35
Shakespeare's Reading (Miola), 121
Shakespeare & Violence (Foakes), 134–35
"Shards" (Cannon), 164
"Shells" (Cannon), 160
Showdown: Confronting Modern America in the Western Film (Lenihan), 130–31
Six Shooter (film, McDonagh), 114, 128
Skull in Connemara, A (McDonagh), 113, 125
Slotkin, Richard
    on Peckinpah, 128
    on violence in the American West, 118
    on the Virginian, 132
    on *The Wild Bunch*, 134
Smyth, William J.
    Robinson compared to, 23–24
    on tracing, 24–25, 43
Snow Leopard, The (Matthiessen), 13
Snyder, Gary, 11
    Cannon compared to, 171
    ecocriticism and, 54
    influence on Meehan, 64
    Murphy compared to, 52, 59, 60, 68
    on Native Americans and settlers, 67
    on walking, 6
    and wilderness, 67–68
    See also Turtle Island (Snyder)
"Solitary Reader, The" (McGahern), 95

Solnit, Rebecca, 6, 7
Somerville, Edith, 31
Songlines, The (Chatwin), 42–43
　Enzenberger on, 45
Song of the Earth, The (Bate), 54
Songs of Innocence and Experience
　(Blake), 90
space, ecological reimagining of, 59
Standing by Words (Berry), 53
Stegner, Wallace
　definition of the Westerner, 107
　McGahern compared to, 105
Stephens, Michael, 116
stereotyping in McDonagh's plays,
　119, 120
Stevens, Wallace, 54–55
Stones of Aran (Robinson), 1–49, 8
　maps included in, 16–17
　Ulysses compared to, 8, 9
Stones of Aran: Labyrinth
　(Robinson), 1, 14
　as love story, 46
Stones of Aran: Pilgrimage
　(Robinson), 1, 14
　on circular motion, 12–13
　epiphany as beginning of
　　journey, 11
　negative review of, 48
"Stormpetrel" (Murphy), 64
Studies in Classic American
　Literature (Lawrence), 103
suffering, O'Malley on, 84
Sustainable Poetry: Four American
　Ecopoets (Scigaj), 54
Symons, Arthur, 31
Synge, John Millington, 31, 137
　Kiberd on, 33
　Robinson on, 34
Szegö, John, 17, 22

"'Taom'" (Cannon), 163–64
Tarantino, Quentin
　influence on McDonagh, 118,
　　122
　McDonagh compared to, 121,
　　128
　stereotyping in, 120
"tEarrach Thiar, An" ("The
　Western Spring") (Ó
　Direáin), 35–36
television, McDonagh and, 123–24
terra nullius, concept of, 22
"That the Science of Cartography
　Is Limited" (Boland), 79
That They May Face the Rising Sun
　(McGahern), 87, 88, 100,
　110–11
Theatre of Martin McDonagh, The:
　A World of Savage Stories
　(Chambers and Jordan, eds.),
　118
The Clash, 124
Thoor Ballylee, 55
Thoreau, Henry David, 5
Thubron, Colin
　on Leigh Fermor, 40
　Robinson compared to, 41–42
"Timbre" (Cannon), 160–61
"To Colmcille Returning"
　(Cannon), 160
tourism, cultural, 32
tracing, 24–25, 26
　Songlines compared to, 43
"Tracing" (O'Malley), 75
Translations (Friel)
　Deane on, 152
　"High Ground" compared to, 94
　Kiberd on, 151
　on Ordnance Survey, 20, 145

Troubles in Northern Ireland,
television coverage of, 123
Turtle Island (Snyder), 52
bioregionalism and, 175
High Island compared to, 57

Ulysses (Joyce)
Heaney's and Cannon's links to,
160
shaped by Dublin, 8
Stones of Aran compared to, 8, 9
Untilled Field, The (Moore), 92
"Untitled" (O'Malley), 77
Utley, Robert M., 130

Victory (Conrad), 103
View from the Horizon, The
(Robinson), 6, 47
"Vigil, The" (O'Malley), 73
"Village Tailor, The" (Lysaght), 153
Viney, Michael, 69
"Viola d'Amore" (Cannon), 164–65
violence
in the American West, 118
in McDonagh's plays, 114–15,
118, 119, 120, 125
in McGahern's works, 109–10,
114, 131
in Shakespeare, 134–35
toward children, 126
Virginian, The (Wister), 104–5, 109
Voous, K. H., 141–42
Voros, Gyorgi, 54–55, 65

Walcott, Derek, 78
walking
connection with writing, 5–8
as enabling and framing device
in Robinson, 1, 10

and form, 8–9
importance for Chatwin, 45–46
as liberating, 15
and mapping as decolonizing
act, 25–26
Robinson on, 46
Snyder and, 6
"Walking" (Thoreau), 5
Wallace, Clare, 120
Wanderlust: A History of Walking
(Solnit), 6
Watkins, Vernon, 168
*Way That I Went, The: An Irishman
in Ireland* (Praeger), 139, 146
Way to Rainy Mountain, The
(Momaday), 3–4
Weekes, Ann Owens, 72
West, the
as frontier area, 107
as sacred space, 60
See also American West; West of
Ireland
Westbrook, Max, 104–5
Western-ness
of Jeffers and Yeats, 55
of McGahern, 88
West of Ireland
growth of Galway, 85
in McDonagh
—as dysfunctional and
hyperviolent society, 114
—view of County Galway, 127
in McGahern, 80
—on religion, 96
—on the splendor, 110–11
position of vulnerable women in,
99
reimagining by contemporary
women writers, 81

West of Ireland (*cont.*)
  version of English-language
    writers, 137
  wordwide developments and, 84
  writer's attitudes toward, 79–80
Wheatley, David, 79
"Wheels" (McGahern), 88
Whelan, Kevin, 17, 28
Where the Rocks Float (O'Malley), 71
  boat poems in, 73–74
White, Richard
  on myth, 137–38
  on mythologizing of American
    West, 105, 133, 136–37
  on roots of violence in American
    West, 118
Whybrow, Graham, 117
*Why I Can't Read Wallace Stegner
  and Other Essays* (Cook-
  Lynn), 81
Whyte, James, 103
Wild Bunch, The (Peckinpah), 128,
  134
wilderness
  ecocriticism and, 67
  Snyder and, 67–68
Wilderness and the American Mind
  (Nash), 53
Williams, Raymond, 6
Wilson, August, 122–23

Wister, Owen, 105
  character of the Virginian, 107
  McGahern compared to, 104–5,
    109, 131
women
  McGahern on violence against,
    109–10
  O'Malley on, 72, 77, 84
women writers
  and reimagining of the
    American West, 81–82, 83
  and reimagining of the West of
    Ireland, 81
"Woodcock" (Lysaght), 153
writers, paradigm of British, 39–40
writing, movements of the body
  and, 16

Yeats, William Butler
  Cannon and, 158
  McDonagh's life compared to,
    116
  Murphy compared to, 55–56
  Ó Direáin compared to, 35
  scarecrow in, 155
  Western-ness of, 55
"Yellowhammer" (Lysaght), 140,
  149–50

Zimmerman, Michael E., 175

EAMONN WALL

is Smurfit-Stone Professor of Irish Studies and Professor of English

at the University of Missouri-St. Louis.